(Pvt)
SH PRAIRIE
290 — 28

R

089°

ARRIVING VFR AIRCRAFT SHOULD
CONTACT PORTLAND APPROACH CONTRO
WITHIN 20 NM ON 133.0 360.8

FLY FOR FUN (W56)
275 — 21 122.8 C

(Pvt)
GREEN MOUNTAIN
280 — 20 122.75 C

44

V 5

12

40
20

VER MALL

3

EVERG...
310 L

GROVE (WA10)

WASHOUG

25

294
(276)

281
(265)

283
(247)

236
(210)

40
SFC

229
(203)

12

125°

84

PORTLAND
TROUTDALE (TTD)
CT—120:5 C
35 °L 54 122:95

LAKER
332 IA

PORTLAND APPROACH

40
17

substations

See NOTAMs/Dire

SKYJACK

SKYJACK

THE HUNT FOR D.B. COOPER

GEOFFREY GRAY

 CROWN PUBLISHERS | NEW YORK

Copyright © 2011 by Geoffrey Gray

Published in the United States by Crown Publishers, an imprint of
the Crown Publishing Group, a division of Random House, Inc., New York.

www.crownpublishing.com

CROWN and the Crown colophon are registered trademarks of
Random House, Inc.

Library of Congress Cataloging-in-Publication Data

Gray, Geoffrey.
Skyjack: the hunt for D.B. Cooper / Geoffrey Gray.
1. Cooper, D.B. 2. Hijacking of aircraft–United States. 3. Criminal
investigation–United States. I. Title.
HE9803.Z7H5352 2011
364.15'52092–dc22   2010047655

ISBN 978-0-307-45129-3
eISBN 978-0-45131-6

Printed in the United States of America

Design by Leonard Henderson
Map by David Lindroth
Jacket design by David Tran
Jacket photograph (man) by Getty Images
Endpaper maps: Courtesy of National Oceanic and Atmospheric
Administration (NOAA)

10 9 8 7 6 5 4 3 2 1

First Edition

For Nana

CONTENTS

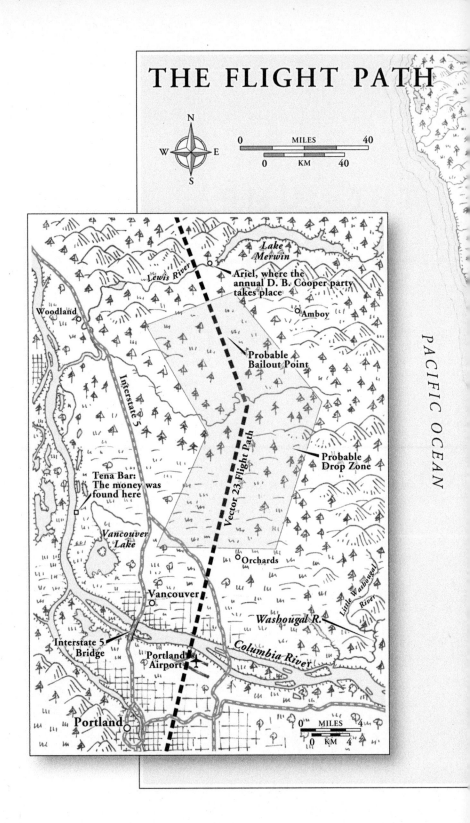

THE FLIGHT PATH

N
W E
S

MILES
0   40

KM
0   40

PACIFIC OCEAN

Lake Merwin

Lewis River

Ariel, where the annual D. B. Cooper party takes place

Amboy

Woodland

Probable Bailout Point

Interstate 5

Vector 23 Flight Path

Probable Drop Zone

Tena Bar: The money was found here

Vancouver Lake

Orchards

Little Washougal River

Vancouver

Washougal R.

Interstate 5 Bridge

Columbia River

Portland Airport

Portland

MILES
0   4

KM
0   4

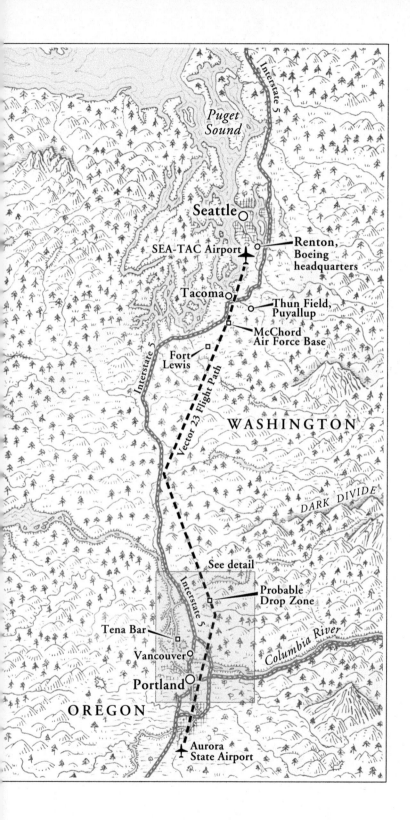

Bombproof and crowded with oxygen . . . terrace, volcallure at casa Cugat, Abbe Wants Cugie Gets.

We're up against an enemy, a conspiracy. They are using any means. We are going to use any means. Is that clear?

–Richard Nixon

THE JUMP

Skipp Porteous wants to talk and says can we meet and I say fine. He arrives in a suit that is South Beach white, and between the wide lapels is a T-shirt that is snug and black. He has leather sandals on his feet, no socks. His hair is curly and brown. His goatee is trimmed and gray in spots. He removes his sunglasses, which reveal hooded eyes, and gives the room a looky-loo.

The bistro is typical midtown Manhattan. A fruit basket of martinis on the menu—mango, peach, Lillet. The clatter of voices at the banquettes and the clank of dishes ricochet over the roar of lunch talk. In the gilded mirrors on the walls are reflections of Windsor knots, hair gel, six-figure cleavage.

I have dealt with Porteous before. He had a few story ideas; none worked. I can't remember why now. Porteous was his own story, and maybe I should have written about him.

He used to be a preacher before he became a private investigator. In the late 1960s, Porteous ran a church in Los Angeles and worked the Sunset Strip with his Bible. He preached to hippies, the homeless, anybody who would listen to his salvation pitch. "Excuse me," he would say, "if you died tonight, where would you spend eternity?"

The game for Porteous then was to win souls for the Church, until he lost his own. He saw corruption in the Church and started digging around. What he found was that he was good at digging around, often in disguise. Porteous liked undercover work so much he made a second career out of it. For a small-town sheriff, he bought drugs as a narc. For the FBI, he infiltrated gangs and groups wearing a wire. It was a decent living. The feds paid on time, and in cash.

His style is not tough-talking or pushy. Porteous has a holistic approach toward PI work. Some retired cops flash badges or guns. Porteous starts each investigative day with a meditation session.

He also hires mostly women to do PI work.

"Women have better instincts than men," he told me when we first met.

Sherlock Investigations, his agency, had the gimmicky type of title that attracts a lot of attention on the Web. It snared me, and countless others needing help solving problems of an unusual kind. Like the disappearance of Captain Jack, an iguana that was stolen through an open window in Greenwich Village. Or the woman who called because she was convinced the actress Lily Tomlin was stalking her (she wasn't). Or the man convinced his wife was having an affair with his father (she was). Or the runaway from Israel they found living under a bridge in Arizona. Or the mother from India who wanted to spy on the man her daughter was dating, and all the suspicious spouses and suits who are convinced (and wrongly so) that their phone receivers are tapped and their offices are bugged. Sin and paranoia form the backbone of his business.

It's loud in the bistro and I can't hear the private investigator so good. I lean over my *moules*, anxious to hear what case has come over Porteous's transom. Another missing pet? Another teenage runaway? Gypsy scams?

Nope. It's a new client, Lyle Christiansen.

His intel is sparse. From what the private detective has pieced together, Lyle Christiansen appears to be a kooky old man, an eccentric, and prodigious. He is eighty years old, and lives in Morris, Minnesota, a prairie town closer to Fargo, North Dakota, than it is to Minneapolis. Lyle grew up in Morris and worked for the post office there. In retirement, he has become an inventor. He is in the process of patenting a hodgepodge of household contraptions: the Yucky Cleaning Wand (it slips into the neck of a bottle to clean the tough-to-reach places), an egg breaker that cracks eggs perfectly every time, and a shirt that disguises the appearance of suspenders (he finds them distasteful—in his version, you wear them on the inside of the shirt).

Christiansen's wife, Donna, has a creative mind, too. Over the years she has assembled a collection of expressions, adages, sayings, idioms, clichés, and senseless American verbiage. The title of her book is *As Cute as a Bug's Ear*. It has 2,270 entries, ranging from "As Bald as a Billiard Ball" to "You've Got it Made."

Great. But so what? What's the story here? Why would a retired post office worker and aspiring inventor from Bumblefuck, Minnesota, need the services of a Manhattan sleuth-for-hire like Porteous?

Porteous was puzzled too. The first e-mail he received from Christiansen was cryptic. It read:

> *Dear Good People at Sherlock Investigations,*
>
> *I would very much like to contact Nora Ephron, Movie Director of the movie, "Sleepless in Seattle". I think she would be interested in what I have to say.*

The Sherlock employee who handled the note was Sherry Hart. Before she became an investigator, Hart tried to make it as a singer-songwriter and actress. Her training in the dramatic arts now helps with her undercover work. She's handled hundreds of cases for Porteous, and as she read over Christiansen's e-mail she thought, *Here we go. Another whackjob.* She wrote back:

> *We would not be able to give you a famous person's address. If you want to write a letter to Ms. Ephron, we would deliver it to her ourselves. The fee would be $495. Proceed?*

Proceed. Christiansen's check and letter arrived shortly thereafter. Porteous handled the letter with caution, as if it contained a nuclear code. He held the envelope to the light to examine it. He rotated the edges. He peered through the fibers of the paper and checked the pockets for powders.

The note was clean.

He read it. Lyle's letter to Ephron was a pitch for a movie. Lyle wanted to base the film on the life and times of a person he knew. The language was vague. The person he knew was quiet and shy. *Bashful* was Lyle's word. Mr. Bashful also happened to be a culprit to a major unsolved crime, Lyle said.

He also suggested a title for the film: *The Bashful Man in Seattle*. A tip of the hat to Nora Ephron's blockbuster, *Sleepless in Seattle*.

Reading the bizarre note, Porteous did not attempt to understand it. He wasn't getting paid to understand it. He hailed a cab to Ephron's building on Park Avenue and approached the doorman.

"Nora Ephron live here?" he said.

"Yes," the doorman said.

Porteous placed Lyle's envelope in the doorman's white-gloved hands. He then hailed a cab home. Easy money.

As the weeks passed, Lyle Christiansen was patient. Did Ephron know he was a retired civil servant living on little income, and paid so much money to send her a note? Ephron's films were so warm and tender. How could she be so cold and rude as to not respond with a note of her own?

In her home on Park Avenue, Ephron did receive Christiansen's letter. She saw his note on her kitchen counter and maybe later in the office. Or did it land in the wastebasket with her junk mail? She couldn't be sure. It disappeared.

In Morris, Christiansen was flustered. He decided to write Ephron again. Did she not receive his first letter? Would Porteous deliver it for him? Whatever the fee was, he'd pay it.

Porteous was baffled. Why was Christiansen so desperate to reach Nora Ephron? And what was he talking about when he said he knew a person connected with a famous crime? Which crime? How famous?

In e-mails, Porteous prodded for more information. The old man was cagey. He wanted to tell his story to Nora Ephron, give her the exclusive. But Ephron never wrote him back. Lyle finally gave up. He told Porteous everything.

His hunt started on television. Flipping around the dial, Lyle settled on the program *Unsolved Mysteries*. The topic of the episode was D.B. Cooper: the famous hijacker who in the fall of 1971 parachuted out the back of an airplane with $200,000 in stolen cash—and was never seen again. D.B. Cooper had become a famous American outlaw, the legendary Robin Hood of the sky. The subject of poems and ballads and rock songs, D.B. was up there in the crime annals with Billy the Kid, Bonnie and Clyde, and Bigfoot.

D.B. Cooper, where are you now?
We're looking for you high and low.
With your pleasant smile
And your dropout style,
D.B. Cooper, where did you go?

His identity is a mystery. For four decades, agents, detectives, reporters, treasure hunters, amateur sleuths, and others have quested for clues that might reveal who the hijacker was. But no effort has yielded definitive results. Cooper remains only a face seen in sketches composed by FBI artists. And what a face!

Lyle Christiansen perked up in his chair when he saw it. The face was familiar. The receding hairline, the thin lips. The sloped forehead. The perky ears. The smile—that mischievous smile.

A cold and queasy feeling swept over him as he looked at the face. Could it be? It could. Lyle wrote to Porteous:

Yes, I knew the culprit personally. . . . He was my brother.

✗

The PI looks discouraged as I slurp up the garlicky broth at the bottom of my bowl of *moules.* Cooper? Sky pirate? Never heard of the guy.

The name is alluring, though. *D.B. Cooper.* It's fun to say out loud. It has a royal ring, a rhythm, with those stately initials that look so good in history books. J. P. Morgan. D. H. Lawrence. J. S. Bach.

Back at the office, I look up the case. The headlines continue, forty years later: VANISHED INTO THIN AIR. THE PERFECT CRIME. THE WORLD'S MOST DARING CRIMINAL.

Cooper was a genteel thief, according to legend. He wore a suit and tie. He was polite—caring, even—to his hostages. He developed his own cult following. On the anniversary of his crime, in the forests of southwest Washington State, where many believe his parachute came down, worshippers toast his feat and keep the legend going at a party that has been running for forty years.

"He comes off as a kind of curious Robin Hood," a sociologist said. "Taking from the rich, or at least the big and complex. It doesn't matter whether he gives to the poor or not." The symbolism of the skyjack was "one individual overcoming, for the time being anyway, technology, the corporation, the establishment, the system."

And the posse. Cooper spurred one of the biggest manhunts in law enforcement, as spy planes orbited over search areas and soldiers and generations of FBI agents on the ground waded through snow, mud, and rain in the most remote forest in the nation looking for him. Some lawmen were so impressed with the cleverness and courage of the getaway, they hoped the hijacker was never caught.

"If he took the trouble to plan this thing out so thoroughly, well, good luck to him," one sheriff said after the jump.

"You can't help but admire the guy," another federal agent on the first search teams said.

Cooper's crime transcended crime. In one jump, the hijacker was able to make the good guys root for the bad guys. So who was he? Why did he do it? And what happened to him?

Over the decades, the number of suspects and persons of interest in the Cooper case has grown to more than one thousand. Buried in the basement of the Bureau's field office in Seattle, the file runs over forty feet long. Inside are dossiers, letters, photos, interviews from witnesses, airline officials, parachute packers, tipsters, fraudsters, psychics, suspicious neighbors, business partners, conspiracy theorists, parents, jealous lovers. Some suspects disappeared. Some suspects faked their own deaths. One man nearly died in a custom-built submarine, scanning the bottom of a lake for the hijacker's ransom. One renowned reporter attempted suicide after his suspect was proven to be a fraud; only a steady program of electroshock treatment jolted him back into coherency. Countless impostors emerged. Men went to prison. The hijacking became myth, and over time the myth became truth. It was no longer clear what information was fact, or what was legend.

Like the quests to find the Holy Grail and the Lost Dutchman Mine, the hunt for the hijacker is an odyssey that tests the boundaries of obsession, and the farther along the path one gets, stranger and stranger things happen.

The Cooper Curse is what those who have felt it call it. But is the Curse real? Or something we create, then blame when we fail to find out what happened? Or the by-product of a moment in time defined by chaos and paranoia?

When Cooper jumped in the fall of 1971, the nation was at war with itself. In government buildings and on college campuses, bombs went off. In cities, looters roamed as riots raged and buildings burned. At demonstrations against the war in Vietnam, protesters were arrested by the tens of thousands. A defeat in Vietnam was imminent. The nation was also mired in recession. Labor strikes crippled the workforce. Unemployment soared. So did the crime rate. Prisons were overcrowded and taken over in riots. Communes were built. Cults formed. Otherwise normal teenagers ran away from home, and had to be "deprogrammed" after they were brainwashed.

"The music is telling the youth to rise up against the establishment,"

Charles Manson said during his trial for murder. "Why blame me? I didn't write the music."

A mob had formed. The underground was rising. Terrorists were homegrown. Communist fears were reborn. Inside J. Edgar Hoover's FBI, a campaign was afoot to compile information on protesters and anarchists. Phones were tapped.

At the center of the spookfest was President Nixon, whose motorcade was pummeled with rocks and surrounded by protesters.

"I just want to ask you one favor," Nixon told top aide H. R. Haldeman. "If I am assassinated, I want you to have them play Dante's *Inferno* and have Lawrence Welk produce it."

The president feared blackmail from so many different directions, both in and outside his administration, that his aides formed the Plumbers, the White House's own dirty tricks brigade. The Plumbers' black-bag jobs eventually led to Watergate and Nixon's resignation from office, perhaps the lowest point in the nation's political history.

Skyjacking was then a national epidemic. Throughout Nixon's term, there had been roughly a hundred hijackings of American airplanes, and over half the attempts had been successful.

The airplane had become the next stagecoach, a crime scene for dangerous jet-age robberies, and the skyjacker a momentary cultural hero. Like no other innovation, the invention of the airplane in Kitty Hawk and the evolution of American airpower were testaments to the nation's technological virility and essential to the American ethos. Air-power had been instrumental in winning the World Wars, in ushering in the jet age, in developing the space program. America had put man on the moon. Boeing had built the 747, the jumbo jet. And yet, in one impulsive action, the lone skyjacker was able to show the fallibility of the costly flying machines. What good was the power of the Air Force in a country like Vietnam where American soldiers were slaughtered under the canopy of the jungle? What good was flying a jet to vacation in Miami when so many flights were getting rerouted to Castro's Cuba?

The skyjacker himself was a kind of schizo-transcendentalist. Onboard a jet, taking all passengers and the flight crew as hostages, the skyjacker was able to create his own society. He became his own head of state, directing others—the pilots, the stewardesses, the lawmen, mayors, governors—to act upon his whims. In one flight, the skyjacker went from nobody to somebody. And with reporters from newspapers, radio, and television stations monitoring the drama in the air, the culprits achieved celebrity. Dr. David Hubbard, a psychiatrist interviewing nearly a hundred airplane hijackers in the late 1960s and early 1970s, described taking over an airplane as a holy experience. "The skyjackers," he once wrote, "seemed intent to stand on their own feet, to be men, to face their God, and to arise from this planet to the other more pleasing place." To date, hundreds of skyjackers and terrorists have taken over airplanes. Only one remains unknown.

Shit. Porteous and Lyle Christiansen are on to something. The Cooper case is a big deal. Uncovering the identity of the hijacker is a major story (Pulitzer, hello!), and it's mine so long as I don't mess it up. Of course, I'll have to prove Lyle's brother was actually the hijacker. How hard could that be?

Back at my office after lunch, I call Porteous. I want to read the file he's put together on Lyle's brother. I want to see it fast, before Porteous decides to call another reporter. As a general rule, PI's can get giddy over the prospect of publicity. Breaking the Cooper case would make

Porteous the most famous PI in America. At least that's what he must be thinking. That's what I'm thinking.

I race over to Sherlock headquarters. The office doubles as Porteous's one-bedroom co-op apartment on the Upper West Side. He opens the door and the classical piano music noodling away on the stereo oozes out. The place is like a zen palace for gumshoes.

I sit down at the dining room table. Porteous slides me the file. I pull out a few papers. One is a photo. The image is of a gravesite, for Lyle's brother. I read the name.

KENNETH P. CHRISTIANSEN
TEC 5 US ARMY
WORLD WAR II
OCT 17 1926–JUL 30 1994

So Lyle's brother's name was Kenny. I wonder what he died from.

Cancer, Porteous says. The pancreas. That's what Lyle told him.

I read Kenny's military record.

PARACHUTIST'S BADGE, ASIATIC PACIFIC THEATER.

So it was true. Kenny knew about parachutes. He could have jumped out of that plane just like D.B. Cooper had.

I pull another photo. In this one, Kenny is in uniform. He wears a skinny tie with a clasp. He is standing in the aisle of an airplane.

Kenny worked for Northwest, the airline Cooper hijacked, Porteous says. He wasn't a flight attendant. He was a purser. A purser is a senior flight attendant who handles the money and immigration issues on international flights.

In the photo, I can see Kenny is grinning. Or is it a smirk? It looks as if Kenny knows something—a secret he is keeping. Kenny, what is it? Why the smirk? What is your secret?

Porteous hands me a sketch of the hijacker.

I place the image next to Kenny's face. Time to compare.

Whoa. Porteous is right. The resemblance is spooky.

"Oh, I think it's him," Sherry Hart says. Porteous's ace is typing away at a computer terminal next to the kitchen.

If Hart's femme instincts are so good, what is she sensing?

"Oh, coincidences lining up," she says.

I'm not convinced. But I'm getting there.

I flip back to Kenny's military records. In the far corner of one form I see his thumbprint, taken May 25, 1944, when he enlisted. I place my own thumb on it. I close my eyes. I imagine what Kenny's hands must have felt like. I imagine my own thumbprint on his—to summon a feeling, an out-of-body clue that would tell me if Lyle's brother was indeed D. B. Cooper.

I feel something. Really. I swear. *Kenny?*

Or do I feel anything? Am I trying too hard and making it all up?

I look at another paper in Porteous's file. 18406 OLD SUMNER BUCK-LEY HIGHWAY, BONNEY LAKE, WASHINGTON. That's Kenny's address.

Where's Bonney Lake?

"About forty miles from Seattle," Porteous says. He's seen the town on Google maps. He's also noticed that Bonney Lake is strategically located. It's only twenty miles away from SEA-TAC, the airport where the Cooper hijacking took place. The authorities suspected Cooper was familiar with airlines and the area.

Coincidences, as Hart said, are lining up.

Do I have a choice? I have to fly West. I have to go to Kenny's old house, feel around for more spirits, knock on the doors of his neighbors, find old friends, colleagues from Northwest. I write to Lyle for more information about his brother. I want to know him as Lyle did. I want to understand the way his mind worked. I drop all assignments. I do more research on the case. I read several books, newspaper clips. Soon I am leaving for the airport and now I am on the plane and I can't get the ballad out of my head. I can hear guitar strings. I hum along to the chords.

With your pleasant smile
And your dropout style,
D.B. Cooper, where did you go?

I know exactly where: 18406 Old Sumner Buckley Highway.

November 24, 1971
Portland International Airport, Oregon

She is a specimen of red. Red lipstick. Red nail polish. Red uniform. It is not a candy apple red or a fire truck red, but the coral red you find on a necklace. Red is a central component of the "new look" campaign Northwest Orient Airlines launched the previous year. The makeover means new menus, mottos, ticket jackets, logos, and lots of red. Blue is out. Blue is conservatism and depression. And red? Red is passion, strength, arrogance.

Flo Schaffner hates Northwest's new-look uniforms, designed by Christian Dior. She has to wear the Carnaby Street cap with a duck bill and ear flaps. The dress and jacket ensemble are too mod. All the straight lines make her look fat. She feels like Elmer Fudd.

Now she stands on the top of the aftstairs, and cold wind off the tarmac blows through the silk of her stockings and into the maw of the cabin. She looks out and sees the last passengers for the 305 flight. Huddled in their coats, they had been waiting at Gate 52, Concourse L. Now they are on the tarmac in Portland, lining up to board under the giant red fin of the Northwest Orient jet. Above them are clouds that are dark and heavy with rain. Heavy storms are predicted for the next few days.

The first passenger in line walks up the stairs.

Flo meets him. Two years working for Northwest, her lines are automatic.

"Hi. Welcome aboard. Can I check your ticket?"

She reads the name on the boarding pass. Finegold, Larry.

He has frizzy hair, chunky eyeglasses. He does not look like a federal prosecutor. He spent the day in Vancouver, Washington, on the border of Oregon, to watch his colleagues prosecute the mayor of San Francisco on corruption charges. Finegold needs to get home. He and his wife, Sharon, have an event at their synagogue later in the night.

Finegold is nervous about the flight. Only two months before, the same type of plane, a Boeing 727, disappeared. Preparing for a descent into Juneau, the navigational system on the Alaska Airlines jet malfunctioned. The pilots and passengers were never heard from again.

"It apparently crashed into a sheer wall of mountain," an airline official said.

The Alaska Airlines crash was the worst airline accident to date in the country's history: 111 fatalities. Officials still haven't figured out what mechanical failures caused the crash of such a big plane. Flight computers can't be trusted. Or pilots. Or passengers.

The fear of flying is pervasive. To ease nerves, passengers on morning flights drink breakfast martinis with their cornflakes. Others use hypnotists or take tranquilizers before boarding. A group of psychologists recently started the Fly Without Fear Club, whose members are so petrified of airplanes they can't look at them on the ground. The underlying causes of the fear, psychologists say, are feelings of claustrophobia, a lack of control, a fear of achievement. "There you are, up there, strapped in, trussed up, unable to affect your own destiny in any way," one passenger told the *New York Times*. "If the plane goes down, so do you. What a perfect place for God to get you."

To quell the nerves of passengers, airlines invest in advertising campaigns. "Hey there! You with the sweaty palms," read the copy for a Pacific Air Lines ad. "Deep down inside, every time that big plane lifts off the runway, you wonder if this is it, right? You want to know something, fella? So does the pilot, deep down inside." At Northwest Orient, one early idea was to stage a photo with a group of Crow Indians. In front of a Northwest plane, the Indians wore headdresses and moccasins and posed for the camera stone-faced and bare-chested. "If the Indians aren't afraid of the white man's bird, nobody else should be," a Northwest pilot said.

The ads weren't enough to put passengers at ease. Stewardesses are the new panacea; they've become sex objects, redirecting passengers' fears. At Southwest, the stews wear white leather boots with porn-star laces and tangerine hot pants.

For Braniff, Italian printmaker Emilio Pucci designed the Air Strip, uniforms that come off during the flight. "Introducing the Air Strip," the Braniff ads read.

> *When she boards our airplane, she*
>   *Zip*
>   *sheds these outer garments to greet you in a raspberry suit and color-coordinated shoes. This ensemble is too expensive to risk soiling during dinner, so at the appropriate moment, she*
>   *Zip*
>   *Snap*
>   *Zip*
>   *changes into a lovely serving dress which we call a Puccino (named for its creator, Emilio Pucci, who believes that even an airline hostess should look like a girl).*

Braniff stews were then nicknamed "Pucci Galores" after the Bond girl in *Goldfinger*. At United, the ads are generous: *"Every passenger gets warmth, friendliness and extra care. And someone may get a wife."* At American, ads boast that the airline's stews are marriage material. *"A girl who can smile for five hours is hard to find,"* the brochure says, *"not to mention a wife who can remember what 124 people want for dinner."* At National, the pleasing spirit has been taken to the next level. Last month, the airline spent nearly $10 million on this Madison Avenue campaign: *"I'm Cheryl. Fly me."*

National's stews also appear in their airline's television commercials. They stare lustily into the camera as they deliver their punch line: *"I'm going to fly you like you've never been flown before."*

To boycott National, protesters have formed picket lines in Washington, D.C., and New York. Women's libbers are filing papers in court and demanding judges ban the Fly Me ad campaign. On the streets they march behind barricades.

"Go Fly Yourself, National," their pickets read.

At Northwest, petitions are going around for the stews to sign. The flight attendants want to unionize. Flo hasn't signed them. She's happy to have her job, after what she's been through.

"Hi. Welcome aboard. Can I check your ticket?"

Kurata, George. A steel importer from Japan.

Next in line. Zrim Spreckel, Cord. He runs a printing company in Seattle.

Flo checks more boarding passes. Her head itches. It's her wig. The bob is brunette and shaped like a space helmet.

Next passenger. Pollart, Les. Big feller. Could have been a tackle. He owns a trucking company. Next: Labissoniere, George. Pollart's lawyer.

"Hi. Welcome aboard. . . ."

The wig. Flo needs it. She never has time to do her hair before flights. She keeps it long and black, like Cher. Cher is number one on the charts. Flo knows the lyrics to her songs.

I was born in the wagon of a travelin' show . . .

Flo knows a bit about fame herself. She won several beauty prizes as a child. She was voted Miss Pink Tomato, Miss Swimming Pool, Miss Fordyce. Freshman year she made Redbug varsity cheerleading. She barked out the letters so loud—*Gimme an R! Gimme an E!*—she could barely speak the next day. It was cadet-style cheering: lots of straight arms and snaps of the black and red pom-poms.

Fordyce is the name of the town where she grew up. It is a speck on the Arkansas map, located on the way to New Orleans. It was too small for her. After high school, she wanted to go to the most exotic place she could think of. Tahiti. She wanted to stick her feet in the black-sand beaches and learn the hula dance.

She applied for work at eleven airlines. Her pa drove her to Little Rock and to Nashville for interviews and told her not to worry, Flo, this was the one, he could feel it. She got the same letter back eleven times: "Dear Miss Schaffner, We are sorry to inform you that . . ."

Flipping through *Glamour* magazine, Flo saw an ad for a flight training school in St. Paul. She enrolled. It felt like the military. There was a giant pool and she had to dive in the water and save dummy passengers. She was given instructions on beauty. How to apply foundation, how to sit, how to talk. Guidelines for stews had been printed in manuals.

1. *Be a good, sincere listener. Ask leading questions and show interest in conversation. This allows the passenger the feeling of importance.*
2. *Avoid talking about yourself and encourage passengers to talk about themselves. This procedure will make their trip pleasant.*
3. *Avoid argumentation. The aim of Stewardess work is to please passengers. Argument creates opposition and disgust and will not please, therefore defeating the aim of Stewardess work.*

The airlines were not the Great Escape she imagined. It was a cruel and lonely journey without a destination. To pass time, she ate. Doughnuts disappeared by the glazed dozen. Empty buckets of chicken and pizza boxes stacked up by the garbage. Flo tried to disguise the weight by wearing her serving apron, but her bulging hips bumped passengers in the aisles. On the way to Fargo, she was caught.

Spotters. Flo was called into the Northwest management office and told to step on their scale. This time she shocked herself: *185 pounds!* Northwest placed her on unpaid probation. She went to a doctor who prescribed diet pills. The pills made the pangs of hunger disappear. She starved herself and got her job back.

Next passenger. Mitchell, Bill. University of Oregon sophomore. He wears a paisley shirt, shows his ticket, and sits in 18B. It is the last row of the jet, port side, middle seat. Mitchell is looking forward to Thanksgiving weekend. His old friends will be back home in Seattle, and they will all party by the lake like they did in high school. He looks over the rows of seats in the cabin. The flight is half-full. He notices her immediately.

Tina Mucklow is the youngest stewardess on the crew. She has simple looks. Her blond hair is not shaped or sprayed or styled. It is long and clumped together into a ponytail. The ribbon holding it together is as basic as the string on a bakery box.

Mitchell wonders about her. Maybe she is as lonely as she looks or as lonely as he wants her to be. She is standing in the galley now, preparing the drink cart. What will he say to her when she passes? The flight to Seattle is only twenty-eight minutes long.

※

"Hi. Welcome aboard."

Flo looks at the name on the ticket.

Cooper, Dan. His suit is dark and his raincoat is black. He is holding a dark attaché case. He shuffles into the cabin and sits in the last row, 18, starboard side. The row is empty. He places the attaché case on the seat next to the window. He keeps his raincoat on.

"Hi. Welcome aboard."

Gregory, Robert. The passenger is out of breath. He ran to catch the flight, almost missed it. He sits across from Cooper in 18C, aisle seat, port side. Gregory is the last passenger to board. He is part owner of a paint company in Seattle.

The engines turn. The captain is speaking over the intercom.

"Uh, ladies and gentlemen . . ."

Flo pulls the lever, and the aftstairs bend and creak and tuck themselves into the fuselage. Located in the rear of the plane, these stairs are a signature feature on the Stubby, as the Northwest stews call the Boeing 727. Pilots do not require a boarding gate or airway to load passengers. They don't even need an airport. Passengers can board or deplane directly onto the tarmac. The aftstairs run on a simple hydraulic system. Pull the lever inside the jet, the stairs descend. A pull in the other direction, the aftstairs retract. The engines on the Stubby are so powerful and the design so nimble, stewardesses joke they'll land behind every tree to pick up passengers.

The model is popular with airlines. The aftstairs allow the 727 to land in small and mid-size cities that have not yet upgraded their airports. Or in jungle fields. In the mid-1960s, the Central Intelligence

Agency relied on Stubbies to conduct secret missions over Laos. Through CIA front groups like Air America Inc., the aftstairs were used by operatives to drop cargo. "Soft rice" was food. "Hard rice" was arms. It wasn't only gear. The CIA also used the Stubby to deploy American operatives who parachuted off the aftstairs and down into the jungles of Indochina.

He looks at Flo. She is ready to take Dan Cooper's drink order. What will it be?

"Bourbon and Seven-Up," he says.

The price is a dollar. He hands her a twenty.

"Anything smaller?"

"Nope."

"Well, I can't give you change until I finish," she says.

She moves up the aisle. In row 12, Pollart, the trucking company owner, is talking with his lawyer, Labissoniere. The trucking business is suffering in the recession. Pollart is now using his refrigerated trucks to ship blood. The samples come from the junkies at the Seattle missions, who sell their blood for drug money.

Pollart feels a lurch. The wheels of Northwest 305 are moving. He hears a stewardess's voice. It's Alice Hancock, the flight attendant in first class.

"All carry-on baggage must be stowed under the seat or in the overhead compartments," she says. "Please check your seatbelts in preparation for takeoff."

At five two, Alice Hancock barely passed Northwest's height requirement. Her hair is chestnut and bobbed. You look like Mrs. Spock, her friends tell her. She has soft eyes and speaks in a voice that is playful and light and trails into a honey-dipped giggle.

She recently got engaged. Jim, her husband-to-be, is a Northwest pilot. He is also flying to Seattle, on another flight. Thanksgiving dinner will be at Jim's uncle's house in Seattle. The uncle has a hothouse. He raises orchids. Alice is eager to see them.

She goes through the preflight announcements. Flo is done serving drinks. She stands next to Alice and inhales and exhales into a dummy oxygen mask. The captain is on the intercom again.

"Uh, we've been cleared to taxi, so if the cabin attendants will take their seats, we'll be on our way."

A front is moving in. The reports are calling for sleet, fog, snow, and rain. Some Thanksgiving, the pilots think. At least for now, the weather is clear. The sun has come out from the clouds and casts a beam of light against the aluminum belly of the jet and N467US, its registration number.

Inside the cockpit, Capt. William Scott and copilot Bill Rataczak go over the takeoff checklist once again.

"Window heat?"

"High."

"Pitot heat?"

"On, checked."

Flight 305 is a milk run. The route made Northwest Orient. When the airlines were controlled by the post office, the route across the empty northern lands of the country was barren and dangerous. Planes just disappeared. Flying through mountain crevices, with gusts of freezing wind sweeping down off the plains of Canada, Northwest pilots proved (with the navigational help of a sheep herder and Amelia Earhart) that a direct route from Minneapolis to the Pacific Northwest was safe. Now, decades later, the airline flies to Seattle across the northern Midwest each day.

This morning, the first stop was Great Falls, South Dakota, then Missoula, Montana, then Spokane, in eastern Washington, then over the Cascades to Portland. The last leg is Portland to Seattle.

Harold Anderson, flight engineer, monitors the wall of instruments behind the pilots as they prepare for their final takeoff. Other than talking about sports, the custom of most airline pilots is to stash a *Playboy* magazine in the cockpit. Miss October 1971 has filled her cleavage with beads and draped her torso in a tasseled buckskin bikini. Miss November 1971 is kneeling on a bear rug, her skin as white as the snow piled up in the ski cabin window behind her. She has doll lashes, and between her legs, draped from her belly just so, dangles a red scarf.

NAME: Danielle De Vabre, 36,25,34, Montreal, Quebec.
AMBITIONS: To become an airline stewardess.
IDEAL MAN: Age does not matter, as long as he has character.

Northwest Capt. William Scott has character. He has brown and gray-flecked hair and combs it full. His cheeks are jowly and smooth. Everyone calls him Scotty, even his kids.

Up close, the captain's body tells the stories he won't. He's missing his ring finger. He was working in his garage when his band saw snagged onto his wedding ring and lopped the finger off. Some muscles and ligaments never healed. His middle finger went so stiff he can't move it. Even when he's sleeping, Scotty looks like he's flipping people off.

Like many of Northwest's senior airline pilots, Scotty learned to fly during the war. He was assigned the least desirable route. The Hump, historians called his mission. Operation Vomit, the pilots called it.

In Allied freighters, Scotty and other Hump pilots lugged cargo over the Himalayas to the Chinese. In the mountain labyrinths, gusts of wind would blow the freighter planes into rock walls. Temperatures in the cockpit dropped to forty below. The navigation systems on the planes were so poor that pilots drew their own maps. The best way to get to China through the Himalayas, Hump pilots said, was to follow the glimmer of airplane wreckage below. Down in the valleys, the charred parts of Allied planes were used by nomads as shrines.

Coolies, laborers hired by the Chinese army, believed the wind from the propellers of the huge American cargo planes had magical powers. To rid themselves of evil spirits, they planted their faces in front of the giant engines, and many were fatally sucked in.

Scotty's base was in Assam, India. He slept in a *basha,* or bamboo hut, and kept a panther as a pet.

Supplies ran thin, especially during monsoon season. Electric wires doubled as shoelaces. Shoelaces doubled as hat straps. Pilots hunted for wild pigs and cooked the carcasses on makeshift spits.

Scotty doesn't talk about India. He is quiet and reserved, rarely speaks at the dinner table. Says what needs to be said. That's all.

His kids would like him to say more. A few weeks ago, Scotty's daughter Catherine asked him to come to her high school. Catherine wanted Scotty to talk about what it was like to be a Northwest Orient captain, but she worried. She knew Scotty did not like to speak in public. Would he clam up and bore her friends?

Scotty arrived in his Northwest uniform and cap. He waited for the questions.

"Ever been hijacked?" a student asked him.

"Ah, never," Scotty said.

The wheels of the jet are moving across the tarmac. In first class, Alice takes her seat near the front door. In the rear, Flo and Tina sit next to each other and wait for a month of flying and living together to finally be over.

The tension started their first night in the hotel room. Flo was getting ready for bed. Tina asked her a question.

"Are you a Christian?"

Flo was taken aback. Where were they, church? Flo also noticed that Tina carried a Bible with her in the hotel and on flights. Tina would say things to her like, "Have you been saved?" Tina also spoke to passengers about Christianity, Flo noticed. Was Tina some kind of undercover missionary? Was she deployed by the Church to cleanse the airlines of sin?

Twenty-eight minutes to Seattle . . . Twenty-eight minutes to Thanksgiving vacation. Soon Flo will be in the hotel room, and the hot scalding water of the shower will massage her itchy scalp. By this time tomorrow, Flo will have flown back to Arkansas to reunite with her ma and pa in Fordyce. After Thanksgiving dinner, she will cruise to the Dixie Dog with her old friends.

"Miss?"

A man is talking to her. She looks up. It is the same man who ordered a bourbon and Seven. He is holding a white envelope in his hands. Flo takes the envelope and drops it into the pit of her purse. She'll look at the love note later. Or never.

The jet moves faster along the runway. The fuselage shudders. Northwest 305 will be in the air any moment.

"Miss?"

Him again. Mr. Bourbon and Seven.

"I think you better have a look at that note."

She reaches into her purse. She retrieves the envelope.

The Northwest jet barrels down the runway. Seventy knots. Eighty knots.

In the cabin behind the pilots, passengers cross themselves and close their eyes. Some grip the armrests bracing for liftoff, hoping the jet doesn't explode.

Flo opens the note. She can see the words are written on a thick piece of paper. The ink is black. The words look printed by a felt-tip pen. She can see the curls of the letters—neat, crisp. The words are pretty to look at. Is this man an artist? She looks into his eyes. She reads the words again.

> *MISS,*
> *I have a bomb here and I would like you to sit by me.*

August 25, 2007
New York, New York

His eyes are not dark and demonic. They are soft and compassionate. Sad. No, tragic. They are the eyes of a loner, a man on the lam from his own secrets.

I have compiled my own dossier on Kenny Christiansen. I've spoken and written to his brother Lyle every day for the past month or so, and now I have my own collection of Christiansen family photos.

Here Kenny is, maybe eight years old, curling up to a cat and gazing into its eyes and petting its fur. Here in black and white is the family farmhouse outside of Morris where Kenny and Lyle grew up, and around it there is snow and barren flatlands. Here, another black and white: Kenny in his Northwest Orient uniform, wearing a captain's hat as if he is the pilot. His legs are short and his arms are long and dangle below his waist. Here is his passport photo. He wears a crew-knit sweater like a high school social studies teacher. And here, in color, is the front door of 18406 Old Sumner Buckley Highway. It's a small house, slightly larger than a trailer. Its country door is painted blood red, and above it is an American eagle clutching a quiver of arrows in its talons. One panel in the front door is missing. In its place is a black, medieval-looking grate. That way, Kenny could see who was at his door without opening it. It's creepy.

I look at more photos. I look into his eyes again. They appear darker now. Did I miss something before? I must have, because behind the sadness, especially in his passport photo, I now see a quirk.

Lyle told me about growing up on the farm outside of Morris. Kenny was second oldest. Lyle was youngest. Their pa was always frustrated with Kenny. He was not good at farmwork, at least not as good as their older brother Oliver. When they were boys, the Dust Bowl of the Great Depression hit. Grain prices collapsed.

"Our folks were so busy," Lyle wrote me. "Pa in the field and Ma, cooking, sewing, washing clothes. All of us kids did not get lots of hugs . . . I think it made us all a little bashful and made us long for the hugs."

To entertain them, their pa built toys. One invention he called the Perpetual Motion Machine. It ran on marbles. The weight of the marbles pushed the others through and kept the wheels of the machine spinning. Kenny spent hours in the attic marveling at how the machine worked. Kenny's mind was like a puzzle, always hunting for the missing piece, always looking for the answer.

As boys, they were also taught to be tough. At the county fair, one attraction was the strong-man competition. Last a round with a prize-fighter, collect $100. Their pa took that challenge, stepped in the ring, and came home with five $20 bills.

Kenny didn't like to fight. His passion was theater. He was the lead in school plays. He and their sister Lyla developed their own acrobatic act and performed at the county fair. Kenny also tap-danced.

"He could really snap those shoes around," Lyle told me.

Kenny received several scholarships for college, but had to postpone his journalism degree. In the spring of 1944, as the Allied troops prepared for the D-Day invasion at Normandy, Kenny enlisted in the Army. For basic training, he was sent to Fort Leavenworth, Kansas. Here, he joined the Paratroops. It was a prestigious detail, an elite fraternity of aerial invaders. Training was arduous. By the time he strapped on his harness and gear—rear chute, front (or reserve) chute, crash helmet, canteen, cartridge belt, compass, gloves, flares, message book, hand grenades, machete, M-1 Garand rifle, .45 caliber Colt, radio batteries, wire cutters, rations, shaving kit, instant coffee, bouillon cubes, candy— he could barely walk. The load weighed nearly a hundred pounds. His fellow Paratroops had to push him onboard.

Kenny was 11th Airborne Division, the Angels. He trained for parachute jumps over jungles and jungle warfare. The Angels were fighting in the Philippines. When he arrived overseas, the war was over. On base, Kenny worked as a mail clerk. For extra money, he volunteered for parachute jumps. He wrote about them in letters he sent home.

> *I went to church this morning. I went last Sunday also, but I had more reason to go, as after ten months of hibernation I once again donned a chute and reserve and entered a C-46.*

I looked up C-46. It was a massive military transport plane. Curtiss Calamity, troops called it. Kenny and twenty-nine other Paratroops jumped out the side door.

> *I cringed a good deal but I managed once again to pitch myself into the blast. That jump was worth $150. The nicest thing about this whole affair was that I never had time to worry about it. . . . I had only an hour to get into my harness. The first thing I knew I had jumped and was on my way back to the trucks that were to carry us into camp. Don't get the idea that I didn't get that certain stomachless feeling, because I did.*

He spent a week on vacation in Numazo, an ancient Japanese city known for its hot springs.

> *I lived in a hotel, which sat only about fifty yards from the shore. I spent most of my time up on the roof during the day; nights I usually lounged in a beach chair down by the water's edge. They had a group of Hawaiian guitar players down there. With the music, the breeze off the ocean, and the waves crashing the shore, I felt like a millionaire enjoying his millions.*

Every time I read the letter, I get stuck on that line. *Like a millionaire enjoying his millions.*

More coincidences lining up. Not only did Kenny know how to parachute, like Cooper did, Kenny did it for money, like Cooper did. Maybe his request of $200,000 was an echo of the $150 he made from the military during his test jump? I wondered how much $200,000 was worth in the fall of 1971. It didn't sound like much. I punched the numbers into a historic currency calculator. The return: $1,080,054.

Like a millionaire enjoying his millions.

Throughout his life, Kenny was not a heavy earner. He was a gutsy laborer, willing to work dangerous jobs that paid a few dollars more an hour. He was also restless, aimless, as if trying to escape. But from what?

After the war, Kenny went on the road and sold encyclopedias for the Continental Sales Corp. He also worked the ticket booth at Charley Dobson's circus in Minnesota. In 1949, he was hired by Northwest Orient and sent to work on Shemya.

Schmoo—that's what Northwest employees called the island. Living here was like living on the moon. Located on the far tip of the Aleutian Islands, a few hundred miles off the coast of Russia, Schmoo was a pit stop for Allied planes that needed to refuel in the Northern Pacific. The island was small and lonely and flat. The winds were vicious and cold. After the war, Schmoo became a garbage heap for the U.S. military. It was cheaper for Allied forces to dump surplus from the war here than transport it back home. The beach was littered with rusted-out tanks and old bullets.

On the island, Kenny was a grunt. He cleaned airplanes and dumped the toilets. He also drove a bus that carried Northwest stewardesses and pilots to Quonset huts, which were used as sleeping quarters.

Kenny worked on Schmoo for five years. Somehow, he then managed to find even more isolating work. In the summer of 1955, he left for Bikini, a remote island in the South Pacific.

The government was testing hydrogen bombs on Bikini. Villagers had lost their hair. The radiation caused vomiting, diarrhea. Women could not get pregnant. Layers of ash covered the houses and turned the drinking water yellow. During testing, villagers saw two suns as bombs exploded in the sky. Debris turned the afternoon black. Kenny worked here as a telephone operator.

He was then rehired by Northwest as a flight attendant and for the next three decades as a purser. He kept to himself, a ghost in the cabin of Northwest planes.

Through the union, I found pursers who worked with Kenny. "He was almost invisible," Harry Honda told me. "If you asked somebody on his plane who was the purser on that flight, they couldn't tell you, that's how quiet this guy was." Lyle Gehring flew with Kenny, too. "You ask people and say 'Ken Christiansen' and they'll say, 'Who?'"

When Kenny was diagnosed with cancer, in 1991, his family suspected the source was the radiation he suffered on Bikini Island. When his condition deteriorated, he retired from Northwest. Kenny was so sick he asked his family to spend his last days with him in Bonney Lake. One day, in the hospital, his eyes weak and his lips dry, Kenny motioned to his young brother.

Lyle rushed to Kenny's bedside.

"There's something you should know," Kenny said. "But I can't tell you!"

"I don't care what it is," Lyle said. "You don't have to tell me about it. We all love you."

Now, almost two decades later, Lyle has been ruminating about what Kenny said on his deathbed. Was he about to confess to the Cooper hijacking? Did Lyle deny his brother a chance to clear his conscience? What was Kenny trying to tell him? What was his secret?

November 24, 1971
Aboard Northwest Orient Flight 305

The jet banks and climbs. In first class, passenger Floyd Kloepfer, an electronics specialist, pushes his nose against the window and looks down at the Columbia River. Explorers Lewis and Clark paddled through here in canoes, marveling in journals about Native American women wading in the waters, wearing only "a truss or pece [sic] of leather tied around them at the hips and drawn tite [sic] between their legs."

Across the border into Washington the elevation changes. The sandy river banks of the Columbia turn into a storybook forest with trees as tall as buildings. These forests are where the nation's logging industry was based, where miners searched for gold, where Bigfoot lives. One remote area is called the Dark Divide. Outside of Alaska, the Dark Divide is the largest stretch of uninhabited land in the country. There are no street signs, no roads. Backpackers and hikers disappear trying to find a way out. The land is so dense and untouched it is said to possess a brain of its own.

Kloepfer now watches the Columbia River shrink into a stream. He looks at the dark clouds and worries about the weather. Tonight he and his wife are driving to her folks' place across the border in Canada. In the slushy rain, it will be a long drive in his Plymouth Fury.

Some Thanksgiving, he thinks.

The passenger next to him is drunk. The guy's been drinking whiskey since South Dakota. Kloepfer looks over the seat behind him and finds the sergeant he was talking to earlier. The sergeant is in uniform. He is coming home from Vietnam. He will be spending Thanksgiving with his family, the first time since he shipped out.

The sergeant is not alone. All throughout the fall, soldiers have been lingering in airports and bus stations. Two weeks ago, President Nixon promised that an additional 45,000 American troops stationed in Vietnam would be coming home, too. The promise would be a blessing, except that troops are not the same when they return. Roughly a third of American soldiers in Vietnam are addicted to heroin. The antiwar sentiment is so strong, the soldiers have also become targets for loud-mouths and longhairs. What are they fighting for, anyway?

Troops are refusing orders, turning on their commanders. In 1970, there were at least 109 reports of fragging, incidents where soldiers killed officers. Others refused to enter Laos, and scribbled antiwar sentiments onto their combat helmets. "The unwilling, led by the unqualified, doing the unnecessary, for the ungrateful."

The body counts in Vietnam are staggering—almost 60,000 dead, more than 150,000 wounded. Only months before, details of the Pentagon's covert bombings in Laos and Cambodia were leaked to the *New York Times*. In Congress, legislators read the so-called Pentagon Papers into the public record to ensure the Nixon White House could not cover up the scandal. Anyone with access to a newspaper or a television set now has proof: their government is lying to them about Vietnam. How many other lies are there?

"I'll say modestly that our country will be gone very shortly," H. L. Hunt, the San Francisco oil magnate, said earlier in the week. "The communists are much smarter than freedom-loving people. America doesn't want to do anything else except make a profit."

Even the weather in 1971 seems to contribute to a feeling of looming Armageddon. In the South, fifty tornadoes blew through towns and cities in one week, leaving one hundred dead. Los Angeles was rocked with its biggest earthquake in four decades, leaving sixty-five dead.

A mob has been forming. In Detroit, the city zoo had to hire extra security guards because animals were getting attacked. A baby wallaby was stoned to death. A duck was shot with a steel-tipped arrow. Firecrackers were thrown at a pregnant reindeer. A hippopotamus was found with a tennis ball stuffed down his throat.

Cops are getting killed. In Syracuse, the police chief complained that black teenagers were using cars to conduct "guerrilla-type warfare" against his officers via "hit and run." During the first nine months of the year, ninety-one cops were reported to have been killed on the job.

The war—cultural, political, generational—is raging. Throughout the year, the authorities reported 771 bomb threats in federal buildings. Over the summer, 200,000 protestors descended on the capital. In one day, 12,000 people were arrested. In Miami, anti-pollution activists shuttered a Pepsi bottling plant by pouring cement over a drainage pipe. In Chicago, college students and members of an activist group were arrested for plotting to poison the city's drinking water. Their plan: inoculate themselves, and create a superior race.

Prisons are overcrowded. Riots break out. In early September, in the upstate New York prison of Attica, inmates armed themselves with shanks, chains, broomsticks, baseball bats, and hammers. They seized the exercise yard. They burned the schoolhouse and chapel. They gagged prison guards at knifepoint, ordered them to strip naked and navigate a club-swinging gauntlet. Gas was released. Shots were fired. Inmates were stripped naked and beaten.

"The Attica tragedy is more stark proof that something is terribly wrong with America," said Maine senator Edward Muskie, who's campaigning for president. "We have reached the point where men would rather die than live another day in America."

To combat violent hippies and homegrown terrorists, a new conservatism has been born. Just this past September, a twelve-year-old boy called the police to turn in his own father for smoking pot.

"There is such a feeling of powerlessness in this country," said John Gardner, who resigned as the Secretary of Health, Education, and Welfare. "We all have the feeling that we want to complain to the manager, but the manager is invisible. Nobody knows who he is and where to find him."

The manager is President Nixon, who sounds most powerless of all. Over the summer he made a speech referring to the ornate federal buildings in Washington. He forecasted a gloomy future. "Sometimes when I see those columns I think of seeing Greece and Rome," he said. "And I think of what happened to Greece and Rome, and you see only what is left of great civilizations of the past—as they have become wealthy, as they lost their will to live, to improve, they became subject to the decadence that destroys the civilization. The United States is reaching that period."

The words. To her. Pay attention, Flo. Pay attention. The words glare at her as bright as lightbulbs.

I have a bomb. Sit by me.

He's kidding, right?

"No, miss. This is for real."

She gets up and sits in 18D next to him. She drops the note. It flutters to the floor.

"You're kidding, right?"

"No, miss."

He reaches over to the window seat and puts his fingers on his attaché case. He opens the mouth. She peers inside.

The sticks are red, about eight inches long. She sees a battery. It is bigger than a battery you might put in a flashlight.

He's teasing Flo now, holding in his fingers the naked copper tip of a wire in front of her. This *is* for real. She turns.

There's Tina.

Tina can see Flo's lips moving but the words are not coming out of her mouth. Flo gasps.

"Tina. *Tina.*"

Tina picks up the note near Flo's feet. She reads it. It's too late to turn back. The wheels are up. Flight 305 is already in the air.

Tina reaches for the interphone hanging outside the lavatory. The interphone is her direct line to the cockpit. She speaks into the receiver.

"We're being hijacked," she says. "He's got a bomb and this is no joke."

May 27, 1969
University Hospital, University of Washington, Seattle

"Nothing I do is phony," Bobby Dayton would say.

It was true. When he wanted to go on a hike to clear his mind, he left with his dog, Irish, and came back three weeks later. He prospected for gold in the Yukon and nearly died from starvation. In the Merchant Marines, traveling the world in the hulls of the big ships, he went hunting in the Philippines and lived among the Māori warriors, who were famous for their guerrilla battle tactics. Back on the boat, he was nearly shot for being a deserter. Bobby spent plenty of time in the brig.

He could be nasty, a savage. He'd punch you in the face if you looked at him wrong. He'd spit on your shoes to get a reaction, then slug you. Bobby talked about robbing banks because there was never any good work around, and he once rode with the Hells Angels as they terrorized the State of California. He never killed anybody, but he could have and almost did several times. Once in Mexico. Once in Seattle, where he lives. A taxicab driver cut him off. In the dispute, Bobby got out of his Dodge, removed a chain from the trunk, and beat the cabbie to within inches of his life.

✕

"Evidently, I'm a transsexual problem," Bobby tells his doctor before the surgery. "My wife tells me I'm two people. She tells me when I'm Bob I seem bitter, but when I'm Barbara I'm a much nicer person."

He is in the hospital for a psychological evaluation, which is necessary before sex change operations. He is wearing a long-sleeved blouse (to cover his tattoos) and high heels. There is lipstick on his cigarette.

The doctor studies his appearance and mannerisms. His teeth are in poor shape. His hands are rough. His speech is quiet and soft, and his gestures and hand movements are mildly effeminate.

The doctor asks what Bobby does for a living.

Until recently, Bobby was working on the Lockheed shipping yards, as an electrician. He was foreman to twenty men. It was uncomfortable for him to be in charge; men shouldn't take orders from women, he thought, and so he quit.

"I feel better away from people," Bobby says. "I feel they can see through me for what I am. I don't feel like the other men. I feel if I was a woman I could let myself go."

The doctor has a test for him, a game really. Free association, no wrong answers. The way it works is the doctor starts a sentence and Bobby finishes it.

The doctor starts.

"If I had ten thousand dollars . . ."

"I would buy myself an operation," Bobby says.

"If I were invisible . . ."

"I wouldn't do anything."

"If I were an animal I'd be . . ."

"Bird. I like birds and flying."

One early memory. Bobby is five. He wants to be Tinkerbell, from *Peter Pan*. She is trailed by magic dust. She can always fly away.

Even as a boy, looking in the mirror at his legs, which he thought were too shapely, Bobby thought he could see the woman inside him. He snuck into his mother's dresser and placed his hands among her bras and panties to feel the fabric. Alone in a room he tried them on. Later, he slept in them.

His dreams were of men on top of him, pushing themselves into him. Sometimes Bobby put the family dog on top of his groin. He told the dog to sit and imagined the weight of the dog was the weight of another man.

Another early memory. He can see the airfield in Long Beach. The planes have propellers, fins, and wings—just like birds. He can see them coming in for landings and can hear the scream of their engines. He watches them scurry around the taxiway. How can these aluminum contraptions manage to fly?

Bobby looks through the airport fence. An older man is cleaning his plane. Bobby shouts to the man through the fence.

"How about a ride?"

The man shakes his head.

The next day Bobby comes back. The next day too.

Finally the old man hands Bobby a rag and Bobby wipes down his plane. In exchange, Bobby gets his ride and discovers a purpose in life: to fly.

"I don't like being under someone else's control," Bobby says years later. "In my plane, I feel like I'm totally inside the sky, totally free."

During his psychiatric evaluation, the doctor asks Bobby to describe his employment history.

"I'm a job jumper," Bobby says.

He dropped out of high school and picked lemons with migrant workers for a quarter a day. He drove to Oregon to pick tomatoes and then found higher pay in the logging camps of the Pacific Northwest. When he was old enough he enrolled in the Air Force. He wanted to learn how to fly for free. But the exams required a background in mathematics. Doctors also noticed a problem with his eye. He didn't qualify for flight school.

He vowed revenge. He would not give the military the satisfaction of good service. He would be a terrible, incorrigible soldier. He joined the Merchant Marines.

On Merchant ships, Bobby wrote home from ports that were hard to pronounce, names he tattooed onto his arms and chest. Eniwetok, Alang Alang, Kara Gara, Barugo, Batangas, Cagayan, Agoo, Tabao. He was in the South Pacific. He was in South America. He swam in shark-infested waters. He hunted with natives.

He was a violent case. He drank fifths of bourbon in gulps to impress other sailors (then wandered off to vomit). He followed other sailors into brothels and forced himself to have sex with women. Anything to protect his secret. In the dead of night, under the moon and adrift in the ocean, Bobby would crawl out from his bunk and sneak toward the front of the ship, where he would slip on his dress and his heels.

"You can't live if you don't do it," Bobby tells his doctors about his cross-dressing. "It's like medicine."

After the Merchant Marines, Bobby changed jobs every month or so. He's had more than 150 over the years, he tells the doctor. He can fix cars, washing machines, vacuum cleaners. He was a mechanic at Ford, Bethlehem Steel, Continental Can. He worked at Yosemite National Park.

He knows how to plaster and cement too—just like his father, Elmer.

"I can do anything he can do," Bobby says about Elmer.

In the hospital, Cindy Dayton is interviewed about Bobby. Cindy is Bobby's second wife. If she felt Bobby was a woman, the doctor asks, why did she marry him?

"I'm not sure why I married him," Cindy says. "I wanted a husband and he seemed like a good provider. I like him as a person. He doesn't lie or swear."

Recently, Bobby tried to commit suicide, she says. For months they lived in Baltimore because Bobby was on the list for a sex change operation at Johns Hopkins. He was rejected. The doctors in Baltimore felt it would be too much of a challenge for Bobby to adapt in society as a woman. How could he pass with his bad teeth, his chain smoking, and his tattoos covering his body?

"I say he is a woman," Cindy says. "He thinks like a woman. . . . He's beautiful as a woman. He doesn't overdress or over-makeup. As a man, he's sloppy, and it's a little embarrassing."

November 24, 1971
Aboard Northwest Orient Flight 305

The jet is climbing. Ten thousand feet, fifteen thousand feet. In the cockpit, Scotty and copilot Bill Rataczak aren't sure how to respond. A bomb? Is it real? Does it matter?

In total, there are thirty-six passengers in the cabin, six crew members. As captain, Scotty is in charge. What to do?

Scotty radios Northwest Orient flight operations in Minnesota.

A man in the back says he has a bomb, Scotty says. He doesn't know who the man is or what he wants. Not yet.

"Take this down."

Flo Schaffner reaches into her purse and retrieves her pen. She can no longer see the man's eyes. He's put on sunglasses. The frames are dark. The lenses are brown.

"I want two hundred grand by five p.m., in cash," he says.

She writes down the words on the envelope he gave her.

"Put it in a knapsack," he says.

The pen scratches paper and the words she writes appear in a messy swirl of cursive. Anything else?

"I want two back parachutes and two front parachutes. . . . When we land, I want a fuel truck ready to refuel."

Anything else?

He wants meals for the flight crew, in case anyone gets hungry.

"No funny stuff, or I'll do the job."

She writes down those words, too.

"No fuss. After this we'll take a little trip."

"No fuss," she writes and her mind reels and her chest heaves. No, Flo, no, don't do this. Do NOT panic. The images of the airplane in the sky are easy to conjure. KABOOM! Smoldering debris bobbing in the water.

Charred bodies. She is a corpse. Her pa is getting calls in Fordyce . . . from the newspapermen . . . from the morgue. This isn't happening, Flo, this isn't happening. Focus on the details. No, no. Details are worse. Parachutes? What did he want parachutes for? Is he taking a hostage? Is that hostage her? A fuel truck? Where are they going? What is this "little trip"?

The word flashes in her mind. RAPE.

How would she know how to pull the parachute cord? Would he pull the cord for her? They could parachute into a dark forest. He could steal her uniform and leave her there—with cougars, bears. She would have to run through the woods in bare feet and find a road. A pair of headlights would flash against her naked body, and she would have to scream out into the headlights, Stop, stop. Please stop.

"I have to go to the cockpit," she tells him

He does not want her to leave. That is his rule. *Sit by me.*

His rule does not make sense, she says. If he wants his demands met, she has to take the note to the captain, no?

Kneeling in the aisle, stewardess Tina Mucklow is eavesdropping on the conversation.

"Do you want me to take the note?" Tina says.

"No," he says.

Flo is pushy.

"I have to go to the cockpit," Flo tells him.

He thinks it over.

"All right. Go ahead."

"Do you want me to stay here?" Tina says.

He looks her over.

"Yes," he says.

Flo steps out of the seat and into the aisle and strains to walk toward the cockpit. The jet is still climbing. The gravitational pull forces her back toward the lavatory. She pushes off the armrests and propels herself forward. In first class she passes Alice. The first-class stew can see the fear on Flo's face. Alice looks back into the tourist cabin to see the hijacker. Tina, she can see, is sitting next to him. He is wearing sunglasses. Tina was right. This is no joke.

As the oldest stew, Alice has to do something. She wants Tina away from this man. She walks to her.

"Tina, can you help me find a deck of playing cards?"

Tina is not listening. Alice walks away. Is Tina in shock?

Inside the cockpit, the Northwest pilots hear the door open. Flo slips in. The envelope with the hijacker's instructions is in her hand.

"Did you get a good look at the bomb?"

"What was in the briefcase?"

"Red sticks," she says.

"Dynamite?"

"They looked like dynamite."

"What else?"

"Lots of wires, a battery."

Copilot Rataczak reads the hijacker's note. He notices the fine lettering, the felt-tip pen. The hijacker could be a master criminal, he thinks. The pilots better play his game. No funny stuff.

Scotty reaches for his radio. He calls Northwest Flight Operations back in Minnesota. His words are recorded via Teletype.

PASSENGER HAS ADVISED THIS IS A HIJACKING. EN ROUTE TO SEATTLE. THE STEW HAS BEEN HANDED A NOTE. HE REQUESTS $200,000 IN A KNAPSACK BY 5:00 PM. HE WANTS TWO BACK PARACHUTES, TWO FRONT PARACHUTES. HE WANTS THE MONEY IN NEGOTIABLE AMERICAN CURRENCY. DENOMINATION OF THE BILLS IS NOT IMPORTANT. HAS BOMB IN BRIEFCASE AND WILL USE IT IF ANYTHING IS DONE TO BLOCK HIS REQUEST.

Dispatch is calling.

"PD 32, PD 32."

PD 32 is the number of Special Agent Ralph Himmelsbach's unmarked '68 Plymouth. He's driving back to the field office from Yaw's

Top Notch, a drive-in burger joint on the outskirts of Portland. He had a light lunch—grilled cheese, chased down with a glass of milk—because his wife is cooking a pre-Thanksgiving dinner and he needs to be home with a healthy appetite. There is tension in the marriage. Himmelsbach is never around, either working cases or flying his airplane. He suspects she is having an affair with her boss.

"164 in progress, Portland International."

In the Bureau, each crime has a code number. 164 is an airplane hijacking. Is it real or a prank?

"Verified," the dispatcher says. "Report to Northwest Airlines Operations Office."

Himmelsbach reaches for the radio.

"PD 32," he says. "Ten four."

He slams the brakes, banks into a U-turn, cuts off traffic, and heads toward the Portland airport. He places the sirens on the car roof. He wants to drive faster. Can't move. Traffic.

"Damn, this is a long light," he says.

Himmelsbach hates what Portland has become. His city has been sacked! From the East, the liberals have come from New York and Boston, purchasing property and running for office. From the South, the hippies come from Northern California. He can see them in bus stations begging for money or rides. The spoiled kids don't have the decency to cut their hair. The women don't shave under their arms. They do drugs and sell drugs. They don't believe in relationships. Only a short drive from Portland, a group of girls has built the first lesbian commune. The girls have rules. Monogamy is forbidden. Imagine that!

Ralph Himmelsbach can't. In the rearview mirror of his Bureau squad car, the agent's reflection is all straight lines. His jawline is sharp and angular. His Wyatt Earp mustache is full and trimmed. His eyebrows are hawklike, fitting for the hunter he is.

It is elk season and he could be hunting elk on a day like today. Elk can be invisible creatures. One of the best places to hunt them is in the eastern part of Washington, up in the Blue and Wallowa Mountains.

Himmelsbach and his brother, a district attorney there, set up camp in waist-high snow, crouch near the trees, look for tracks, and wait. But in ten years hunting them, Himmelsbach has never taken an elk.

"PD 32, PD 32."

Dispatch again.

"On the 164 . . . we've learned the suspect has an explosive device."

Himmelsbach leans on the horn. Bastards, let's move. The guy has a bomb!

Another one? Was this a copycat? Ten days ago, a Canadian man slipped on a mask, brandished a shotgun, and threatened to blow up an Air Canada flight with forty pounds of plastic explosives. The man, Paul Cini, told the flight crew he was a member of the Irish Republican Army (he wasn't) and wanted the plane rerouted to Ireland. He also demanded $1.5 million in cash. He couldn't make up his mind though. He wanted the pilots to refuel in Saskatchewan and then changed the location to Great Falls, Montana, where the governor negotiated a lower ransom of $50,000. On the ground in Great Falls, the hijacker listened to the news of his hijacking on the radio in real time, and in glee, passengers later reported, as if he had achieved his fifteen minutes of fame.

Cini then demanded the pilots fly him to New York. In the air, Cini then shocked the crew and passengers by stepping into the harness of a parachute. The plane was a DC-8, which like the Boeing 727 had aft-stairs that could be opened during flight.

Cini nearly made it. As he was planning to jump, according to news reports, the Air Canada purser on the flight "let him have it with a fire ax."

The story of Cini, who was rushed to the emergency room after the plane landed, was national news. Images of the bloodied hijacker, who was too foolish and deranged to execute his daring escape with $50,000, also ran on the national news.

Agent Himmelsbach cursed the media outlets for publishing them. Like bank robbers, Cini could inspire others to board planes with bombs and crazy demands, hold the passengers hostage, and attempt to make a getaway via parachute.

In Seattle, the Bureau field office is located in an old bank downtown, a few blocks from the piers off Alaskan Way. The boss, J. Earl Milnes, steps out of his office.

The first agent he sees is Bob Fuhrman, a recent transfer. Fuhrman is trained as an accountant. Hoover wants only lawyers and accountants to be G-men.

Milnes points a finger at Fuhrman. "You," he says. "Drive me to the airport."

Fuhrman follows Milnes out to an ummarked car and turns over the keys. The radio is on. Voices are on the frequency. What is the procedure for hijackings? Should the feds cooperate with the hijacker and give him $200,000 and parachutes? Should they storm the plane, take him out? Is it even their responsibility to make the decision?

The airlines and agencies are feuding over how to handle skyjackings. Who is in control? At the FAA, officials argue that it is the pilot who is responsible for the plane and its passengers. At the FBI, Hoover argues that once a plane lands, the hijacker has violated federal air piracy laws; therefore, he is within the Bureau's jurisdiction and should be apprehended immediately. It's too dangerous to think otherwise. What if the hijacker had a manic episode, killed the pilot, and crashed the plane into downtown Cleveland? Hundreds of bystanders would die in the explosion. Or worse. What if hijackers demanded that pilots fly airplanes into skyscrapers?

In New York, tenants have already moved into the North Tower of the World Trade Center. Construction on the South Tower is almost finished. With a hijacker at the controls, a domestic airplane becomes its own bomb. Thousands could die.

The jockeying over who controls a hijacked plane unfolded only weeks before on the front pages. A charter jet to the Bahamas was taken over by a man with a gun and a bomb.

Onboard, the flight crew could see the man was delusional. The captain begged Bureau agents to let them refuel. He felt that if the plane was back in the air, the armed hijacker would relax and nobody would get injured.

After landing in Florida to refuel, the request was denied. Agents fired gunshots at the plane's tires. The skyjacker panicked. He fatally shot the captain, his wife, then himself.

Hoover's lawyers raced into court to keep the transcriptions between the pilots and Bureau agents sealed. A federal judge tossed out the request. The transcript made national news.

Pilot: This is fifty-eight November. Uh, this gentleman has about 12.5 pounds of plastic explosives back here and, uh, I got no yen to join it right now so I would please . . . appreciate it if you would stay away from the airplane.

Tower: This is the FBI. There will be no fuel. Repeat. There will be no fuel.

Pilot: Uh, (gasp) look, I don't think this fellow's kiddin'—I wish you'd get that fuel truck out here.

Tower: Fifty-eight November. There will be no fuel. I repeat. There will be no fuel.

Pilot: This is fifty-eight November. You are endangering lives by doing this, and for the sake of some lives we request some fuel out here, please.

Skyjacking had a twisted history. Early on, passengers who hijacked planes wanted to flee Communist countries and come to America. The skyjack was a means of escape, and the United States welcomed political dissidents from Eastern Europe and later Cuba. By the late 1960s, the direction had turned.

Since the United States cut off ties with Fidel Castro and banished travel to Cuba in 1961, eighty airplanes had been successfully hijacked to Cuba. The frequency of hijackings to the island was so high, airline pilots began to carry approach maps for the Havana airport. "Take me to Cuba" became a catchphrase. One government plan was to build a replica of the Havana airport near Miami as a decoy to hijackers.

Around the world, an airplane was taken over once every week. In newspapers and on television, passengers reported live from the new war zone: airplane cabins. "We had no control," one passenger said after a grenade went off on an Ethiopian Air flight. "We were weaving all over. When that bomb took off I thought, *This is it.*" On a flight out of Sacramento: "I counted twenty-two shots. There was a pause and a man shouted, 'I'm shot.' The bullet went through the back of his seat and out his chest. The wound—it was as big as a fist. He said good-bye to his wife. She embraced him and said, 'God have mercy on him.'"

Struggling to keep their companies afloat during the recession, airline presidents don't want to spend millions to install magnetometers, or metal detectors, in airport terminals. Won't the devices be an inconvenience to their customers, most of whom are businessmen? Executives would cringe at having to walk through the detectors and have each bag checked for weapons and explosives. President Nixon, who counts several airline presidents among his supporters and contributors, does not want to force the airlines to comply with costly security mandates. Nixon prefers a voluntary approach, and has introduced the sky marshals, a new breed of armed undercover agents who travel on airplanes to deter hijackers. At the Federal Aviation Administration, officials have also developed a secret psychological profile of hijackers, and brief airport officials on what types of passengers to look for. As effective as the program is, it is left up to airline officials to screen passengers. Security is now a judgment call, and somewhere along the flight path of Northwest 305, a hijacker was allowed to board.

At Northwest Orient, the decisions on how to handle the hijacker—comply with his requests, or turn him down—go to the airline's president, Don Nyrop.

Nyrop. A bit to the left of Genghis Khan, one executive calls him. Nyrop is stubborn, abrasive, unpredictable, cheap, a brilliant administrator.

According to company legend, Nyrop popped into a hangar one afternoon to check on Northwest's mechanics. After inspecting the work, Nyrop used the hangar bathroom and heard the rustling of paper in the stall next to him. Reading a newspaper on company time! All men's bathroom doors in Northwest buildings were removed henceforth.

In turn, the thousands of Northwest stewardesses, pursers, mechanics, pilots, and ground crewmembers rob his planes blind. After flights, they steal toilet paper, booze, pillows, blankets, silverware. They went on strike last year over pay and working conditions. Picket lines formed. Nyrop wouldn't budge. President Nixon had to help negotiate a settlement. Nyrop's stinginess made him a hero to Northwest management and the company's stockholders. During the recession, other airlines tanked. Northwest Orient posted profits.

Nyrop's decision is swift. At the airport in Minnesota, Nyrop tells the feds he wants to comply with the hijacker. The airline has insurance. They will cover the $200,000 ransom. Now the feds in Seattle need to find parachutes.

Throughout Northwest's facilities, officials listen to the radio. In the hangar, mechanic John Rataczak, father of copilot Bill Rataczak, can hear his son's voice on the frequency. Who is the man in the back with a bomb? What if it detonates?

X

In the cockpit, the phone is ringing. It is Tina.

The hijacker is getting nervous, she says.

About what?

About the radio currents on the plane.

Why?

He thinks the radio currents might be too strong, she says. They could accidentally detonate the device he's packed in his briefcase.

Is he sure?

No.

On the radio, Scotty and Rataczak hear new voices. It's the feds.

"Do you know where he wants to go . . . ?"

"Negative. Have asked him once and so we don't want to ask him again. . . . Would suggest we wait and see where he wants to go."

"Can bring out the manuals to Alaska if you think so."

Outside the cockpit window, it is getting dark. The weather is changing. The storm should hit any minute.

"Approach, NW305, ah . . . a little rain up over here. We'd like to hold it at about . . . ah . . . turn back on the radio now and go out to about, oh, thirty would be a little better."

On the ground in Seattle, officials are concerned about the radio communications. Can the hijacker hear the conversation between the pilots and the authorities on the frequency?

"I don't know. I think it's free to call us. Nobody's giving us any trouble up here. He's in the back."

August 25, 1977
Hilton Airport Hotel, Atlanta, Georgia

It is her birthday. She sits at the bar alone. She wears a brown jumpsuit and a white handkerchief around her neck, wrapping herself up like a present. She is out of work. She has two children at home, and she has saved all week to splurge on a glass of champagne or two for herself. She thought about going to the Admiral Bimbo, but that airport bar is a meat market and she isn't with her girlfriend tonight. Besides, she isn't in the mood to be picked up anyway. So she drove here, to the Hilton. If she's going to celebrate, she might as well do it classy.

The bartender places a bucket of ice on a stand beside her. She looks inside the bucket. Inside is a bottle of champagne.

"From the gentleman," the bartender says.

The man is in a suit. He is sitting at the far corner of the bar, nursing his drink. He has dark eyeglasses and dark eyes.

She nods. She smiles. Wow. Champagne!

"I think you better look closer," the bartender says.

She looks. Wrapped around the neck of the perspiring bottle is a hundred-dollar bill.

The man in the suit gets up from his seat and walks toward her. She can see his suit is gray and wool, a sophisticated cut, not like the plaid flannel jackets her ex-husband wore. This suit is tailor-made.

He says his name is Duane, Duane Lorin Weber.

Her name is Josephine Collins. Call her Jo.

He is an older man, older than she is used to dating. She would never consider him as a suitor except that she is alone now and the pangs of emptiness have pierced her for months—*so alone!*—and she has two daughters to support and so what if the man in the nice suit is a little old.

He asks her what a woman like her is doing here by herself.

It's her birthday, she says.

He is celebrating too, he says.

She raises her glass of champagne. So, sir, what are you celebrating?
"Divorce," he says.

They talk for most of the night.

Before she started selling real estate, Jo was a Sunday school teacher. She was raised on the family farm in Kentucky. She learned the verses of the Bible and how to call a pig. She was the only child in her family to smoke and drink, even if it was only a few glasses of light wine.

He tells her how attractive she is. He walks her to her car, holds the door. He is a gentleman. Of course he can have her number and call her, she says.

Jo's parents don't want her to marry Duane when she brings him home. He is too old, her father says. She has doubts about his age, too. He is sick. A kidney disease, he tells her. He doubts he will live five more years. Still, Duane is fun. He croons to her. She sits on the couch and he stands in front and turns his hand into a microphone. He is a baritone. The songs he sings are etched in her mind.

If you don't know me by now,
You will never never never know me.

Duane sells insurance. They work on the road together. Jo makes the appointments, he closes the customers, she collects the checks. They sleep in motels in different states and spend hours in the car together. He tells her about his past. Of course he doesn't tell her much. The rest she will piece together later on.

He was a bad child. He stole. He hurled rocks at the school windows. He pushed a boulder down a hill. He pushed a grand piano down a flight of stairs. He tells her his mother forged his birth certificate so she could get him into the service and out of her house a year early.

After he was discharged from the Navy for misconduct, Duane enrolled in the Army. Here, he also found trouble. He was in detention at Camp Sibert, Alabama, where the Army was testing chemical weapons like mustard gas. In one note home, written in 1943, Duane begged his mother to send him his watch. "I sure do need it out in the field as I have a lot of time prevision [*sic*] and I need something to tell what time it is," he wrote. "I only have one more week of detention and then I can go anywhere on the base."

Duane has had three other wives Jo will come to know about. Edna she cannot escape. Duane tattooed her name onto his arm.

Mary Jane Ross, Duane's second wife, is his obsession. He spends so much time talking about Mary Jane that Jo once told him to go see her and resolve any feelings he might have before they got married. Jo rarely hears about Margie, Duane's third wife. Years later, Jo will call her and ask her what she thought of Duane.

"He was a bastard," Margie says.

Jo loves him anyway. Duane makes her laugh. He's a jokester. His handle for his CB radio is "World's Greatest Jock Carrier." Immature, but he makes her smile. That's the secret to selling insurance, he tells her. No matter what you tell them, make sure you make them smile.

Duane's business stays on the books. He wins free cruises. His name is inked on company plaques. She has the certificates of praise from the companies he's worked for. In 1973, Duane was first runner-up in selling life insurance policies for American Income Life. In October of 1974, another company he worked for, Life Investors, in Charlotte, North Carolina, made him Agent of the Month. He earned a complimentary dinner. At one meeting for Family Life, about 150 salesmen were asked what they thought of the company's new plan to ban the use of phones and pursue all leads door-to-door. Duane walked up to the stage to address the crowd. He turned around, bent over, and farted.

When Duane retires, he and Jo move to Pace, a city in the Florida panhandle near Pensacola. They open an antiques store, the Peddler. Duane runs it for a few years and sells antiques at flea markets on the road until his kidneys stop working. His kidneys are so swollen, his abdomen balloons. At night, he vomits. He is so weak he breaks bones turning over in his sleep.

Jo drives him to West Florida Regional Medical Center. The dialysis is too much for him. Without the treatments, he will die.

"Is this a body you would want to live in?" Duane tells his doctor. "I can't even hold my own cigarette."

November 24, 1971
Aboard Northwest Orient Flight 305

In the back row of the jet, he fishes a pack of cigarettes from his pocket.

"You smoke?"

Quit, Tina says. The word is out. Smoking kills. This past summer, Congress banned smoking ads from television and radio.

She offers to light the cig for him. The matchbook he has is blue. The words *Sky Chef* are on the cover. He leans in close as she flicks the cardboard stick against the strike pad and watches the sulfur fizzle into flame.

"Want one?"

He holds out the pack.

Why not? Tina takes a butt and sticks it in her mouth. She lights it.

"Where are you from?" he asks.

She grew up in Trevose, a small city outside of Philadelphia. She now lives with roommates in an apartment near the Minneapolis–St. Paul airport. The stew zoo.

"Minneapolis is very nice country," says the hijacker.

Tina takes a drag of her smoke. She knows where they are going: Cuba, where all the other hijackers want to go. She jokes with him.

"You know Northwest Orient has strict policies against traveling to Cuba. Can't bring home rum or cigars. Customs confiscate them in the airport."

The hijacker laughs.

"No, we're not going to Cuba. But you'll like where we're going."

In the seat across from them, Bill Mitchell, the college sophomore, waits for his chance. What is the young stew doing talking to such an older guy? Mitchell notices that as the man talks to the stew, he spills his drink. What is that stewardess thinking wasting her time on him? When will she get up so he can make his move?

The jet banks into a turn around Seattle, circling the city twenty miles to the south. The hijacker wants to know the time. His deadline is 5:00 p.m. He peers out the window.

"We're over Tacoma now."

✗

In Portland. Special Agent Ralph Himmelsbach sprints into the terminal. In the doorway, a lady is lugging hat boxes. Himmelsbach nearly knocks her over. He heads for the management office of Northwest Orient. His boss, Julius Mattson, special agent in charge of the Bureau's field office in Portland, is listening to a panel of radios cued in to the cockpit of the hijacked plane.

"There you are, Ralph," Mattson says. "Where you been? We got a hot one going here."

"Got here quick as I could. Damn traffic on Sandy was fierce. Dispatch said the guy has a bomb. What else do we know?"

"Not a lot more," says Mattson. "He wants money and a parachute. So far that's about all that we've been able to put together."

"How much cash?"

"Two hundred thousand," says Frank Faist, a Northwest official.

"Whew. That's a hell of a hit, Frank. Are you going to make it?"

"I imagine so. He's holding all the high cards."

"Any idents on the guy with the bomb?"

"We've asked the crew to pass on anything they can, but so far no info."

"Have your people found out anything more?"

"We got the ticket lifts and the flight manifest. We know there are twenty-nine men aboard that aircraft. He could be nine or ninety for all I know now."

Over the radio, there is a crackle of sound. It is the Northwest pilots on the frequency. Himmelsbach and Mattson strain their ears.

"Our future destination not yet advised . . . Name of man unknown . . . About six feet one inch, black hair, age about fifty, weight a hundred and seventy-five pounds. Boarded at Portland."

Portland! He was here, Himmelsbach thinks. But who was he? How did he get here? Taxi? Car? Did he stay overnight? Walk from a hotel? Take the bus?

Agents fan out across the terminal, searching for witnesses. The day before Thanksgiving is one of the busiest travel days of the year. Agents approach airport officials, security personnel, passengers, taxi drivers, bus drivers, parking lot attendees, rental car agents, gift shop employees, coffee shop employees, bartenders in the cocktail lounge, waiters and waitresses in the restaurants, and salesmen working in the insurance stands.

See anybody suspicious? About six foot one? Black hair?

"Yes, as a matter of fact, there was a gentleman that looked awfully suspicious," Hal Williams says.

Williams is a gate clerk for Northwest. He noticed the gentlemen. He was odd, not like the others. He boarded Flight 305.

What was so odd about him?

He was dressed in black, all black, Williams tells the feds.

Anything else?

The man was a lone wolf, Williams says. Before the flight, other passengers on the 305 gathered by the terminal window. With the storm coming, they joked about how they would all have to run across the tarmac. Everybody would get drenched in the rain. The man in black was not part of the group. His attitude was different.

How different? How would he describe the attitude?

"Blah," Williams says.

The agents have the passenger list for Flight 305. Recognize any names?

Williams looks at the list.

"No," he says.

The feds hunt for more eyewitnesses. To get on the plane, the hijacker must have purchased a ticket. Who sold it to him?

Dennis Lysne was working the ticket desk that afternoon, agents learn.

Where is Lysne?

He's left for the day, Northwest officials tell the feds.

In Portland, agents race to Lysne's home. They find his wife. Where is Lysne?

The supermarket, she tells them. Doing some Thanksgiving shopping.

In the supermarket parking lot, Lysne loads up his car with groceries. He gets in the driver's seat. His engine won't start. He walks to a pay phone and calls his wife.

"Better hurry home," she tells him. "The FBI wants to talk to you."

At his house, Lysne is briefed. Flight 305 was hijacked. The man says he has a bomb. Does Lysne remember selling a ticket to anybody suspicious?

"Yes," Lysne says. There was one suspicious passenger.

Does Lysne happen to remember the passenger's name?

He does.

"Cooper. Dan Cooper."

Cooper was the last passenger to buy a ticket for Flight 305.

What did Cooper look like?

He was wearing dark clothes. Had darkish skin. Olive in color.

Anything else?

Lysne remembers snippets of their conversation. The man asked, *Can I get on your flight to Seattle?* He asked, *That's a 727, isn't it?*

Does Lysne remember anything else?

The fare was $20. Cooper paid with cash.

Did Cooper display any nervous behavior or fidgeting?

He did not.

Did Lysne notice what Cooper was keeping his money in?

He did not.

Could he recognize Cooper again if he saw him?

Lysne isn't sure.

It is raining. It is unclear how powerful the storm will be. On the ground in Seattle, homicide detective Owen McKenna gets a call from Seattle's chief of detectives. McKenna is briefed on the hijacking. The chief wants McKenna to fetch the $200,000 ransom for the hijacker and bring it to SEA-TAC airport.

In his unmarked car, McKenna races to the Seattle First National Bank downtown. Two employees from the bank's security department are waiting for him. They have a leather satchel. Inside is a canvas bag that contains $200,000, all in twenty-dollar bills.

The money is not coated with powders or rigged with exploding packs of dye. But the bills are marked. To prepare for a robbery, Seattle First National has set aside a cache of bills, and each serial number of each bill has been recorded on microfiche. They count out a hundred stacks of twenty-dollar bills, each stack worth $2,000. The load must weigh twenty pounds, maybe more.

McKenna drives the bank officials and the satchel to SEA-TAC. He thinks about the man with the bomb on the hijacked plane circling above them.

As a detective, McKenna has little respect for the airlines. One cold case haunts him. He found her body on a houseboat near the University of Washington. She had been beaten, strangled, raped. She was a stewardess, and he suspects the killer was a passenger she met. The airlines are selling sex in their stewardesses, but what are they doing to protect them? So many of the stews tell the same story: small-town girls, left home to see the world before they got married. What about the creeps? The killers? And now parachuting hijackers?

On the police radio, there are more voices on the frequency. The feds want to know where the parachutes are.

With sirens flashing, state troopers descend on Issaquah Skyport, a parachute jump center twenty miles east of SEA-TAC airport. Inside, proprietor Linn Emrich hands the troopers two front or reserve chutes. These front chutes will clip onto the harness of the rear or main parachutes. A trooper puts them in the trunk of his car and speeds off to SEA-TAC.

The rear parachutes are already at the airport. Norman Hayden, a local pilot, sent them in a taxicab. Hayden recently purchased the chutes from Earl Cossey, a local parachute rigger.

Inside the airport, the bank officials from Seattle First National lug the ransom into the Northwest flight operations office. The bank officials cut open a seal of the leather satchel and hand FBI boss J. Earl Milnes the canvas bag inside. Its dimensions are roughly a foot by a foot, and eight or nine inches tall. Milnes looks at the money. He does not count it. He hands the bag to Al Lee, Northwest's director of flying. Lee lugs the sack of cash into the trunk of McKenna's unmarked car, along with the rear parachutes, eight meals for the crew, and instructions on how to use a parachute.

Thousands of feet above them, in the cockpit of the Northwest jet, Scotty worries about the passengers. Won't they get edgy when the plane doesn't land? Won't they start asking questions? Should he tell them the flight has been hijacked?

"You know, Scotty, I don't think it's a good idea," Rataczak says. "I know we picked up some good old Montana mountain boys and they're pretty good sized, and they're sitting up in first class and they're on their second and third martinis. We don't need them to look at each other and say, 'Hey, let's go back and get a hijacker.'"

The pilots have an idea. Why not ask *him* what he wants to do?

They call back to Tina. She asks the hijacker if he wants the passengers alerted.

"No," he says.

She relays the message back. Now the crew needs a ruse to explain the delay. Rataczak switches on the in-flight intercom system.

"Ladies and gentlemen," he says, "there's been a slight mechanical problem. We've been asked to circle Seattle, to burn off excess fuel."

A clap of thunder. The storm has hit. In the jet windows there are flashes of lightning against the dark sky. In the bulkhead row, prosecutor Larry Finegold can see them. He tries to make sense of what the pilot had just said. It doesn't make sense. How could any mechanical problem on a jet be *slight*?

He thinks, This is the one, oh boy, here we go, get ready to crash. He thinks about his wife. Sharon was in law school at Berkeley when they met. She had such long hair. He was a preppy in jeans and penny loafers. Once they started talking, he didn't want the conversation to end. He couldn't stand to be apart from her. After they met, he went with friends on a three-day fishing trip. After the first night, he made his friends dock. He hitchhiked to her dorm room and proposed. Now she's pregnant with their first child. A boy, they've learned. His son.

The jet is shaking. More lightning. The cabin drops in spasms. His stomach is rolling like a waterbed.

Across the aisle, passenger Barbara Simmons wakes up from a nap. She looks out the window and sees the lights of the Space Needle. The futuristic structure was the tallest west of the Mississippi when it was built for the 1962 World's Fair in Seattle. It is located several miles north of SEA-TAC.

"Oh my gosh," Simmons says to her husband. "Either we're on the wrong plane or we're being hijacked."

One passenger gets out of his seat and marches toward the back. Tina gets up and intercepts him at row 14.

"I'm bored," he says. "You have any sports magazines to read back there?"

She escorts him to the rear. She looks for a sports magazine. She can't find any.

"How about the *New Yorker*?" she says.

In a nearby seat, passenger Labissoniere, the trucking lawyer, gets up to use the lavatory.

When he comes out, another passenger is blocking the aisle. He's a cowboy type, wearing a Stetson. He's furious, demanding that Tina tell him more about this "mechanical difficulty." Why do they have to burn fuel? When will they be on the ground? Does Tina know *anything*?

Labissoniere notices the man in sunglasses sitting next to Tina. He seems amused by the cowboy's antics. Then he gets annoyed when the man won't stop. He tells Stetson Man to go back to his seat. The hijacker and Tina are alone again.

"If that's a sky marshal, I don't want any more of that," he says.

"There aren't any sky marshals on the 305 flight," she says.

He remembers something: his note. Flo has it. He wants it back.

Tina picks up the phone and tells the captain. She eases back into her seat. She asks the hijacker if he wants anything to eat or drink.

"No."

She asks him about the passengers. When can they get off?

He goes over his instructions again. She needs to pay attention.

First, the fuel truck; he wants it out at SEA-TAC and ready to pump gas when the plane lands.

Second, the money; he wants the car carrying the ransom parked so he can see it from the windows at all times.

Third, her; he wants Tina to get out of the plane and fetch the bag of money.

She worries. The bag may be too heavy for her to carry.

"You'll manage," he says.

Once the money is on board, the passengers will be released. Then Tina will get the parachutes and meals. He also has Benzedrine pills in his pocket. He doesn't want the crew to get sleepy.

The jet banks another wide loop.

Tina tries to chat him up.

"So, where you from?" she says.

He won't tell her. He's not that stupid.

She wants to know his motive. Why hijack this plane?

"Do you have a grudge against Northwest?" she says.

He looks at the stewardess, the sunglasses shielding his eyes.

"I don't have a grudge against your airline, Miss," he says. "I just have a grudge."

December 7, 1942
Cove City, North Carolina

Ever since he was born, the old folks in the tobacco town said there was something about Richard Floyd McCoy Jr. that was not right. He could not speak properly. The cord under his tongue was too taut, so doctors snipped it and left him with a lisp. As a boy he got picked on and was always in fights. One reason for the birth defects, townsfolk surmised, was that the boy's parents were first cousins.

The marriage was not stable. In town, it was an open secret that when Richard's father, who went by the name Floyd, enlisted in the war, the boy's mother, Myrtle, had an affair with her boss, Richard Edward Holland, who owned a local sawmill. When Richard's father came home after two years in Belgium, Myrtle was pregnant. They eventually divorced, but there was tension in the house as they tried to raise two boys with different fathers.

Floyd would spank the younger boy, Russell. Myrtle protested, thinking Floyd was punishing him for her affair.

"That boy may not be your boy, Floyd McCoy, and you might not like him being around here! But he's my boy, and from this day forward, you'll never again lay a hand on my son," Myrtle would say.

Instead of beating Russell, Floyd beat Richard. He could beat his own son, couldn't he?

⚓

"During my formative years, it was still the in-thing to serve one's country so at nineteen I followed my father's footsteps and enlisted in the army," Richard McCoy would later write. "After completing parachute school and volunteering for the Green Berets, then came two more years of advanced demolition and guerrilla warfare."

When McCoy first arrived in Vietnam, in 1963, the country was already chaotic. In the streets, Buddhist monks were lighting themselves on fire. The Green Berets conducted clandestine missions to stop the North Vietnamese and contain the spread of Communism throughout Indochina. President Kennedy deployed more troops and was assassinated later in the year. In the jungles, McCoy developed an ear fungus. Later, he was nearly killed in combat. Awarded the Purple Heart for his valor, McCoy was sent home to Cove City and spent a year recovering in a wheelchair. The fungus infection in his ear would not heal. Doctors could not figure out how to treat it.

Richard wanted to work in law enforcement. His family was Mormon, so after his recovery he moved to Utah and enrolled in Brigham Young University, majoring in criminal studies. In school, he met Karen Burns, a pretty blonde who was taken with McCoy's war hero image and his ruggedly handsome good looks. They married and had two children, Chante and Richard Jr.

The marriage was tense. Money was tight. Richard was in school. He had National Guard duty. He was a Sunday school teacher on weekends. He didn't have time for a job. Karen's younger sister Denise was living with them, too. Richard was frustrated. He needed to escape. He decided to re-enlist on the condition that he be sent back to Vietnam. He missed the adrenaline of combat.

His first training was in helicopter flight school in Texas. Later, he went through six months of advanced training in Alabama. When he arrived in Vietnam, McCoy was like an aerial Rambo. He earned combat medals for his missions. In the summer of 1967, an American observation helicopter had an engine malfunction and was forced to land in enemy territory. American soldiers were stranded, waiting for the rescue helicopters. From the Army report:

Suddenly, the rescue aircraft lost power and crashed near the first aircraft, causing them both to erupt in flames. Due to the extreme danger caused by the burning aircraft plus the added danger of enemy intrusion, MCCOY placed his helicopter as near as possible to the downed aircraft. With complete disregard for his own safety,

MCCOY leaped from the aircraft and worked his way through the dense jungle to his comrades. He immediately located the two survivors and led them to his waiting helicopter.

In combat, there was a madness to Richard, who conducted his own bomb runs in his armored chopper. In November of 1967, an American compound had been overtaken by Vietcong. A thick layer of fog covered the ground, and low clouds covered the trees. Visibility was extremely poor, and there were no tactical maps of the area. From another Army report:

Flying by instrumentation and radio alone, MCCOY located the compound and came under automatic weapons and small arms fire. With the position of the compound marked by a flare and the firefight marked by tracer rounds, MCCOY began a series of firing passes, launching rockets until his ammunition was expended. Due to his courageous flight and highly accurate fire, the enemy was completely routed, leaving twenty bodies behind.

His head. Back home again at Brigham Young, Richard suffers from migraines. He can't think. He blacks out. He undergoes a series of medical tests and X-rays. Richard has a possible tumor in his brain, doctors find.

The prognosis is devastating. After so many years in school, and with his skilled training as a helicopter and fixed-wing pilot, Richard would have been highly employable in the FBI, or another law enforcement agency. Now Richard can never be hired. What if he suffers a blackout at the controls? His helicopter or plane could crash.

He's lost everything. His marriage is fragile. His career is ruined. What can he do?

He considers suicide. Too cowardly, he thinks.

He becomes absorbed in school work. Better at least get his degree.

In one of his classes, Richard has to write a paper on how to deter the increased number of airplane hijackings.

"In working on the project, it was necessary to play the roles of the people involved," Richard will later say. "The person I identified most with was the skyjacker."

November 24, 1971
Aboard Northwest Orient Flight 305

In the air, the jet banks another turn. In the bulkhead row, prosecutor Finegold looks out the portal window for the roof of his house. In the rain, in the dark, he can't find it. Behind him passengers shift uneasily in the powder blue fabric chairs and flip through Northwest Orient's in-flight magazine.

Sitting in his seat over the wing of the plane, passenger Patrick Minsch, a heavy-equipment operator from Alaska, worries about his connection. In Seattle he is changing planes to go to his grandmother's house in the San Juan Islands. The plane has been circling for three hours. He'll miss his flight. He'll have to spend the night in SEA-TAC. He looks out the window and sees the lights on the wing illuminate the rain streaking by. He feels the plane move.

Another loop. The jet banks again, over Everett, where Boeing's 747 factory is located.

The 747 was a gamble that nearly bankrupted the company. In the recession, Boeing has been forced to lay off more than half the workforce. A company town, Seattle has the highest unemployment rate of any American city since the Great Depression. It's over 12 percent. Aeronautical engineers with advanced degrees are forced to mow lawns to feed their families. Foreclosure rates skyrocket. Homeless shelters are at full capacity. Across the board, local budgets are slashed. Police officers in Seattle are placed on unpaid leave. Dope is sold outside drive-in restaurants.

Down near the piers off Puget Sound, the homeless sleep in wet bundles under the freeway as smack junkies warm their hands by oil-drum fires. An exodus is under way. A new billboard is up: "Will the last person to leave Seattle please turn off the lights?"

Outside the city, in old logging towns, the government is collecting on back taxes. Auditors snake through the maze of country roads in rural Washington where many loggers and their families are living off the grid. The tax bills are higher than what many homes are worth. Laborers are forced to move, forced to sell. Locals vow to get back at the government for stealing their homes.

The hijacker wants to know what time it is.

After five, Tina tells him.

Five was his deadline. What are the feds trying to do? Stall?

For the first time, Tina sees panic on his face.

"They're not gonna take me alive," he says.

Tina calls the cockpit. The hijacker is starting to lose control. What's the delay?

The front chutes are not at the airport yet.

"Ask him if he wants to start our descent without the chutes present."

She asks him.

"Yes," he says.

She relays the message. The phone rings again. It's Scotty.

"The front chutes are now at the airport," he says. "We're going down."

At SEA-TAC, agents rush to the windows of the terminal to watch the jet come in. Along the wet runways and on the rooftops, Bureau snipers get into position. In Washington, D.C., officials at the FAA and the FAA's psychiatrist listen to the drama on the radio frequency. In Minnesota, Don Nyrop and other Northwest officials pray the feds in Seattle will let Scotty handle this and not storm the plane. At his lakefront home outside Minneapolis, Scotty's wife is crying in the upstairs bathroom. Scotty's young daughter, Catherine, has gone to the sock hop at her high school. Her friends and the music are a blur. Who is the man in the back of the jet? Why does he want to kill her father?

"Seattle Approach, we're ready to make our approach."

"Okay Northwest 305, would you have any objection to a right turn from your present position?"

"That should not present any problem and we understand we're landing at 1606. Is that correct?"

"Correct. . . . If you want some light we can turn the high-intensity runway lights up after you land, and they're pretty bright."

The airport is closed. Planes are told to circle. Air traffic controllers in the towers monitor the loops at different altitudes, careful not to cause a collision. Other jets are rerouted.

On the tarmac, on a domestic flight to Denver, pilots listen to the hijack unfold on the radio frequency. The conversation between the Northwest pilots and the FBI is so entertaining they play the radio over the cabin's intercom speakers so their passengers can follow what is happening in real time.

In his unmarked car, police detective McKenna and Northwest flight director Lee wait for Flight 305 to land. The high beams of the detective's car carve tunnels of light in the falling rain. McKenna and Lee look into the dark sky for the plane. First they see the lights on the wing, then the landing gear; now the jet is landing. Its wheels deflate on impact against the slick runway. From the car, McKenna and Lee can see the caps of the Northwest pilots in the cockpit. Through the cabin windows, they can see the heads of passengers.

Lee speaks into a hand radio. "305, this is Al. If you want to stay on the runway, that's fine with us."

"We might pull off to the right side just a little bit off the runway . . . until we make contact with our friend in the back."

Down on the tarmac, McKenna wants to storm the plane, take this guy out. He is carrying his service weapon.

"Okay, Al, can you hear me?"

"Yes sir."

"Okay, he at the present time is in the lavatory and apparently desires to stay there."

"I'll go back and get the fuel truck started."

"Okay, fine. Okay, be sure to get the fuel out here right now."

The jet rolls to a stop. The passengers are anxious to get off. In row 15, passenger Nancy House looks toward the back of the jet. She sees the man in sunglasses coming out of the lavatory. She sees that he is holding an attaché case on its side with both arms, like a pizza box. On top of the attaché case is a bag. The bag is about four inches tall and about the same size of the attaché case. The bag is a light color, made from manila, or perhaps burlap. It is yellow, with a tinge of pink. What is in this bag?

Passengers scramble to collect their luggage. They want off. In the front row, prosecutor Finegold can see flashing beacons of a fuel truck out the window.

"They care more about the fucking gas than they do about the passengers!" he screams.

A pickup truck appears. A set of airstairs is attached to the rig. The stairs connect to the jet's front door. The pressure seal is cracked. It's time. The man in the back wants Tina to get the money. *Now.*

Tina moves up the crowded aisle, through the passengers, to the front exit door. On the tarmac, the SEA-TAC ground crew has set up klieg lights. The runway is illuminated like a movie set.

Al Lee scurries out of the detective's car and around to the trunk. He opens it. He grabs the canvas sack of money and waits for Tina in the rain.

Tina peeks her head out of the airplane and slinks down the wet steps. In the rain, she is a smear of blond and red.

She walks up to Lee. She is talking.

Lee can't understand a word. The stewardess must be in shock. He hands her the money bag.

In the driver's seat of the unmarked car, McKenna watches.

Last chance to storm the plane. He can sneak under the pickup's stairs, slip into the cabin on his belly, slither under the seats, and take out this motherfucker.

Tina clutches the canvas bag in her arms, like a giant sack of mail. She clinks back to the jet in her heels and up the wet stairs into the maw of the cabin. She drops the money bag on the floor—it *is* heavy—and drags it down the aisle.

The hijacker is waiting. The sack has no drawstring, no handle, no straps. The mouth is loose.

This isn't right. He asked for a knapsack—with straps. What are the feds trying to do?

He peers inside.

"Looks okay," he says.

He plunges his hands in the bag, and his fingers swim around the tightly wrapped twenties.

"There's a lot of cash in that bag," Tina says. "Can I have some?" She is joking.

The hijacker pulls out a stack of bills and hands it to her anyway. He wants her to have the money.

"Sorry, sir," she says. "No tips. Northwest Orient policy."

She asks about the passengers.

"Why not let them go now? You've still got the crew and the plane."

He agrees. The passengers can go.

Soon the announcement is made. The passengers flood the aisles, retrieve their bags, hats, coats. Flo Schaffner is out of the cockpit and stands near the front door with Alice Hancock. From the rear, Tina Mucklow joins them, helping the angry, hostile passengers off the jet and into the rain.

"Happy Thanksgiving!" she says.

The cabin is clear. The hijacker wants Tina to get the parachutes. She protests. She is not strong enough.

"They aren't that heavy. You shouldn't have any trouble."

She turns for the front exit door again. That's when she sees him.

A passenger! He's snuck back on board. What is he doing?

"Forgot my briefcase," he says.

Tina follows him back to his seat, stuffs the briefcase in his arms, and escorts him out the door. The Northwest pilots are flustered.

"Is this Al?"

"Yeah."

"Okay, please go stand by the bottom of the stairs and secure that area. We just had a passenger that came back up the steps because he forgot a bag. We just had to literally push him back off the steps."

Scotty checks the fuel gauge. It hasn't moved. What's going on?

"We want as rapidly as possible another fuel truck and a third fuel truck to stand by. We've got some difficulty in pumping at the present time and we're not able to take on fuel. Understand? . . . Two fuel trucks, and get them out there as fast as you can."

In the Northwest Orient operations office at SEA-TAC, agents ask the Northwest pilots about the bomb.

"305, as long as you're free to talk, can you give me any more information and type of device or anything about it that you can talk now?"

"Ground stand by."

"This is Al again."

"Yes, Al."

"Yeah, the fuel truck should be on the way."

"Okay, is this the other fuel truck now with the flashing headlights?"

"No, there's a school bus running around there with flashing amber lights."

"You better alert him and get those things off."

"305, this is Al. . . . Are you going to let those girls out?"

"Well, that's what we're working on now. What we're trying to figure out is some way that we can get everybody up here and down those stairs, and we're kept still on the backend."

"Well, how many girls you got trained?"

"A good bunch."

"That one that came down here, she's pretty sharp; get her and then make a mass exodus and leave this sonofabitch. *Go!*"

"Right now, that's our contingency plan. . . ."

"He's just hanging out there on the edge."

In the empty cabin, Alice Hancock inches toward the hijacker. She wants her purse.

"Sure," he says. "I'm not going to bite you."

Flo Schaffner wants her purse, too. As she walks down the aisle toward him, she notices the hijacker's mood has changed. He is giddy, almost boyish, clutching the money bag.

He asks Flo to hold it. Feel how heavy the money is?

She puts her arms around the bag. She lifts.

"It is heavy."

She heaves the sack back to him.

He fishes around the pockets of his pants for the $19 he received from Flo nearly four hours ago, on the tarmac in Portland, for the bourbon and Seven he ordered and spilled. He offers the change.

Flo and Alice shake their heads.

"Sorry."

"No tips."

The stews turn and scurry off the plane.

Tina does not leave. She stands with him in the rear. He is angry. The fuel has not been pumped. What is taking the feds so long?

"Close the shades," he says.

She shutters each window, closing them like heavy eyelids.

When she returns, he is grumbling about the knapsack he asked for. The canvas money bag is useless. What will he stuff the ransom in now?

Think.

The front reserve chutes. He grabs one. He pulls the ripcord. The pink canopy of the chute bursts open and covers the seats like popped bubblegum.

The hijacker reaches into his pocket and retrieves a pocket knife.

He cuts the knots that tie the canopy to the chute. Finally, the chute is free and the container is empty. Maybe he can stuff the ransom bills in here.

No. It won't work. The container is too small. What else?

Think.

The parachute canopy. The shroud lines.

He uses the knife to cut a cord. Then one more.

Tina watches him.

He takes the shroud lines and wraps them around the canvas money bag to secure it. Next: he wraps the shroud lines around the mouth of the bag and ties a nooselike knot into a makeshift handle.

"305, this is Al."

"Go ahead, Al."

"I just talked to the stews here [Flo and Alice] and if you'll call back there and tell him everything is under control then he'll let this other one [Tina] off."

"Whose word is that? Whose idea is that?"

"This is the two stews that got off. They were saying the guy don't really care if she stays on or not, but they suggested to call back and tell him everything is under control and that he'll let that third stew off."

"That's contrary to what's going on up here, Al. He's not going to let her come off right now and we're trying to work out a way that we can get her up here somehow before we go. Right now he wants her to sit back there with him during takeoff."

"Okay, I was just wondering, you know. About the fuel, how much do you want on board or how much more can you take?"

"Well, we got a long way to go and he's getting antsy and that's our problem right now."

"Have you been able to get in the back end of that cockpit or won't he come out?"

"He doesn't want any of us in the aisle. The only one he negotiates with is the stewardess and he doesn't want anybody beyond that first curtain. We've never left the cockpit."

"Did you get the maps I sent out there?"

"Yeah, we got all that stuff."

"And you got that deal from Boeing on how to get out of there?"

Inside the cockpit is a rope ladder. To exit the plane and escape, the pilots and flight engineer can open the cockpit windshield and shimmy down the rope onto the tarmac.

"Yeah, we got that. If we could get the gal out, well, we could make tracks ourselves."

"Is it possible to communicate with her to have her come forward to get food?"

"No, we tried that. . . . We don't want to try that kind of stuff."

"Seattle-Tacoma Tower now for one—stand by. Fuel truck just crossed in front of Northwest hangar."

"Alpha Two, go on."

"Stand by."

"What did he say now?"

"He was giving instructions there."

"We're going to Mexico City," the hijacker tells Tina. "Or anyplace in Mexico. Gear down, flaps down. You can trim the flaps to fifteen. You can stop anywhere in Mexico to refuel, but not here in the United States. Cabin lights out—no one behind the first-class curtain."

The pilots must also keep an altitude of 10,000 feet. No higher.

There is more.

"The aft door must be open and the stairs must be down."

Tina picks up the interphone and relays the instructions to the Northwest pilots: Mexico City, gear down, flaps at fifteen degrees, altitude of 10,000 feet, no higher.

In the cockpit, the pilots are talking to the feds. There's an update.

"305, is the individual in the back? He can't hear?"

"You can have all the conversations you want."

"Okay. 305, did you hear the message from Washington, D.C., from the FAA's chief psychiatrist? He believes the second parachute is for the stewardess to use with him to go out, and after he leaves the airplane will be blown up."

On the tarmac, a bus approaches. The name on the bus is Western Tours. The passengers file in. The bus drives the passengers across the airfield to the SEA-TAC terminal. Here, two federal agents board. One says he's going to take a roll call and if you hear your name on the list, say something or raise your hand.

Menendez. Minsch. Pollart.

The hands go up. Larry Finegold raises his hand. George Kurata raises his hand. Cliff McDonald, a real estate salesman, raises his hand. George Labissoniere raises his hand.

Cooper?

Dan Cooper?

The bus is dark. The agents look for a hand, a face. They wait for a sound.

Dan Cooper?

In Portland, reporters hear the news of the hijacking over police scanners. Clyde Jabin, a stringer for United Press International wire service, asks a Bureau agent in Portland if they have any suspects. As a matter fact, they do.

"D. Cooper," the agent says.

Jabin does not hear what the agent says.

" 'D' as in dog, 'B' as in boy?" Jabin says.

"Right," the agent says.

Jabin scribbles down the "D" and "B" and the name "Cooper."

He calls in the story. The name of the hijacker–D.B. Cooper– hits the wires.

Mexico City?

In Portland, Special Agent Ralph Himmelsbach goes over the flight path in his mind. As a pilot, he knows the most sensible route south at the low altitude of 10,000 feet is Vector 23. The flight path would follow the Interstate 5 freeway and take the hijacked plane back to Portland.

"What do you think?" his boss, Mattson, asks. "Do you think he's coming back to us?"

"I sure hope so," Himmelsbach says. "I'd like to take him here."

Himmelsbach calls around. He learns there is a Huey helicopter at the National Guard hangar at Portland International. His idea is to chase the hijacked plane in the helicopter. He races over to the hangar, where the on-duty Guard pilots are waiting.

Himmelsbach also considers another detail. The request to have the plane flown at the altitude of 10,000 feet was telling. At 10,000 feet, the cabin would not be pressurized. If Cooper cracked the rear door of the jet, he would not get sucked out. Clearly, the man the agents were after knew airplanes.

✦

In the cockpit of Northwest 305, pilots consult with the company's engineers. The hijacker wants to take off with the aftstairs in the down position. Is that even possible?

It isn't, the engineers tell them.

And what about the aftstairs down? Can they fly that way?

Northwest calls Boeing. Engineers there inform them that the Boeing 727 was used by Air America, the CIA cutout, in Vietnam.

"The plane has been flown this way. There's been large boxes of two to three thousand pounds dropped through the door in this configuration."

Another concern is fuel. Under the configurations the hijacker wants—flaps at fifteen degrees, landing gear down—the jet will be moving extremely slowly. The fuel burn will be tremendous. The Northwest pilots will need to land several times to make it to the Mexican border.

"Reno makes a better choice for a wise hijacker."

"Roger. Will plan Reno first stop."

"Roger. A second stop would be Yuma, Arizona."

"Roger. Fuel truck has left. Stairs removed. Forward door has been closed. He has agreed to let us take off with the stairs in the full upright position."

"Okay, we'll start you out here heading toward Portland and then we'll get you clearance."

"Okay, fine. And we've got the company working on the flight plan, so if we don't answer you right away, we're trying to work a couple of free frequencies."

The interphone is ringing. The pilots pick up. It's *him*.

"Let's get the show on the road," he hollers.

In the rear, Tina hands him a piece of paper: instructions on how to use a parachute.

"I don't need that," he says.

She wants to know why she is still with him. Why won't he let her go to the cockpit?

He doesn't know how to release the aftstairs. He needs her help.

She is scared. She imagines herself getting sucked out of the plane once the door is opened and the pressure seal is cracked. She asks him if she can secure herself to something in the cabin. Perhaps the pilots' escape rope in the cockpit?

No. He doesn't want her going to the cockpit.

She asks about the flight engineer. He can bring it back.

"Nobody behind the curtain," he says.

Tina looks at the cannibalized parachute. He cut shroud lines to tie up the money bag. Can he cut a shroud line for her?

"Never mind," he says.

He'll lower the aftstairs himself. He asks her to show him how to use them. Then she can leave.

She goes to the panel. Push the lever this way, the stairs go down. Easy. They have oxygen on board, too, she says.

"Yes, I know where it is. If I need it I will get it."

He looks around the cabin. It's too bright. He wants the lights off.

The switches are hit. The cabin turns as dark as the inside of a glove. He reaches for the reading light above his seat. He turns it on and the light spills onto his hands.

The plane is not moving. Why aren't they moving?

Tina calls Scotty. The pilots are filing their flight plan.

"Never mind," the hijacker says. "They can do that over the radio once we get up."

Tina wants to know what he will do with the bomb.

"Take it with me, or disarm it," he says.

Tina worries about the aftstairs. If he doesn't put them up before they land, they could get damaged.

"Go to the cockpit," he says. "Close the first-class curtains. Make sure nobody comes out."

She leaves. In first class, she looks back. She can see he is standing up. He has a shroud line in his hand. He is tying the money bag to himself, running the rope around his waist. She closes the curtain.

⚔

The rain is light. The wind speed is ten knots, from the southeast. Clouds are scattered at 2,500 feet. Visibility is seven miles. The night is black.

From the cockpit, the pilots can see the high beams of the detective's unmarked car.

"Yeah, say, this is Al again. I'm down here in a car."

"Yeah, Al. We're all set. We're going to crank the engines. You've probably heard me say he's indicated that he wants the show on the road, so we're going to get her cranked up here and pick our clearance in the air."

"Or maybe you can get him downtown toward Portland. He might get homesick and want to land there again, I don't know."

"Well, we'll hope for something to happen here, that's all. You go ahead and pull out. We're going to get cranked up here now. So we'll see you later."

"Yes sir."

"Ground, no force on 305. Be advised that I will be trying to make her up to altitude any way we can. Any other restrictions that may be imposed upon us?"

"No restrictions at all. You fly in the best way you can do her."

"And, 305, there'll be people with you all the way down."

The company is a pair of F-106's, interceptor turbojets designed to shoot down bombers with air-to-air missiles. If the Northwest pilots lose control of the jet and Flight 305 is headed into a populated or residential area, the F-106 pilots could be ordered to unlock their weapons systems and take the jet out.

At SEA-TAC, agents are busy debriefing passengers and Flo and Alice about the hijacker. What color was his hair? Did he speak with an accent? Was he wearing a wedding ring?

On the runway, Flight 305 picks up speed. Soon the nose is up and the wheels are off the ground.

In Portland, outside the Guard hangar, the giant blades of the Huey are spinning. Himmelsbach and a partner hop in the cockpit. As they rise, winds from the storm bully the chopper around the airfield. Himmelsbach can see the lights of the Portland suburbs. He thinks he sees his house. His wife and daughters are probably inside preparing a turkey. He was supposed to have been home hours ago.

Happy Thanksgiving, he thinks.

The chopper picks up speed. They try the radio, but the frequencies are different. There is no way to communicate with the Northwest pilots. Himmelsbach looks out into the night. He can see nothing. They are moving 120 knots into the storm. They are moving too slowly to catch Flight 305. Above the chopper, somewhere, the F-106 fighter jets are moving too fast. To maintain any radar reading on the passenger jet, the fighter pilots are forced to carve wide turns, snaking through the night sky. As they make these S-turns, Northwest 305 comes in and out of their radar screens. They are losing him.

Other jets join the aerial posse. In Boise, Idaho, a pair of F-102 interceptor jets is dispatched. The F-102's cannot make contact with Flight 305, either.

To the west, Norman Battaglia, a National Guard flight instructor, is on a night training mission in a T-33 reconaissance fighter plane. The training mission is canceled.

"We want you to tail an aircraft," an air traffic controller says.

"The one that's hijacked?"

"That's the one."

In the sky, Battaglia positions the T-33 about three quarters of a mile behind Flight 305. It's hard to keep up. The Northwest jet is moving so slowly. And, every forty-five seconds or so, the plane changes courses. Battaglia tries his radio to contact the Northwest pilots. It doesn't work. The frequencies are also different.

In the cockpit of Northwest 305, the phone is ringing. It's *him* again.

He needs help with the aftstairs.

The pilots relay the message over the radio.

"Fourteen miles on Vector 23 out of Seattle. He is trying to get the door down. The stew is with us. He cannot get the stairs down."

"After a while, someone will have to take a look back there and see if he is out of the aircraft."

"Miss Mucklow said he apparently has the knapsack around him and thinks he will attempt a jump."

The pilots notice a change in their instruments.

"We now have an aftstair light on."

Copilot Rataczak picks up the receiver to use the jet's intercom. The air swirling around the cabin must be fierce, a tornado of wind twisting up and down the aisles. Rataczak calls back into the cabin as if trying to reach a man trapped in the belly of a mine.

"Can you hear me? Is there anything we can do for you?"

The hijacker picks up the cabin phone.

"No," he says.

With the aftstairs released, the temperature in the cabin must be far below freezing. In the cockpit window, pilots look at their thermometer. The reading in the sky is minus seven.

It's also loud. The jet's engines are blasting away.

Rataczak calls back into the cabin again.

"Everything okay back there?"

"Everything is okay."

The jet is moving south. The flight crew notices another change in reading.

"We're getting some oscillations in the cabin. He must be doing something with the air stairs."

Harold Anderson, flight engineer, checks his instrument panel. The cabin pressure gauge is spiraling out of control.

Rataczak calls back again on the interphone.

"Sir?"

There is no response. Tina picks up the plastic receiver.

"Sir?"

Underneath the jet, the lights of the cities in Oregon pass: Portland, Salem, Eugene. The configurations of the plane keep the jet moving slow and strain the engines. In Northern California, an HC-130 rescue plane is dispatched from Hamilton Air Force Base, as well as another pair of F-106 interceptor jets. At Red Bluff, California, the pilots and the jets following them turn east, approaching Reno on the Nevada border.

Time to descend. Time to refuel. Tina calls back into the cabin.

"Sir, we are going to land now. Please put up the stairs. We are going to land anyway, but the aircraft may be structurally damaged. We may not be able to take off after we've landed."

Northwest officials in Minneapolis and air-traffic controllers in Reno want to know if the hijacker has jumped from the plane.

Tina uses the intercom phone again.

"Sir?"

The screech of the dangling aftstairs against the runway in Reno sounds like a car crash. Police cars trail the jet to ensure the hijacker does not roll out onto the tarmac. The Northwest pilots are talking with Reno Approach.

"See any sparks coming off the tail at any time on touchdown?"

"Negative. None at all. The only thing that's visible on the tail is lights on your ramp."

"Roger."

"I do see some sparks now, just a few, trailing you as you're taxiing in."

The plane rolls to a stop.

Scotty turns and unlocks the cockpit door. He calls out into the cabin.

"Sir?"

Tina is behind him. She calls out over his shoulder.

"Sir?" she says. "Do you want us to refuel?"

Scotty inches into first class. The seats are empty. He creeps forward into the cabin. He is facing the first-class curtain. He unhinges the clasp. He pulls the curtain back.

"Sir?"

The so-called Bing Crosby sketch was the first composed by the FBI.

The Bing Crosby sketch with sunglasses.

Another FBI sketch. Notice the differences?

What an aged Cooper would look like now, according to the FBI.

Private eye Skipp Porteous and Cooper suspect Kenneth Christiansen. Notice Christiansen's smirky grin.

Northwest Orient Flight 305, hijacked shortly after leaving Portland en route to Seattle. The model was equipped with aftstairs for loading passengers. The CIA also used the aftstairs of the 727 to drop cargo and parachutists during Vietnam.

Stewardess Tina Mucklow. She spent nearly five hours with Cooper. "He was never cruel or nasty in any way," she said after the hijacking. She later became a nun. ASSOCIATED PRESS

Row 18. The hijacker sat in the middle seat.

The aftstairs of Northwest 305, which Cooper leaped from at 10,000 feet.

Suspect Bobby Dayton.
COURTESY OF RON AND PAT
FORMAN

Suspect Barbara Dayton,
post-surgery.
COURTESY OF RON AND PAT
FORMAN

Army soldiers search for
Cooper near Lake Merwin
in the spring of 1972.

Cooper suspect Duane Weber, photographed by his wife Jo Weber in 1979, after they married.
COURTESY OF JO WEBER

After digging into her husband's past, Jo Weber discovered that Duane was a career criminal who spent much of his life in prison, often under the alias John C. Collins.

A military parachutist tests the air-stairs of the hijacked Northwest Orient Boeing 727 during a test flight to see where Cooper landed on January 6, 1972.

Designed for the CIA, the SR-71 was the most advanced spyplane of its era. Its cameras and sensors failed to locate the hijacker. THE NORM TAYLOR COLLECTION/THE MUSEUM OF FLIGHT

Former Green Beret Richard Floyd McCoy Jr. was a suspect in the Cooper case after he hijacked another 727 five months after Cooper's jump, for $500,000. SALT LAKE TRIBUNE

McCoy later escaped from federal prison with a gun made from dental plaster.

Special Agent Ralph Himmelsbach quizzes Dwayne and Patricia Ingram after they claimed their son Brian found the Cooper bills on Tena Bar, the most significant development in the unsolved case.
MAX GUTIERREZ © BETTMANN/CORBIS

Brian Ingram, age fourteen, after winning back a portion of the Cooper bills in a six-year legal war with the FBI.
MICHAEL LLOYD, THE OREGONIAN

FBI agent Larry Carr went undercover in a cyber forum under the code name Ckret; he was later reassigned.
ANDY ROGERS, SEATTLE POST-INTELLIGENCER

Scientist Tom Kaye tests the buoyancy of money in the Columbia River at Tena Bar, where the Cooper bills were found.
RANDY L. RASMUSSEN/THE OREGONIAN

Vietnam veteran and retired drill sergeant Jerald Thomas has been hunting for Cooper for more than twenty years; recent theories suggest he might be looking in the wrong place.
MARK HARRISON/SEATTLE TIMES

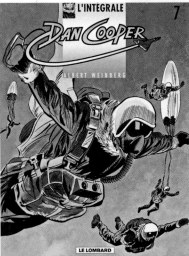

The mystery of the hijacker's alias, Dan Cooper, may finally have been solved—as the name of an old French comic book hero who was a Royal Canadian Air Force pilot.

THE HUNT

I must ask you, who in the hell do some of
you people think you are, and what in the hell
do you think you are doing. I have succeeded
in pulling off one of the most successful,
talked about crimes of today. . . . No one
was endangered, the caper was only committed
to show the unbelieving world that a PERFECT
crime was possible.

NO HARM DONE

```
        the perfect crime
grant me amnesty
        money will be returned
   no harm done
answer by way of public announcement
        within 48 hours
    i've won, admit you've lost
                —d.b. cooper
```

i am alive and doing well in home town PO.
The   system   that   beats   the   system.
db cooper

   ATTENTION!
Thanks   for   hospitality.   Was   in   a   rut.

                    D.B. Cooper

you will never find me
give up

db cooper
               i am right here portland and the
$200,000 is for revolution

dear manager,
much of the credit for my success is yours,
thanks.
I am departing very soon for foreign soil, flying
naturally, thanks again.

D.B. Cooper

I am on the plane and I am thinking of the Pulitzer prize. What is the prize? Is there a trophy? A plaque? Anything I'll be able to keep? A check to cash? And how will I apply? Or will they just know about my exposé unmasking the real D.B. Cooper as bashful Northwest purser Ken Christiansen? And how should the story start? With Kenny as a boy, growing up in the Great Depression and running up to his attic to gaze at his father's Perpetual Motion Machine?

Now I am wondering about a metal detector. Before I left, Lyle was insistent: Bring a metal detector to Bonney Lake. If Lyle knew his brother Kenny, he told me, Kenny would bury the loot in his backyard like the family dog buries gnawed-up bones.

How can I take Lyle seriously? If Kenny was Cooper, why would he have kept the evidence on his property? Then again, if Kenny actually planned out the hijacking—if he was gutsy enough to jump out of a plane over the remote forests of southwest Washington with $200,000 in twenty-dollar bills tied to his chest with a pair of parachute shrouds—then he was capable of anything. To prove the case, I would have to consider the most unlikely scenarios, stretch the limits of my own logic.

My first interview is forty miles south of Portland, with the man considered to be the world's foremost expert on the D.B. Cooper case, Ralph Himmelsbach. The retired special agent is now in his eighties, and there is talk about how he became "obsessed" with the case after the first call ("164 in progress") came over the radio. He's chased Cooper for decades and still failed to identify him. They say Cooper ruined his first marriage.

I have come for his blessing. I have photos of Ken Christiansen in my bag and copies of his military records from the Paratroops. I have my arguments all mapped out. If I can convince an expert like

Himmelsbach that Ken Christiansen is a worthy suspect, I'll be on my way toward making my case.

Ｘ

His ranch is set back from the main road. I drive down the gravel moat and across fields that sit in the shadows of Mount Hood.

Himmelsbach opens the door and the face I see is the same as in the old newspaper clippings. High, arching eyebrows. A mustache trimmed just so. Cheeks so closely shaven they look pink. He wears light stiff jeans and a bolo tie. I follow him out to the back porch. This is where Himmelsbach lines up his .22 rifle and snipes varmints sneaking into his garden.

Himmelsbach—or, H, as Cooper sleuths call him—is the voice of reason in the Cooper case. Since the night of the hijacking, he's been interviewed by countless news outlets—print, radio, television, local, national, international—and he always shoots down the Robin Hood analogy. How, he snuffs, could the hijacker be a hero when he put thirty-six passengers at risk? And the six brave crew members? And what about the hundreds of airline officials and cops and agents whose Thanksgiving was ruined, and who later spent tens of thousands of hours hunting Cooper down? In one interview, Himmelsbach called the hijacker "nothing but a rotten sleazy bastard."

The sun is out. Himmelsbach hears the distant buzz of an engine. He squints up and the sun beams off his blue eyes like flashes of light against the bottom of a swimming pool.

"AT-6 Texan," he says of the plane. "A North American AT-6."

Despite his age, there is an exactness to Himmelsbach, a German-reared thoroughness and competency that only enhances his credentials as the official granddaddy of the Cooper case. Before we start talking, Himmelsbach has ground rules.

No problem. Fire away.

There is one fact that he wants to make sure I understand.

"I *was* not and I *am* not obsessed with the Cooper case," he says.

His eyes gaze over me.

Got it. Not obsessed.

I ask him what he remembers about the hunt. I want to know about the first morning.

November 25, 1971
West Linn, Oregon

It is dawn. His wife is a bundle under the black and orange silk sheets of their bed, the same bundle as when he came home late from the airport the night before. Ralph Himmelsbach puts on jeans, a shirt, his leather bomber jacket, aviator sunglasses, and drives to the hangar.

The sky is wet. The air is cold. Snow today. Snow any minute. Better get up before he gets socked in, he thinks.

His airplane is a single-engine, recreational Taylorcraft. He flies over the Willamette Valley and crosses Vector 23, the flight path of the hijacked plane. He buzzes the treelines of vast areas of remote timber, the streams and lakes and crags that form the border of the Dark Divide.

Himmelsbach flies a grid. Seven miles one way, seven miles back. Back and back again. Where did the hijacker bail out? He must be in these woods somewhere. But where?

The agent squints down into the trees. He looks for a plume of smoke from a campfire, a snare of parachute, a pool of blood.

Back and back and back again. Whoever Dan Cooper is, Himmelsbach is confident he and his fellow Bureau agents will find him. The skyjacker will test the agency. He will prove how good J. Edgar Hoover's FBI really is.

Within the Bureau, the Cooper hijacking is given a name: NORJAK. At headquarters in Washington, senior agents are processing the microfilm that contains the serial numbers to every twenty-dollar bill the hijacker was given. The numbers will be printed in a booklet and released to the public. Field offices in Portland, Reno, Las Vegas, San Francisco, and throughout the Pacific Northwest have been asked to investigate and submit daily NORJAK updates to headquarters via teletype.

In Seattle, agents re-interview witnesses. They need to know what the hijacker looked like, so Bureau artists can create a sketch.

About how old was he?

George Labissoniere, the truck driver's lawyer, says he had a clear view of the hijacker because he went to the bathroom so many times during the flight.

He was no older than thirty-five, Labissoniere tells the feds.

He was about fifty, Cord Zrim Spreckel, the printer, tells agents. Spreckel had a good look at the hijacker too. The man looked so suspicious. Why was he wearing sunglasses?

And what kind of facial features?

He had a square jaw, Spreckel says.

He had a saggy chin, Bill Mitchell, the college sophomore, says.

The details are conflicting. Other than stewardess Tina Mucklow, the only witness who was in close proximity to the hijacker is stewardess Florence Schaffner. Flo tells the feds she saw the hijacker without his sunglasses. She was the only one to see Cooper's eyes. What color were they?

"Brown," she says.

And about how old was he?

"Mid-forties," she says.

Tina Mucklow agrees. But Cooper is shorter than what Flo thinks. Tina pegs the hijacker to be between five foot ten and six feet tall.

Flo says six feet tall, no shorter. And his hair was black, just like his suit and his shoes, Flo says.

His hair was dark brown, and so was his suit, which may have had a black stripe, Tina says.

And what about his shoes? What kind?

Also brown, Tina says. Ankle-length leather shoes, pebble grain, no laces.

To compose the sketch, Tina and Flo and Alice Hancock and other witnesses are shown the Facial Identification Catalog, the Bureau's bible of ears (average? protruding? close set?) and noses (hooked? snub?

downward tip?) and chins (cleft? dimple?). Flo likes face type KK5-1, except for the ears and hair. Alice likes KA3-9 (eyebrows, OC1-10; mouth, KE9-11; cheek and cheekbones, KJ1-1).

And what about the hair?

"Straight, parted on the left side," Flo says.

"Straight, narrow sideburns," Tina says.

Alice saw the hijacker's hair differently.

"Wavy, short, and trimmed in the back," Alice says.

"Marcelled," Robert Gregory, the paint company owner, tells the agents who interview him. The marcel wave is an old French hairstyle created by hot irons.

As co-owner of a paint company, Gregory pays attention to details, especially colors. Gregory says the hijacker's suit was not brown or black. The color was russet, a reddish brown. And the suit, he tells the feds, had wide lapels. Which was strange. Wide lapels are out of style.

Gregory also noticed the hijacker's hair. It was jet black, and had a greasy patent leather shoe polish shine to it. The hair was so dark it could have been dyed. The man's skin was also "swarthy." Perhaps he was Mexican-American, or had American Indian blood.

And about how tall?

Not that tall, Gregory tells the feds. About five foot nine.

✗

In Reno, in daylight, agents can see inside the cabin. Northwest 305 is wrecked. Food from the meals the hijacker requested for the crew are splattered over the seats and on the walls. Searching for fingerprints, agents dust 18E, the seat the hijacker sat in, the handle of the lavatory he hid in, the cabin phone he used to call the pilots when he couldn't get the aftstairs down, the in-flight magazine in front of the seat.

The agents find fingerprints. Too many. Which are the stews' and passengers'? Which are Cooper's?

In the armrest, agents locate the hijacker's cigarette butts. They look at the label. The brand is Raleigh, a coupon smoke. In total, there are eight butts in the ashtray. The agents search for hairs to analyze. On a seat, they find one limb hair. On the cloth that covers the headrest, they find a head hair. It is brown, Caucasian in origin.

Near the hijacker's seat, agents find another piece of evidence. It is a tie. A skinny tie. The color is black. The knot is fake. It's a clip-on. In the center of the tie is a tack. It is gold in color and features a circular pearl-like stone.

Agents turn over the tie and read the label. "Towncraft, #3, Penney's," it says.

In Portland, Himmelsbach comes home for Thanksgiving dinner thinking about Cooper. Time is running out. With every minute that elapses, the feds lose ground. The weather had been so terrible—rain, fog, snow—that agents and local law enforcement could not search the flight path on foot. The next morning, the search would begin in earnest. That night, Himmelsbach watches the evening news. The hijacking is a lead story. At CBS, Walter Cronkite reads the intro.

> *When he boarded a plane in Portland Oregon last night he was just another passenger who gave his name as D.[B.] Cooper. But today, after hijacking a Northwest airlines jet, ransoming the passengers in Seattle, then making a getaway by parachute somewhere between there and Reno, Nevada, the description by one wire service: Master Criminal.*

September 3, 1969
University Hospital, University Of Washington, Seattle

In the auditorium, doctors, surgeons, and all of the fourth-year medical students wait to hear the speech Bobby Dayton has prepared before going into surgery. Bobby has become a fixture at the teaching hospital, sitting in waiting rooms in a dress and heels, chain-smoking. His doctors told him the name he chose for himself as a woman should be similar to his own. Bobby thought about Roberta. He prefers Barbara.

His remarks are typed. He reads them.

> *After forty-three years, I continue to live with an obsession that has ruined not only my life, but the life of others I have loved. I cannot understand myself, nor can I reason why I must be tormented until I die. I did not ask to come upon this earth, and I have never thanked God for the breath of life. My health is excellent and my appearance is normal enough—a normal male who should find a place in the world, marry, and live out a reasonably happy life. If only it were that simple.*

Every night when Bobby was a boy, his family ate dinner together in silence. His father, Elmer, wanted to listen to the news on the radio, and the rest of the family wasn't allowed to talk. Elmer was a cement contractor in Long Beach, California. He was tough and proud and always walked a few paces ahead of his wife, Bernice. "Squaw follow chief," he liked to say.

Bobby was jealous of his younger brother, Bill, who was taller and better-looking. Bobby made his own stilts from wood and stuffed them into his shoes. He practiced walking with the stilts until no one even noticed he was wearing them. Bobby and Bill were close. When they were teenagers, they fled to Mexico to mine gold. Short of money, they camped in a cave for shelter. Bill started complaining about the aliens.

They were watching him, he said. They had taken him into space on a spaceship and returned him here.

His brother was cursed. The curse ran in their family. It was placed on their grandfather by an Indian woman. She decreed that all the men in the Dayton family would suffer from pains in their minds. Bill was later diagnosed with paranoid schizophrenia.

Meanwhile, the Dayton family had moved. Bobby's father, Elmer, purchased land on an old ranch in the Mother Lode, where miners pulled out fortunes from the gold-flecked streams of the Sierra Nevada mountains in northern California. The ranch was over seven hundred acres, not large by farming standards but huge for a cement contractor from Long Beach. At first, Elmer knew little about how to run a ranch. There wasn't enough grass for his livestock to eat; many animals got sick and died of starvation.

On furlough from the Merchant Marines, Bobby met Dixie on a blind date. She had big eyes and a flirty, fun way about her. She liked to write poems, just like him.

After the first date, Dixie's parents found out.

"We're just friends," she told them. Nothing sexual happened.

They didn't believe her. Bobby was older, twenty-two. She was only fifteen. Get married, they urged her.

Bobby was stationed in Alaska when his parents began writing to him, encouraging him to marry Dixie.

"It doesn't make any real difference to me," Bobby wrote back. "Either way things turn out is OK with me."

He was distracted. He was trying to get his pilot license, but he failed the written part of the exam. There was a lot of math on the test. He knew how to fly. Why did he need to know math?

He also flunked the physical exam. Doctors noticed a problem in one of his eyes. His vision was off.

All Bobby ever wanted was to fly for a living. That dream was over. The next best thing was gold. He later moved back to the Mother Lode, purchased his own claim nearby, and married Dixie.

They had a son, Dennis. Bobby built a cabin for them on the mining claim. At night, Bobby would wake them with his screams.

The Blanket Monster was after him again, he'd tell Dixie. The Blanket Monster was a phantom that chased him in his dreams. It was big and fast. Bobby ran from it. He'd stop, turn, look back. The Blanket Monster was gone. Then, there it was. To appear invisible, the Blanket Monster merely turned itself sideways. Then it came in front of him . . . the blanket wide like a sail . . . about to swallow him.

One afternoon, Dixie came home and found Bobby wearing one of her dresses. He tried to calm her down. He told her about his sickness. After a while, she came to understand, and they faked the marriage to protect his secret. When Dixie got pregnant again, Bobby knew he wasn't Rena's father, but he treated the baby girl as his own.

The claim he purchased did not yield the gold he hoped. So Bobby traveled. Once, he went to prospect gold in the Yukon. A small plane dropped him into the bush, along with a guide he called the Crazy Indian. After a while, the Crazy Indian got sick. Bobby left to find help.

Alone in the bush, he was without food and shelter. The natural world devoured him. The mosquitoes attacked in swarms. He stripped out of his clothes and jumped in a river to keep them from eating his skin. When the pilots of the rescue helicopter spotted him, Bobby was naked and running toward them. His first postcard home read:

Had to be rescued. Out of food for eight days. . . . Need rest here for awhile. Any money would be appreciated.

A few days later, he wrote again.

I was the last one rescued. They dropped me some food by air and picked me up the next morning. I had gone about 8 miles back to see if there was any of the moose left we had killed about ten days before but the bear had eaten it . . . I had passed out several times that day trying to reach the moose and had wandered aimlessly four miles out of the way . . . All fine now.

When Bobby came home from his trips, the world he left behind had changed. Once he learned Dixie had an affair with his brother, Bill. Another time, Bobby discovered she had taken up with another man from the Mother Lode and was divorcing him.

He moved to Seattle. He found work in the shipping yards and lived in a boarding house. It was liberating for him to be alone, to cross-dress in peace. Then he met Cindy. She was a waitress. Eventually, she and Bobby married. They were a poor family. On the shipping yards the workers were striking and paychecks were scarce. They went bankrupt. The electricity and gas in the house were shut off. They used a gas lantern and camping stove to prepare meals. Finally, Bobby decided to go back into the Merchant Marines for extra pay. It was the summer of 1967, and he shipped out to Vietnam.

When he got off the boat, the poverty was overwhelming. Bobby got jumped by a gang of kids, who stole six dollars from him. He woke up lying on the street in his own blood, watching the Vietnamese walk by. Why had nobody offered to help him up? What was wrong with this country?

When he came home, Cindy was missing. She had taken off with another man. She had cashed all of the checks that Bobby had sent her. She had also taken his car. Bobby filed a report with the police, claiming she stole it. The police refused to file a charge. Isn't she your wife, sir?

Finally, he found her. They agreed to stay together as friends. At night, Bobby would wear a dress and cook dinner for Cindy and her boyfriend. Then they would all sit around the table and play cards.

He moved to Baltimore, to be near Johns Hopkins University, where doctors were performing sex change operations. Bobby had no money. He didn't eat for days. Doctors rejected his application for the surgery. How could Bobby adapt into society as a woman? His features were too manly. His teeth were bad. His body was covered in tattoos. He couldn't be a pilot. He hadn't found gold. He'd lost his family. He was broke. What was there to live for?

Months later, at the training hospital on the University of Washington campus, Bobby finishes his written remarks before his operation.

> *Society dictates that I live and work as a male, but laws cannot bend deep feelings and longings that tear me away from the maleness they stab me with. If I seem rough and coarse, blame it on society. They forced me to live in a man's world. A world I've despised from the beginning. I no longer care what people think when they meet me, for I choose to stay the way I am now. When I venture out into the world again, it shall be as a female.*

November 26, 1971
Woodland, Washington

The morning light is a curtain of gray. The air is damp. The forecast is for more rain and sleet and snow. Seventeen squad cars are parked outside the police station. The sheriffs and their deputies have come from Clark, Cowlitz, Lewis, and Wahkiakum counties. A posse is in place. A media circus is forming, too, as reporters from across the country descend on southwest Washington to document the manhunt for the missing hijacker.

Inside the Woodland police station, the searchers wear Stetsons and boots to navigate the muddy floor of the forest. On the walls are maps of the search area. The air search will be conducted by six fixed-wing planes, flying in a pattern. Helicopters will hover over the treetops. By radio, the planes and choppers will communicate with search teams on the ground. Boats will patrol Lake Merwin, a dammed-up reservoir.

It is still unclear where the hijacker landed. In Minnesota, Northwest officials have their conversation with the Northwest pilots on the company radio transcribed. Within the transcript, they find this line: WE NOW HAVE AN AFT-STAIR LITE ON. The light from the aftstairs in the rear of the jet means the stairs had been lowered during the flight. According to a Teletype copy of the transcript, that report was delivered from the Northwest cockpit before 7:42 p.m. The transcription also bears this line: GETTING SOME OSCILLATIONS IN THE CABIN. MUST BE DOING SOMETHING WITH THE AIR-STAIRS. That report, 8:12 p.m.

This data is at once precise and vague. What does *oscillations* mean? According to the flight's engineer, Harold Anderson, the oscillations in the cabin refer to a "pressure bump" he noticed on the Northwest jet's air cabin pressure dial. But what caused this pressure bump? Was it a change in the jet's aerodynamics? A stormlike gust of wind? Or the hijacker bailing out?

In Minnesota, Northwest's engineers imagine a likely scenario. Hovering at 10,000 feet in the night sky, Cooper walks down the aftstairs. His own weight (plus twenty pounds of stolen cash) pushes the stairs down. But the combined weight of the hijacker and the ransom (roughly two hundred pounds) is not enough to force the aftstairs into a locked position—the slipstream of air running underneath the jet is pushing the aftstairs up. That leaves the hijacker teetering on the edge of the aftstairs, hovering on a perch over the dark forest below.

He leaps. He slips and falls. However it happens, the Northwest engineers believe that after the hijacker departs the aircraft, the weight from the aftstairs is released; then, like a springboard, the slipstream pushes the aftstairs up toward the cabin of the jet. By closing the size of the open hole in the jet during flight, the cabin pressure changes. The meter inside the gauge oscillates. Hence, the pressure bump.

But: when did the pressure bump happen? Was it at 8:12 p.m., the time recorded on the Northwest Teletype transcript? Or was 8:12 p.m. the time when the pilots reported it? How much time had elapsed between the bump and the report? What if the transcription was off? If so, what was the range of error? One minute? Five? Ten?

In other crimes, the preciseness of a singular moment might not matter. But with an airplane moving 200 miles per hour, and thousands of acres of wilderness for the searchers to cover by foot, determining the exact time in which the hijacker jumped from Northwest 305 is critical. Engineers estimate the jet was traveling along the flight path at roughly three miles a minute. Given that the flight path itself is ten miles wide, a conservative estimate that the hijacker jumped between 8:11 p.m. and 8:16 p.m. would mean the drop zone in which the feds had to search for Cooper would be roughly 150 square miles. A drop zone that big is impossible to search by foot. Maybe the military can help?

The largest base in the area is Fort Lewis, a massive Army compound that houses some twenty thousand troops. The military's aeronautical engineers use flight information from Northwest 305 and other data, and with their most advanced computer systems produce a search area that is roughly twenty-five square miles. It is shaped like a diamond, and straddles Clark and Cowlitz counties in southwest Washington.

Using this newly enhanced drop zone, agents dissect the diamond into six sectors—one per search team. At the center of the diamond is Ariel, a logging hamlet that borders Lake Merwin. To get there from Woodland, sheriffs and deputies drive down country roads and pass the welcome sign:

THE WAGES OF SIN IS DEATH: BUT . . . GOD'S
GIFT IS ETERNAL LIFE.

The forest is a fortress. The brambles are thick and untamed. It is hard to keep the line together as the searchers maneuver around fallen logs and sharp crevices. It is dark, even in the daylight, under the evergreens. On the ground, the fronds of giant ferns hide what lies underneath. The plumes of breath come out of mouths and noses like cigarette smoke.

"You've got to look straight down," a police officer says. "It sure limits the possibility of seeing anything."

The rain turns to snow.

"If he was smart enough to plan it out this far," a sheriff says, "he sure as hell won't leave the parachute around for us to find."

"We're either looking for a parachute or a hole in the ground," an agent says.

Overhead, the searchers can hear the engines of the fixed-wing planes and the helicopters. Back and forth and back again.

In the woods, the searchers are not alone. Treasure hunters are after the ransom. At a gas station, a reporter from Seattle finds a college student filling up her tank. She drove up from Portland with two friends to hunt for the missing loot.

"You start thinking about it," she says, "and you realize maybe he didn't live through the fall and there's two hundred thousand dollars sitting all alone in the woods."

"Even a good Christian man" would keep the money, a farmer says. "A lot of people in Clark County are having to go on welfare because they lost their jobs. A man could buy himself a pretty nice farm with that kind of money—even if he had to go to Australia."

A reward is offered. The airline promises $25,000. The *Seattle Post-Intelligencer* is offering $5,000 for information (and exclusive rights to the story) that leads to Cooper's conviction.

Throughout the Pacific Northwest, the hijacker is becoming a hero. One local paper declares: "While the FBI scrabbles for clues, America canonizes its new patron saint of system-fucking." In small towns, civic groups include the hijacker in weekly programming. One sign reads:

Thurs—Pops Concert
Wed—Dad's Club
Tue—
Mon—CONGRATULATIONS! D.B. COOPER

"That guy is smart," a waitress in Woodland says. "He's probably in Mexico laughing about all these federal agents looking all over Washington for him."

D.B. Cooper. The name is everywhere. A bowling alley organizes the D.B. Cooper Sweepstakes. An unknown prankster places a classified ad in *The Barometer*, Oregon State University's college paper: "David B. Cooper will be available to autograph his book *Night Skydiving for Fun and Profit* 8:30 p.m. at the bookstore, weather permitting." Others build a mock grave on a country road east of Woodland, with a corpse fashioned out of driftwood. D.B. COOPER'S GRAVE, the sign says. DIED NOV 24 1971 FROM A FREE FALL. Entrepreneurs manufacture T-shirts. One design: "D.B. Cooper Fan Club." Another: "Cooper Lives!" A local songwriter, Judy Sword, records "D.B. Cooper, Where Are You?" The song gets constant airplay.

With your pleasant smile
And your dropout style,
D.B. Cooper, where did you go?

In Woodland, in Battleground, in Ariel, in the logging towns that make up southwest Washington, agents knock on doors and stop drivers at roadblocks. Strange sightings are reported.

"You don't catch me sleeping very sound," Jess Hatfield says. The seventy-five-year-old has been sleeping with his rifle next to his bed since the night of the hijacking.

"I was up reading when I heard a noise at the side window."

He perked up in his chair. He fetched his shotgun. He watched the back door and saw the knob turn. Then the back door started to move.

Hatfield had his gun up, finger on the trigger.

"One more push and he would have had a bullet through him. I was ready to shoot him right through the panel . . . Yeah, it could have been [Cooper] alright."

The next morning, Hatfield looked for tracks. There were none.

The forest here has a way of keeping its secrets hidden.

"Right outside town is an old cemetery so grown up that the city can't even find it," one Woodland resident says.

Overhead, loggers hear the constant rumble of search planes and helicopters rattle the windows of homes. A young girl listens to her parents talk about the man who jumped out the plane with all that money and is now missing. The girl mounts her horse, meets her friends, and gallops into the woods to find him. Amid the trees the children find a plane, a rusted-out two-seater. The windshield is gone. The cloth on the seats has deteriorated.

"This is D.B. Cooper's plane," one of the girls says.

In Seattle, reporters flood the city for local reaction quotes.

"I hope he isn't caught," a military private says about the missing sky bandit.

"The way I see it, anybody smart enough to take two hundred

thousand just like that ought to make a clean getaway," a taxi driver says. "I'm not saying he's right, understand, but he plain had guts."

"Technically, of course, he should be caught," a sailor says. "But in a way, I'm glad he got away. I can't help thinking: If I were going to do something like that, I wish I could do it as well as he did."

An elderly woman in Seattle compares the skyjacker to John Dillinger.

"Dillinger had a mean streak," she says. "This man fortunately didn't hurt anybody and somehow that seems to make a difference. . . . He was either very talented or very crazy."

At the University of Washington, Otto Larsen, a sociology professor, explains the phenomenon. "We all like adventure stories," the professor says. "That hijacker took the greatest ultimate risk. He possessed real heroic features—mystery, drama, romanticism, a high degree of skill—all the necessities for the perfect crime."

March 1995
West Florida Regional Medical Center, Pensacola, Florida

She does not recognize him. A feeding tube is in Duane's nose. His belly is bloated and big because his kidneys have stopped working. Duane is refusing treatments. His face is ashen and sallow. He sits in a wheelchair in his hospital room. Jo follows the doctor into the hall. How long will Duane live without treatments?

"Five days," the doctor tells her.

She'll have to plan the funeral, call his friends, his brother John, his sister Gwen. When will she pack up his clothes? Sell the antiques?

Jo walks back into his hospital room. Duane's hand is raised.

"Come here, Josephine," he says. "Come here."

He wants to sneak another cigarette, she thinks. She reaches inside her purse for her pack. They're smoking Salems these days.

He does not want a cigarette. He wants to talk. It's important. He needs her to pay attention. Are they alone in the hospital room?

She looks behind the curtain. The other bed in the room is empty.

"I've got something to tell you," he says.

Soon his body will be pumped with morphine. Soon she will be making plans for his funeral. Which funeral home will she call? How many people will come? Who will write the obituary? Will the newspaper even print a story about his life?

"I'm Dan Cooper," Duane says.

Dan who? She is confused. Did the doctors slip Duane a pill while she was gone? His abdomen is so bloated.

Duane says the name again and says it different. He has a deep voice and when he says the name the second time he gives it a *coo-koo* sound, as if imitating the call of an owl.

"I'm Dan *Cooooooper*," he says.

He rambles on about things he says he did, like jumping out of an airplane. She is not paying attention. What will life be like when he is really gone? Will she date again? Five days!

Duane is furious. Jo is not paying attention. Jo always suffered from DBS, he said. Dumb Blonde Syndrome. He is nearly screaming now. The nurses rush into his room.

"Oh fuck," Duane says. "Let it die with me."

She finds the morphine pills under his pillow a day later. Duane is hiding them, fighting the doctors. They place a morphine patch on his back. He gets sleepy. Woozy. Whoa. Out of it.

One afternoon, Anne Faass, who worked for Duane at the Peddler, their antiques store, comes to see him in the hospital. Duane talks about a bucket.

There was money in the bucket, Duane says. A lot of money.

"$178,000," Jo hears him say. "$173,000," Anne hears him say.

The bucket is gone, Duane says. He forgot where he put it.

Day five. Day six. There is a military chaplain in the hospital. Duane wants to confess. Jo wheels him into a room to be alone with the chaplain.

Day ten. Or is it day nine? She is sitting with Duane in the hospice room. He pulls her close.

"I love you," he says.

The way he says it sounds as sincere as anything that has ever come out of his mouth. She cries.

An hour later, Duane is jumpy, paranoid.

"They're gonna kill me, Jo! They're gonna kill me!"

He won't stop talking. What are the doctors giving him?

"Let's get on down the road, Jo! Let's get on down the road!"

"The mommy wants to kill the baby, and the baby wants to kill the mommy."

"Take the baby downstairs. No, bring the baby back up. I can't go until the baby gets here."

Jo sells what she can. After Duane's death, she puts an ad in the paper for the Astro van he used to haul antiques to flea markets. Gets $3,800 for it. She also goes through his papers. She finds a receipt for a safety deposit box. Was Duane trying to hide money from her? She goes to the bank, presents Duane's death certificate and their marriage license. A bank official goes to retrieve the contents of Duane's safety deposit box for her. When he returns, he is holding a magazine.

Now wait a minute. Where's the rest of it? Is the bank trying to steal whatever cash Duane might have had in the box?

No, the bank official says. The magazine is it. He hands it to her.

She reads the title. *Soldier of Fortune.*

It is a magazine for mercenaries and paramilitary types. She looks at the issue date: December 1994. She looks at the cover photo. A man, dressed in snow camouflage, holds an assault rifle wrapped in white gauze.

COLD WEATHER COMMANDOS, the title reads.

Jo leafs through the magazine. She sees advertisements for brass knuckles, lock picks, lead sap gloves. She reads the first page. She looks at the photo. It's a parachutist. He is clutching an object between his legs. It's a bomb. She reads the title of the story.

THE MAN WHO HELD THE SECRETS, it says.

November 27, 1971
Seattle, Washington

The name of the hijacker is kept confidential. This is by design. With the false alias D.B. Cooper in the press, agents now know that all leads that come in about a "D.B." can be ignored, and all leads with the name "Dan Cooper" should be given top priority.

Dan Cooper. What does the name mean? Is it an anonymous cover, like Mike Smith or John Doe? Or is it a clue they are overlooking?

Whoever Dan Cooper was, he knew about parachutes. Agents are assigned to identify every parachute jump center and parachute club on the West Coast. They collect registration cards for more than fourteen thousand skydivers throughout Washington, Oregon, and California.

Agents go undercover over the border. At a skydiving competition in Canada, Bureau agents snap covert pictures of skydivers.

Earl Cossey, the rigger who packed the parachutes, is summoned to the Seattle field office for questioning. The feds ask Cossey to describe the chutes in detail.

Both rear pack chutes are emergency chutes, Cossey says. But different types.

How different?

It's like choosing between a luxury car and an old tank. The luxury model is the Pioneer, Cossey says. The Pioneer was designed for recreational jumpers. The straps around the legs and arms are lined with heavy foam padding that would ease the jolt the hijacker would feel after pulling the ripcord. And using the shroud lines as guides, the hijacker would be able to steer through the night sky.

And the tank?

The NB6, or Navy Back 6, is a military chute, Cossey says. The container is drab Army green. The harness is primitive, and the jolt is so fierce and the padding so weak, the force can break skin.

What color is the canopy of the NB6?

"White," Cossey says.

What is it made from?

"Nylon. Twenty-eight feet, with a conical canopy."

Could the hijacker even control a chute as crude as the NB6?

"Somewhat," Cossey says. It would be difficult to pinpoint a landing. What chute did the hijacker use? Cossey wants to know.

Well, when agents in Reno searched the plane, they found two parachutes. The first was a front chute, the reserve. The ripcord had been pulled. The canopy was loose in the cabin. It had been cut away from the container.

And the other chute?

The Pioneer. It hadn't been touched. So, agents surmised, the hijacker must have jumped with the NB6.

Cooper must be ex-military, Cossey thinks. Has to be. Why else take the NB6?

And what about the front or reserve chutes? the feds ask.

Useless, Cossey says. The reserve chutes the hijacker was given would not have worked with the NB6. The NB6 does not have steel D rings. Without D rings, there is no way for the hijacker to attach a reserve chute to the NB6.

The issue is moot. Even if the hijacker had D rings, the reserve chute that was missing when the plane was searched (which presumably meant the hijacker took it with him) was a dummy. Linn Emrich, the skydive instructor who provided the reserve chutes, tells agents he mistakenly gave the state troopers a training chute. It was designed not to deploy. The folds of the canopy were sewn shut.

So, the feds ask, is it even possible to survive a jump from the rear of a 727, in stormy conditions, at night, without a working reserve, and a main chute he could hardly steer over a forest as remote as the Cascade foothills?

Quite possible, Cossey says. And the hijacker does not need to be a master skydiver, either. Six or seven jumps with an instructor is enough.

What about jumping at night? Is that more dangerous?

It is. The trouble is vision, Cossey says. When you're floating down over a dark forest, it's harder to gauge the distance to the ground. Not easy on the legs, knees, and ankles.

If the hijacker survived, what are the chances he has an injury?

Extremely high, Cossey says. If Cooper is alive, he would be injured. He could have easily broken a leg or an ankle.

The call goes out from the Bureau field office. Search all local hospitals and interview doctors. Find anyone with a limp.

Inside the Bureau field office, agents are contemplating motives. Was the hijacker a rogue Boeing engineer who was terminated from the company and decided to seek his revenge by hijacking the Northwest plane?

Agents travel to Boeing's headquarters in Renton, outside of Seattle, and file through company records. How many of Boeing's workers might have had parachute experience? How many were male, about six feet tall, with dark hair and dark eyes and a dark complexion, and had recently been fired?

A lot. In 1968, there were over 100,000 employees at Boeing. During the recession, the workforce has been slashed to a third. How can the feds fish through tens of thousands of pink slips?

There are clues to follow. The hijacker was specific. He knew about the 727's aftstairs, and knew a parachutist could safely jump from them and not get incinerated by the jet's rear engines. So is Dan Cooper an engineer who worked on the Air America 727s that Boeing made for the CIA? Agents identify between twenty and thirty Boeing engineers and test pilots who worked on the CIA project between 1963 and 1964. The interviews yield no suspects.

How familiar was Cooper with the 727?

According to stewardess Tina Mucklow, the hijacker did not know how to operate the aftstairs. He was so unfamiliar with how they worked, he needed her help. If Dan Cooper was a Boeing engineer who worked on the jets, he would know how to use the air-stairs, right?

And what about the motive? Was it only money? According to Mucklow, Dan Cooper was bitter. "I don't have a grudge against your airline," he told her. "I just have a grudge."

Fall Semester, 1971
Brigham Young University, Provo, Utah

The headaches. The tumor. Is it real? Richard Floyd McCoy Jr. is in pain. What is wrong with him?

He tries to focus on his schoolwork. The research paper on skyjackers interests him. To prevent skyjackings, he needs to understand how they think, what their minds are like. One psychological study, released earlier in the year, suggests that skyjackers are not really motivated by the politics of Cuba or the Irish Liberation Army or the Middle East, despite what they say. The study burrows deeper into the unconscious, identifies what triggers the criminal impulse and the impact of flight on the ego.

It starts, of course, with the father. Dr. David G. Hubbard, a psychiatrist who interviewed dozens of skyjackers in prison to complete his book, *The Skyjacker,* proposed the following theory:

> *It is my overall thesis that these men introjected the fearful image of a father at an early age, a father who would "do them in if they dared to rise and try to act like men," and that image of the impossible father had an intimate connection with the son's gravito-inertial experiences and his definitions of the impossible, revealing a determinant of crime specifically involving flight.*

Gravity is key, Hubbard thought. From the moment of birth until death, gravity governs us all. It cannot be escaped. After birth, when the mind is in the process of rapid development and the strains of personality and ego are formed, babies are at the mercy of gravity. They cannot stand. They need the help of others to transport them. They are pinned by gravity. Slowly, they learn to use their own two feet to rise up, to break the stranglehold the force of gravity has upon them.

Gravity becomes its own impossible father, Hubbard says. "It is violent, inevitable, instantaneous, and unmerciful. It is indifferent and final, and by its physical nature stands in stark contrast to that of the mother who . . . is condemned to live in a world where a physical reality (the father) is holding her and her children down in eternal subjection."

McCoy's childhood was like that. His father beat him. His mother could do nothing to stop it, until she left him for another man. She was also religious and sweet. There was definitely what Dr. Hubbard called a "hostile border" between the father and the mother. And: "The child must clearly stand on one side or the other."

McCoy and Karen and Karen's younger sister, Denise, live in a small red brick house on a quiet street in Provo. The trees that arch over the street are horse chestnut and sycamore. Their neighbors are like them—devout Mormons connected to Provo's educational and economic center, BYU. For extra money, McCoy has been teaching Sunday school. He is familiar with the Mormon Articles of Faith.

> 12.) We believe in being subject to kings, presidents, rulers, and magistrates, in obeying, honoring, and sustaining the law.
> 13.) We believe in being honest, true, chaste, benevolent, virtuous, and in doing good to all men . . .

Along the siding of McCoy's house are bushes that are so overgrown they almost touch the windowsills. The garage is small. His Volkswagen bug squeezes in.

In the house, there is tension between Richard and Karen and Denise. How will McCoy support his children, Chante and Rich, if he has no chance at a career in law enforcement?

For a release, McCoy goes parachuting at the Alta Jump Center with Robert Van Ieperen, a state trooper and a friend from the National Guard. McCoy talks about the topic on his mind. How easy would it be to jump out of a commercial airliner, if you did it the right way? How much cash could you get away with? Where would you land? It would have to be a remote drop zone, away from authorities.

At home, McCoy thinks and talks about skyjackings. Denise, his sister-in-law, later recalled a question McCoy asked her. If McCoy jumped out of an airplane in a remote location, would she be willing to pick him up?

November 29, 1971
Seattle, Washington

The sketches are finished. The Bureau has postcards printed for agents to analyze and for cops to pass out and slide under house doors. The image is printed in newspapers. It runs on television news spots. The face is everywhere.

The face is an honest face, or a once-honest face. The lips are thin, as if from the Midwest. The hair is good-boy hair: flat and parted neatly on the top of his forehead. The expression is empty and pallid and yet there is something determined about his look. Or maybe there isn't. The face is now a blank canvas for the mind to fill. Dan Cooper is now who you want him to be.

The guy looks a lot like Bing Crosby, many say.

There is a second sketch. It is an arresting image. The frames of the hijacker's sunglasses are not ornate or horn-rimmed. They are wrap-around frames with bubble lenses, sunglasses you might wear riding around the German countryside in a motorcycle sidecar.

In Las Vegas, agents analyze evidence found on the hijacked plane. What does the black clip-on tie mean? Towncraft? Penney's? J.C. Penney's? A Bureau agent takes the tie to the department store. He shows it to the manager and the assistant manager. This tie look familiar?

It does. Penney's carries the Towncraft label.

The agent flips over the tie. Can the Penney's employees tell perhaps what Penney's store the Towncraft tie came from?

Impossible, the manager says. All J.C. Penney stores carry the Towncraft label. Also notice the width, he says. The tie is skinny, a slender ribbon of black cloth.

The assistant manager goes over to the tie counter. He retrieves a Towncraft. The tie he is holding is at least two and half times the width of the Towncraft found on the hijacked plane.

Why was one Towncraft skinny and the other wide?

Styles have changed, the assistant manager tells the agent. Men are wearing wide ties now.

How long ago was Penney's carrying the skinny Towncraft?

At least a year, the assistant manager says. A year and a half probably.

What about the gold-colored pearl tie tack?

Penney's doesn't sell that item, the manager says.

Have any idea who does?

No idea.

What about the #3 on the label? What does the #3 mean?

A price indicator, the manager says. The #3 Towncraft sold for $1.50.

The Towncrafts aren't dress-type ties, the assistant manager says. They're usually worn by working people, purchased in bulk.

They're polyester, the manager says. Easy to wash. They're for bus-boys, waiters, bartenders.

The list of suspects is growing. Gary Samdel is a parachute expert from Illinois. Joseph H. Johnston, a steelworker from Alabama. Louis John Macaluso, a racetrack security guard. John Gordon Hoskin, a mechanic from Sacramento. Some tips that come in are mug shots of men with dark hair lacquered with pomade, chins and cheeks dotted with jail-house stubble. Others have scars, tattoos crawling up their arms, and names that sound regal for suspects: Wells B. Van Steenbergh Jr., R. H. Werth, Floyd J. Snider, James Henry Zimmerman, Owen Patrick Moses, William Cameron Warwick.

Throughout Seattle and the states of Washington and California, there are knocks on doors. Suspects are taken into interrogation rooms for questioning.

"I could have done it, yes, but I didn't," says William Whitney, an-other parachutist. "It would be nice to look like a movie star or some-thing, but not the guy who pulled a job."

Jiří Fencl, a country club manager, is detained for three hours at the Sacramento airport after police find $800 in his wallet, and a card that states Fencl was once a parachutist.

"I went through it calmly because I knew I was innocent," Fencl says later.

More names come in for agents to investigate. Merlin Gene Cooper. Daniel Louis Cooper. Marvin John Dooper. Leif E. Hanson. James Raul Wood. John Scott. James Conrad Clifford. Tom Rompot. Leslie Gene Mince. Robert Lee Horton. Delbert Earl Downing. David Ray Mann. Kent Phillips. Harold Lee Dowell. Ralph Vincent Galope. Jesse Edwin Bell. Ben Liebson. Harry William Celk. Jerry Eugene Dodele. William Wilfred Kriegler. William Latham. George Bryn Siegrist. Henry Epperson.

THE HIJACKER IS EVERYWHERE runs one headline in the *Post-Intelligencer*. More letters arrive at newspapers and Bureau field offices.

```
I didn't rob Northwest Orient because I
thought it would be romantic, heroic or any
of the other euphemisms that seem to attach
themselves to situations of high risks. I am
no modern-day Robin Hood. Unfortunately (I)
do have only 14 months to live. My life has
been one of hate, turmoil, hunger and more
hate. This seemed to be the fastest and most
profitable way to gain a few grains of peace
of mind.
```

August 24, 2007
Woodburn, Oregon

I have the proof. It is in my bag. The bag is near my feet, which are tap-tap-tapping away on Himmelsbach's porch.

I go over my argument for Kenny again. First point: the spooky resemblance. Kenny *is* the sketch. The thin lips, the cheeks, the slightly balding forehead, the nice-guy hair, the social-studies-teacher look– it's him. Second, he knew how to jump out of airplanes. He was in the Paratroops. Third, during the war, he jumped out of airplanes for money. Somewhere in his psyche, there was a connection between his jumps out of a C-46 for a $150 bonus and the $200,000 he asked for years later when he hijacked Northwest 305.

Now, more facts. Ken Christiansen was military. Given the choice between the luxury model Pioneer parachute or the clunky NB6, Ken would have felt more comfortable with the NB6. It probably would have looked like the chutes Ken jumped with in the 11th Airborne during the occupation in Japan.

Kenny also knew airplanes. As Cooper did, Kenny knew how to call the cockpit with the cabin's interphone (*"Let's get the show on the road"*), and where oxygen was located on the plane (*"If I need it I will get it"*). He knew commercial pilots can file flight plans in the air. He would also know, as Cooper did, that airplane cabins need to be pressurized only above 10,000 feet. By keeping below 10,000 feet, the hijacker avoided getting sucked out of the plane once the aftstairs were released.

Kenny's knowledge of aviation also mirrored the hijacker's. Kenny was not a pilot, but as a veteran purser he would have access to aeronautical information. From colleagues, he could learn that the way to keep a B727 moving slowly, as Cooper requested, was to keep the landing gear down and flaps at fifteen degrees.

I thought a purser like Kenny would also know how to operate the aftstairs, and wouldn't need assistance like the hijacker. But according to Lyle, Kenny only worked on international flights. He had seniority.

It was possible Kenny never actually had to fly on a 727 and operate the aftstairs.

More facts. Kenny was a chain smoker. Lyle couldn't say if his brand of choice was the same Raleighs the hijacker smoked, but his brother was "always very saving." He was likely a coupon smoker.

Kenny liked bourbon too, the hijacker's drink. Kenny drank bourbon so much, he collected his own bourbon bottles, Lyle told me.

Kenny was also the same age as the suspect. Flo and Tina both told the feds Cooper was in his midforties. Kenny was born October 17, 1926. At the time of the hijacking, he had recently turned forty-five. Bull's-eye!

Now, the motive: Kenny's revenge against Northwest. How far-fetched could that be? Feelings against the airline were hostile, so much so that even Tina Mucklow suspected employee sabotage.

I look over at Himmelsbach. I feel good that I am here. I can finally end the retired agent's uncertainty about the case. I anticipate the moment of monumental joy that will sweep over the old man when he sees a photo of Kenny and looks into the eyes of the man he's been hunting for four decades. *Hallelujah!*

I reach into my bag. I retrieve the mischievous-grin photo of Kenny. I place it on the table, grin side down. I ask Himmelsbach if during the investigation he and his fellow G-men ever investigated anybody at Northwest Orient—say, a lone-wolf employee who had an ax to grind with Northwest management?

"No," Himmelsbach says. "We had an awful lot of suggestions by people who said, 'I think it's an inside job.'"

So why didn't he look in to it?

"It is inconceivable for several reasons," he says. The main one is character. "If you were acquainted as I was with many of the people in the airline industry, they are exceptional people. They are head and shoulders above the standards and values and the character of normal average Americans."

So maybe that's why Kenny was never investigated?

I finger the photo on the table. I ask Himmelsbach to offer his expert opinion on my suspect. He turns the image over and eyes Kenny for the first time.

"Not bad," he says.

I gush. I tell the agent about Kenny's experience in the Paratroops, his jumps for extra money. I can see the ends of the old man's mustache curl.

I pass him Kenny's records from the Paratroops, which prove much of what I'm telling him. They also contain details of Kenny's physical description.

Himmelsbach squints at the military form, ingesting the information. I think of the Pulitzer Prize committee again. Are there acceptance speeches? If so, what will I say?

"Well," he says.

Well?

"He's too short, too heavy, and has the wrong-color eyes."

I leave Himmelsbach's farm in a huff. I haven't gotten my blessing, and the world's foremost expert on the case has dismissed my suspect.

It's true. Himmelsbach has a point. Kenny is on the short side for a suspect. Most witnesses pegged the hijacker to be between the height of five-foot-ten and six-foot-one. According to his military records, Ken Christiansen was five eight. According to an old driver's license that Lyle had, Kenny was as tall as five nine. That jibed with the description at least one witness, paint company owner Robert Gregory, had given. And how much can we trust the descriptions of the eyewitnesses on the flight? Aren't eyewitnesses notoriously wrong, especially in dramatic situations? And how could they really tell how tall the hijacker was when he was sitting down throughout most of the flight? In photos, Kenny also seemed to have a longish torso, which would have made him appear taller than he was.

It was unfair to dismiss Kenny because of his height.

Plus Himmelsbach didn't have all the facts. Kenny was not fat. At least not yet. The mischievous-grin photo was taken years after the hijacking, in the mid-1970s, Lyle said. In the fall of 1971, Lyle claimed Kenny was in decent shape. About 175 pounds, the same as the hijacker.

And what was wrong with the color of Kenny's eyes? On military records, they are described as "hazel." Flo Schaffner reported them to the feds as "brown." On a hijacked flight, who could tell the difference between hazel and brown?

As an expert, Himmelsbach presents his own problems. As a pilot, his bias is toward the airlines. He confesses to not investigating leads about inside jobs because airline people are "head and shoulders above the standards and values and the character of normal, average Americans."

Bullshit. Somewhere in the airline industry, there have to be a few criminal minds. And considering Cooper's familiarity with airplanes, and the venom Northwest employees had against Northwest, how could the feds not look at insiders?

I pull onto the freeway. I follow the signs to Seattle, retracing the flight path of the hijacked plane. The landscape here is not a mythical tangle of impenetrable forest. This is the Willamette Valley, an agricultural wonderland prized for its rich soil, hops, berries, hazelnuts, Christmas trees, and pinot noir.

I can see the land is flat and the grass is thick. The fields of farms are arranged in well-groomed squares. I get it now. This area along flight path Vector 23 is the ideal drop zone for a parachute landing. I imagine the hijacker, forty years ago, driving the same route north to Seattle, planning the hijack and peering out the window at the verdant land, wondering where to parachute down.

Across the border into Washington, en route to Seattle, the landscape changes. Inside the forest, there are mossy thickets and brambles and vines. It's dark and alive, a forest that watches you. I think of a line from a reporter who followed the first search teams into the woods after the hijacking. "The country is like a beautiful and moody woman," he wrote. "It is itself a character in the story of D.B. Cooper."

December 5, 1971
Woodland, Washington

The weather is taking over. The search teams are stuck. Daily Teletypes are sent back to headquarters.

FOR INFORMATION OF BUREAU, TERRAIN IN SEARCH AREA VARIES FROM A RIDGE LINE WHICH AVERAGES SEVENTEEN HUNDRED FEET AND DENSE WOODS WITH EXTREMELY HEAVY UNDERGROWTH. . . . THERE ARE MANY STREAMS AND HILLS AND MUCH OF THE TIMBERLAND IS ALMOST IMPENETRABLE.

AIR SEARCH COMPLETED WITH NEGATIVE RESULTS. A TOTAL OF EIGHT HUNDRED SQUARE MILES WAS COVERED IN THIS SEARCH WITH NEGATIVE RESULTS AND IT WAS NOTED THAT IT CONSISTS MAINLY OF EXTREMELY ROUGH TERRAIN WITH A NUMBER OF LOGGING ROADS IN EXTREMELY POOR CONDITION.

In Seattle, more names come in for agents to vet. Charles G. Whitaker, Donald Lewis Coleman, James Wayne Wallace, Monroe John Wobick, Daniel McCall Allen. In photos, some have greasy pompadours, combovers, long shaggy ponytails, crew cuts, spiky ears, bug eyes, droopy chins, snaggle teeth, cheap suits, ruddy faces, skinny faces, pale faces, hawkish faces.

Bernie Condon is a bridge worker in Wichita with thick forearms. Frank Charles Emhoff has fat lips and a gap between his front teeth. Donald Wayne Vebeck is a Mississippi cop, Highway Patrol. Bobbie Lee Campbell has done time in San Quentin. Joseph Royce Stagg escaped from federal prison. Randall Ralph Snyder was arrested in Las Vegas. John Marl Nealer is another escaped prisoner. He has a paratrooper tattoo.

In family photos turned over to the authorities, it is difficult to decipher the intent of the man on the couch gripping a beer or dressed up for a night out dancing. John Donald Page is cutting up a pumpkin for Halloween. Donald Eugene Collins has a name similar to the hijacker. *D* for Dan, *D* for Donald. *C* for Cooper, *C* for Collins. Someone overheard him talking about how to escape from a hijacked plane via parachute. Collins, the feds later learn, is training to be a sky marshal.

More tips come in.

In Cougar, another logging town, two men are reported to have checked into the Fir Motel late on the night of the hijacking. The men told the night clerk they were going fishing—but the area had been closed down for years. The next morning, they were gone. Who were they?

One tip comes from a hitchhiker. Says he was picked up by a man named Monsebrotten, who was holding a lot of $20 bills. The call is a crank.

Another tip, confirmed and verified, concerns a fixed-wing plane. On the night before the hijacking, the plane took off from a landing strip within the Cooper drop zone. Cooper's getaway vehicle?

"I was a little surprised to see a plane flying so low through the storm," a witness says. "I thought to myself, What's that nut doing up in the air on a night like this?"

The feds locate the plane. It's registered to a local pilot. The pilot is interviewed. He'd gone up for a ride in bad weather.

A hunting cabin is searched. Agents trek deep into the woods to find it.

The cabin is a dump. The walls are falling apart. Dust and grime coat every surface. On a countertop, agents find a receipt. It's dated a month before the hijacking, for a purchase of $23.07 from Tweedy and Popp, a hardware store in Seattle. Maybe Cooper purchased his bomb-making supplies at Tweedy and Popp? The owners of the store (Tweedy and Popp) are questioned and shown the Bureau sketch. They can't identify the hijacker. A lot of customers look like the sketch.

Arrests are made. One night, police pull over a car for speeding. A chase ensues. The driver is pushing 130 miles per hour. His tires blow out. His wheels burst into flames. The car grinds to a charred stop.

Searching the driver in custody, police find an unusual amount of foreign currency: Canadian, Mexican, Chilean, Peruvian, Australian, Brazilian. All together, the foreign notes must be worth the same as Cooper's ransom.

News of the arrest leaks to newspapers and radio stations. Cooper is caught, early reports say. But agents learn the driver is Dutch and speaks little English. Witnesses on the hijacked plane would have detected his accent.

In Portland, Ralph Himmelsbach's house phone rings. A bartender reports another customer buying drinks for the bar and waving around a stack of $20 bills. Improbable. Himmelsbach gets up and gets dressed and checks it out anyway. No surprise. Another prank.

Himmelsbach worries about copycats. If Cooper isn't caught soon, others might hijack airplanes for cash and parachutes. The feds will have to fight off an epidemic of skydiving robbers.

He thinks of D.O. Guerrero, a character in the bestselling novel and hit film *Airport,* which came out last year. A sweaty, nervous passenger, Guerrero is down on his luck, so he loads up on life insurance and tries to blow up himself and a plane on the way to Europe. Like Cooper, he fashions a bomb inside his briefcase. Himmelsbach thought the film shouldn't have been aired. It could inspire imitators. Heck, Cooper himself could have watched it and decided to hijack Flight 305.

In weeks, the agent's fears prove true.

Everett Holt is twenty-five. He made high grades, was the lead in school plays. A Quaker, he attended meetings. On Christmas Eve, roughly a month after the Cooper hijacking, Holt boards a Northwest plane in Minnesota and wields a revolver and fake bomb. He demands two parachutes and a $300,000 ransom, before surrendering.

"It surely couldn't be the same kid," a friend says of Holt. But it was.

Billy Hurst is twenty-two. On a Boeing 727 from Dallas to Houston, he pulls a pistol and claims to have a bomb. He wants parachutes and a ransom of $1 million.

Richard LaPoint is twenty-three. He uses a fake bomb to hijack a DC-9 from Las Vegas to Reno. He demands $50,000 and parachutes. He jumps. On the ground, he is captured.

Merlyn St. George is on parole from San Quentin. He uses a starter pistol and a fake bomb to commandeer a Mohawk Airlines plane from Albany to New York. Just like Cooper, he asks for $200,000 and parachutes. He holds a stewardess hostage by placing a pistol to her head. An FBI agent opens fire with a shotgun. St. George is killed in the blast.

Stanley Speck is thirty-one. He is a National Merit scholarship winner and a Stanford graduate. He wears blue fatigues and threatens to blow up a Boeing 727 with a hand grenade. He wants four parachutes and $500,000. "He must have flipped his lid," Speck's mother says after his surrender. "I just can't understand it."

February 18, 1970
University Of Washington, Seattle

There are complications. Another surgery is planned. That way, she won't have to use a colostomy bag. From the nurse's notes:

> *Talked with Barbara for approximately 2 hours about her concerns. 1) Surgery. She feels that up to now most of it has been a failure. Wonders whether another attempt will be made at creating new vagina— hesitant to question doctors for fear it may anger them. . . . She asked if she could wear [a hat] as she was concerned about the appearance of her hair and the fact that it has gotten so sparse.*

> *8-11p [Patient] doing well. However was somewhat upset tonight after [unclear] phone calls from former "friends" asking that she no longer visit them.*

The second surgery is a success. Barb leaves the hospital to recover. She is living in a small house in Renton, south of Seattle. The sky is filled with Boeing airplanes. Renton is where the legendary 707 and 727 are manufactured. Renton is also where Boeing's engineers are now busy trying to perfect the Supersonic Transport, a futuristic jet that can ferry passengers to London in only a few hours, and at the sound-breaking speed of 1,900 miles per hour.

Designed to compete with the French Concorde and the Russian Tupolev, the Supersonic Transport program is controversial. The jet will fly too fast. Over time, the Supersonic will shorten the life expectancy rate, one scientist warns. Humans are not supposed to live life at those speeds. And the jets will be noisy and dirty. Across the country, activists and environmentalists complain that the sonic boom the jet will create will be a constant disturbance. Already, civic groups are complaining about the noise pollution of bigger planes and new airports.

In Washington, President Nixon wants to keep the program going.

Already, the government has given Boeing $1 billion for development costs. In Renton, the program employs some 1,500 people. Most domestic jets are made from aluminum, but one challenge for the jet's engineers is to build the airplane out of titanium. It is heat resistant, and is a relatively new material for the Boeing engineers to work with. Titanium sponge, which is where the ore comes from, is mostly found in Russia. When Boeing competitor Lockheed was building spyplanes out of titanium in the early 1960s, the CIA used an elaborate network of cutouts to funnel the material out of the Soviet Union.

Barb Dayton does not like the SST or Boeing's planes. They clog up the sky and make it far too difficult for Weekend Warrior pilots like herself to simply take off on an afternoon. Near the giant Boeing fields and hangars, Barb Dayton rarely leaves her house. She wants to wear feminine clothes but can't because short sleeves will expose her tattoos. She wants to wear lipstick but can't because lipstick draws attention to her bad teeth. When she returns to the hospital for checkups, doctors remark how morose she is.

> *She is aware that she is isolating herself from society. Lives alone in house in Renton ($60/mo. Rent), prior to this lived in trailor [sic] but moved when man threatened to kill her after she told him about her surgery "people like you don't deserve to live."*

She is broke. She needs a job but is too ashamed to apply for one. She cashes her welfare checks and shops at the Goodwill. Her clothes don't fit. She considers suicide again.

Volunteer, her doctors tell her. A job—any job—could restore her confidence.

Her clothes aren't nice enough for volunteer work, she says. Besides, how can she volunteer? She can't afford the gas to drive to a job. And no, she doesn't want help, doesn't need any, won't take any, it's not her way.

Her father, Elmer, offers her money to repair her teeth. No thanks, she says. She wonders about her children. Meanwhile, Dennis shipped out. He is in Vietnam. He looks like a boy wearing his Army helmet. He is addicted to heroin. Her daughter, Rena, ran away at age fourteen. She was living in a trailer with her mother, Dixie, and Dixie's new husband. Rena was scared. She feared sexual abuse. She disappeared. Now she is living in Texas with a woman who tries to prostitute her.

A year passes. Spring turns into summer and now it's fall and soon it will be Thanksgiving. Barb has always spent Thanksgiving at home with her family—but as Bobby. How can she go home? Now her brother, Bill, won't even talk to her. "My brother is dead," Bill says.

Barb is truly alone. She writes a letter to her children. She tells her parents to give the letter to them "some day." It reads:

Dennis and Rena,

I know you have both wondered why I've remained so distant and never tried to contact you the last few years. To be brief, no matter how hard I've tried in the past, I have never been able to accept myself as a male, and nearing the brink of possible suicide, I submitted myself to extensive medical and psychological research. It was determined that I was a transsexual. Physically a male, but more basically a female. In December 1969, I underwent conversion surgery for sex reassignment. I am no longer a would-be man and I have my true identity now, and am much happier for it.

Please don't hate me for what I've done. Life is full of the unexpected.

BARBARA DAYTON
ROBERT DAYTON

January 6, 1972
McChord Air Force Base, Tacoma, Washington

On the tarmac, the Northwest jet is waiting. The goal of the test flight is to find out where Cooper's parachute came down. Agents want to determine why the "pressure bump" occurred in the cabin of the hijacked plane, and when, to pinpoint a more accurate drop zone. Harold Anderson, the flight engineer on the Northwest 305 flight, is here to monitor the dials of the cockpit, to see if the reactions are similar.

The original plan was to have a parachutist mimic the hijacker's jump and see where he landed. That plan has been scrapped. What if the test parachutist is speared on a tree? What if his chutes don't open and he dies? And do they need him anyway?

The same results can be achieved, agents feel, with a simulation. They've built two sleds that weigh more than 200 pounds, roughly the same weight as the hijacker plus his cash bundle. The plan is to drop the sleds over the Pacific Ocean and monitor the jet's gauges.

Inside the cabin, agents wear headphones to protect their ears from the blast of engine noise once the aftstairs are released. They snap photos of Air Force personnel as they don parachutes and parachute helmets. Another Air Force plane flies alongside the Northwest jet to record the experiment on film.

It's sunny and clear above the clouds. Over the Pacific Ocean, the jet stabilizes at ten thousand feet. In the cabin, agents watch as the aftstairs are opened and released. A blast of air and noise rips through the cabin. The stairs do not lower on their own. As Northwest engineers predicted, the slipstream under the jet's belly pushes up against the hydraulics. The stairs cannot get into the locked position. They are suspended in midair.

Inside the cabin, an Air Force captain donning a parachute and crash helmet moves to the back of the jet. He places a foot on the stairs, tests it out.

The step moves down.

He takes another step and inches down the stairway, under the scream of the 727's Pratt & Whitney engines. The captain does not feel heavy gusts of wind. The aftstairs act as a shield, a covered perch high above the Pacific.

Dan Cooper could make his jump from here. He would be cold. It would be loud. But he would be stable enough to make a jump.

One sled is lowered. The sled has wood runners. It slides over the stairs and down to where the last step of the aftstairs meets the sky. The rope is cut. The sled falls and drops and sails and crashes into the ocean below. Another sled is brought out, another rope cut. Later in the afternoon, the report is sent via Teletype from Seattle to Hoover's office in Washington.

THE EFFECT OF THESE DUMMIES DEFINITELY RECORDED A CABIN PRESSURE CHANGE AND, ACCORDING TO FIRST OFFICER ANDERSON WHO WAS A CREW MEMBER OF THE HIJACKED AIRCRAFT, THE REACTION TODAY WAS IDENTICAL TO THAT WHICH OCCURRED DURING THE HIJACKING.

The suspicion is confirmed. The pressure bump must have been when the hijacker jumped. Against a map, that places the potential drop zone in the impenetrable forest the feds have been searching.

"Come next deer season some hunter will find him," a cop in Woodland says.

The forest is too thick to search by foot, the winter weather too harsh. If man can't find Cooper, maybe machine can.

Nicknamed the Blackbird for its radar-repelling black paint, the SR-71 spy plane is the fastest and highest-flying aircraft ever produced. Built for the CIA to conduct aerial reconnaissance during the Cold War, the Blackbird flies three times faster than the speed of sound. It's retrofitted with infrared cameras and heat sensors that are like the eyes of God. They cover more than 100,000 square miles per hour, and are so powerful they can identify a car's license plate from as high as 85,000 feet. The film itself is printed on a strip roughly 24 feet long, and requires special training to decipher.

Each time the SR-71 prepares for a run, the weather breaks. Again, the forces of nature seem to be in cahoots with the hijacker. The first report:

DUE TO CLOUD COVER, NO PHOTOGRAPHS TAKEN.

The second, the third report:

PHOTOGRAPHIC OVERFLIGHT USING SR-SEVENTY ONE AIRCRAFT PER-
FORMED . . . ON ALL THREE FLIGHTS, NO PHOTOS OBTAINED DUE TO
LIMITED VISIBILITY FROM VERY HIGH ALTITUDE.

Into the spring, the weather clears. The ground search resumes. Jeeps and trucks from the 3rd Armory Cavalry at Fort Lewis barrel down country roads into Ariel, and troops set up tents on a patch of wet grass at the corner of Lake Merwin. In total, there are 260 soldiers and eight Huey helicopters dispatched from the army base to aid the FBI.

At daybreak, the Hueys drop soldiers and agents in and out of forest clearings. The soldiers wear heavy boots, dark green camouflage, and orange vests to shield themselves from hunters.

A body is found.

The report comes from two sisters. The sisters were hunting for antique bottles near an old grist mill outside of Woodland. Down near the bottom of the mill's cistern a few rotted planks were missing. They looked closer.

It was a body part.

Soon, the police, the feds, the Fort Lewis troops from the search, the medical examiner, and reporters are all in the woods at the foot of the old cistern. A soldier uses a chain saw to cut through the old wood. The body is removed.

She is in her mid to late twenties. She is wearing blue tennis shoes and bell bottom blue jeans. Her jeans have been pulled down to her knees. She's been raped and stabbed, the medical examiner finds.

A few weeks later, another body is found. A collection of bones, scattered on the ground. Cooper? The remains are of a hunter who broke a bone and could not make it out of the woods.

The Army troops search on. Then the spring weather turns. The conditions are so poor they cripple the cavalry.

DUE TO NEAR EXHAUSTION OF ARMY TROOPS, WHO HAVE ENDURED RAIN, SNOW AND OTHER INCLEMENT WEATHER WHILE TRAVERSING TREACHEROUS, STEEP, HILLY, VINE, TREE AND BRUSH COVERED AREAS, LT. COL. BONSELL FEELS FOR TROOPS WELFARE AND SAFETY THEY SHOULD BE GIVEN REST, WILL TEMPORARILY DISCONTINUE SEARCH.

When the weather clears, the Army troops return to Lake Merwin. Now, they number 269. They cannot set up their tents.

DUE TO CONTAMINATION OF JET FUEL, SEARCH NOT COMMENCED.

When the troops return a week later, winter has returned.

SNOW, SLEET AND FREEZING RAIN HAMPERED SEARCH. REMAINING AREAS TO BE SEARCHED CAN BE REACHED ONLY BY HELICOPTER IN-SERTION AND LANDING ZONES IN MOST CASES UNDER SIX TO TWELVE INCHES OF SNOW.

April 1995
Pace, Florida

The phone rings. Jo Weber picks up.

The caller is the man who bought Duane's Astro van from Jo. He was cleaning out the van, he says, and found a wallet.

That's strange. Jo thought she cleaned out the van.

He returns the wallet to her. The color is black and the material is pebbled. "Ostrich skin," it says on the label. She's never seen this wallet before.

She goes through it. She finds a picture. A house and palm trees. "San Marino Sanitarium," it reads.

Strange. Why would Duane have a picture of an old mental institution in his wallet?

She finds another paper, folded up. She unfolds it and reads it: COMMUTATION OF SENTENCE. STATE OF MISSOURI.

Commutation? She doesn't know what the word means. The document says John C. Collins was sentenced to prison in Missouri for four years and released after two. CONVICTED OF THE CRIME OF . . . GRAND STEALING.

John C. Collins?

She finds another card in the wallet, a Florida driver's license. There it is again. The name: John C. Collins. She looks at the photograph on the license. It's Duane. Why would Duane have a license under the name John C. Collins? The name is curious. Jo's maiden name was Collins. Is that why he married her?

She finds a card from the National Rifle Association. Member name: John C. Collins. And one from the Navy. "Honorable discharge," it says. "John C. Collins." Whom had she been living with? Who was Duane L. Weber? Who was John C. Collins?

She goes through the wallet again. She burrows deep into the crevices. She finds two slips of newsprint. One is a classified ad for a rifle—it is for sale. Another bears the following text:

Bombproof and crowded with oxygen . . . terrace, volcallure at casa Cugat, Abbe Wants Cugie Gets.

The words don't make sense. Bombproof and crowded with oxygen? What does that mean? Is it code?

✈

Several months after Duane's death, Jo is on a date. She wasn't interested romantically, so to send the message she starts talking about Duane. She tells her date about the wacky things Duane told her on his deathbed, and how angry he got after he said, "I'm Dan *Coooooooper.*"

Dan Cooper sounds a lot like D.B. Cooper, her date says. What if Duane was trying to confess to the hijacking? What if Jo was too preoccupied with his medical condition to pay attention?

She doesn't remember much about the hijacking. She stops off at the library the following day. She checks out the book *D.B. Cooper: What Really Happened?* by Max Gunther. She reads the first few sentences.

> *He had given his name to a ticket agent as Dan Cooper, but news reports mistakenly identified him as D.B. Cooper, and that is the name by which he became famous.*

Dan Cooper! *Dan Coooooooper!* Jo can't breathe. She goes home. She calls the FBI. She is so hysterical the agent asks her if she has forgotten to take her medication. He won't listen to her.

She reads on.

> *The audacious crime stunned the world. Nothing like it had ever been done before. Others have tried it since, but nobody else has ever succeeded. The man called D.B. Cooper became a legend. Millions*

of people in America, Europe, even Russia wondered who this man was, where he had come from, what had driven him to take such a mad risk.

She reads about the case, everything she can find. She calls the FBI again. She tells them what she heard him say in the hospital. *I'm Dan Cooooper.*

It doesn't matter what Duane said, agents say. They need proof of a crime. Does Jo have proof of a crime?

She does not. She has memories. She remembers the strange things he told her. She remembers the places he took her. When she pieces it all together, the portrait of the hijacker and Jo's memories of Duane are almost identical.

Both were familiar with the Pacific Northwest. He took her there once, in 1978. After they married and moved to Fort Collins, Colorado, they drove west on a trip over the Cascades. Outside of Vancouver, Duane took her on a hike.

"This is where D.B. Cooper walked out of the woods," he said.

"How would you know?" Jo said.

"Maybe I was there," Duane said.

She assumed he was joking.

Another memory. She thinks it was later that year. Can't be sure. She and Duane are sleeping. He wakes up. He is frantic. His right arm is raised.

"I left my prints on the *aftstairs*," he said. "I'm going to die."

Aftstairs? An odd word. Reading books on D.B. Cooper, she learns the *aftstairs* are where the hijacker made his infamous leap from the Northwest Orient 727.

There was also an airline ticket she found in a sock drawer. She thinks it said Northwest Orient on it, and the year 1971. Again: she can't be sure. She asked Duane about the airline ticket. He shrugged it off. When she went to put his socks back in the drawer, the ticket was missing. Why was it missing?

Without proof, the Bureau agents dismiss Jo Weber. How can they be sure she is telling them the truth? How can they be sure she isn't manufacturing her memories?

Jo is bitter. Jo is scorned. She decides to conduct the investigation herself. She follows the clues Duane left her, tucked into the folds of the ostrich-skin wallet.

She starts with his sentence for grand larceny.

When he arrived, the prison where Duane was incarcerated in Jefferson City, Missouri, was considered the most violent, dysfunctional prison in the nation. Built in 1836, the gray stone buildings were described as a "medieval twilight zone," and later "the bloodiest forty-seven acres in America." It was also home, Jo learns, to a small-time crook who rented out magazines in the courtyard.

James Earl Ray was a jailhouse legend at Jefferson City. Before he pled guilty to assassinating Martin Luther King (and later recanted), Ray had reportedly escaped from the prison by hiding in a bread box.

Jo wonders, did Duane (or John C. Collins) know James Earl Ray? How can she find out?

Duane's wife at the time was Mary Jane Ross. Jo finds a number for her in California. Jo is nervous about calling. Eventually, she dials. She has to know: Does Duane have a connection to James Earl Ray? If so, what is it?

Lana picks up. Lana is Duane's stepdaughter. Lana misses Duane. She is sorry to hear he passed.

"We're all family in a way," Lana tells Jo.

Lana has fond memories of Duane. He was an inspiration to her.

"He lived a hard and fast life . . . as a cat burglar. I always thought, Great, my stepfather is a sophisticated criminal. Wow, some of the jewels he brought home. Wow . . . He always worked alone."

Cat burglar? Worked alone?

Jo knew he stole. Once, after selling antiques at a flea market, Duane's friend Jim Stallings went with Duane to a pharmacy. Stallings looked down the aisle and saw Duane pocket a bottle of aspirin.

Jo was not surprised. Before he passed away, Duane would come home from the Piggly Wiggly and she would find packets of Kool-Aid in the pockets of Duane's coat. Duane didn't even drink Kool-Aid. She went to the Piggly Wiggly and spoke with the manager. She wanted to pay for what Duane stole.

"We've known about it for some time," the manager told her. "If he takes anything expensive, we'll give you a call."

Were these signs? Had Jo been in denial about Duane all along?

"He was a real sophisticated person . . ." Lana says, "nothing about him that wasn't first class . . . He was pulling diamonds out of barrettes, big diamonds . . . I learned a lot of lessons from him. He told me never tell a cop nothing."

Jo asks about Mary Jane. Is she around?

"Best time to call her is in the morning," Lana says, "before she's had a few beers."

X

Mary Jane doesn't sound too drunk when Jo calls. "Why don't you come out here and enjoy our earthquakes?" Mary Jane says.

"I wish I could afford to," Jo says.

"You little asshole," Mary Jane says. "Have you ever been in a seven-point-two?"

Mary Jane rambles. Maybe she is drunk. She is hurting.

"I look in the obituary every day to see if my name is there," Mary Jane says.

Jo asks her about D.B. Cooper. Did Mary Jane know anything about the hijacking?

"Never heard of it, Jo."

Really? Or is Mary Jane covering up for Duane? Was Mary Jane involved in the caper somehow?

Jo asks her about James Earl Ray.

"I met the guy," Mary Jane says.

What?

"I met him. His wife stayed with me for a while."

James Earl Ray's wife and Mary Jane were roommates?

"She was Jewish," Mary Jane says. "I'm not Jewish and I don't go for this Hanukkah."

Jo asks Mary Jane about James Earl Ray's escape in a bread box.

"That was a put-on, honey. He didn't escape. That was all a big hoax. They got him to Canada because he was supposed to act like he was the guy who killed Martin Luther King. I know it for a fact."

How does she know it? Jo is trembling. Duane must have known James Earl Ray. Their wives were roommates! Was that the connection? Was there more? Jo is now recording her phone calls to prove she is not making up what others tell her. She is also keeping an audio diary to document her journey into Duane's past. When the call with Mary Jane is over, she speaks into her tape recorder.

"Oh my god! Oh my god! *Oh my god!*" she says.

✗

She writes letters. She calls federal agents, witnesses, private detectives. She spends hundreds of dollars on phone calls, then thousands. She talks for hours, won't get off with people. She asks reporters and editors for help. All shrug her off. Except one.

As a reporter for *U.S. News & World Report,* Doug Pasternak listens to Jo Weber for three years before he publishes a piece on Duane Weber in 2000. During the course of his reporting, Pasternak discovers that Jo was married to a career criminal. Duane's first prison was Mc-

Neil, a federal penitentiary in Washington. His scam had been seducing women during the war and swindling GI checks from them. After the war, Duane did time at the Ohio State Penitentiary, in Columbus, Ohio. In 1953, he was paroled from San Quentin. In 1954, he spent one day in Soledad, south of Santa Cruz. Then he was in Folsom, near Sacramento, until 1959. In 1960, he was arrested in El Paso for burglary, convicted, and sent to Canon City, the federal prison in Colorado.

Later, she stumbles on a newspaper story, printed in the *St. Petersburg Times,* July 29, 1957. The paper calls Duane Lorin Weber a "smooth-talking ex-con." Then 33, Duane had been arrested for flirting with women at a nightclub on Treasure Island, Florida, and stealing their wallets. When the police searched his hotel room, they found, among other things, identification from several people, among them a badge from an investigator at the District Attorney's office in Jackson County, Missouri. Police learned Duane had already spent six years in prison in California and five in Ohio.

"It may take several weeks before we can run down this man's history, even then we may only know half of it," a deputy sheriff told the newspaper.

Questioning him after his arrest, one police officer asked Duane his occupation.

"Crook, I guess," he said.

Jo cries learning these things. Who did she marry? She sobs into her tape recorder.

"Duane, I get chills thinking about what you did," she says.

August 27, 2007
Edgewater Hotel, Seattle, Washington

I wake up under the plaid sheets of the hotel bed. It is dawn, the sky is gray, the window of my room at the Edgewater is open. I hear pelicans and the horns of the passing boats on Puget Sound. Through the window, I see the giant cranes of the port. I smell salt water.

I duck back under the covers. Could I have been wrong about Kenny? How could I so easily dismiss an expert like Himmelsbach? True, he wasn't the lead agent on the case—that was Charlie Farrell, then Ron Nichols, out of Seattle—but Himmelsbach had access to the same case documents they did, and he worked the case the longest. What do I know about a criminal investigation? I'm taking my cues from an 80-something retired postal worker from middle-of-nowhere Minnesota, whose advice to me was to rent a metal detector.

I am ready to cry. I am burning my magazine's money and my own out here in Seattle. Nothing in Kenny's past suggests a propensity toward criminal activity. Still, what are the chances? How many other ex-Paratroopers would have lived near the Drop Zone, knew enough but not all about the aftstairs on a Boeing 727, worked in airplane maintenance, and looked exactly like the Bureau's sketch?

Kenny's grin flashes in my mind. I can't give up on him now. I haven't even been out to Bonney Lake yet. I think of a story his brother Lyle told me about a game he and Kenny played as boys. The Parachute Game, they called it. It required a blindfold and a table board. Their pa blindfolded Lyle and told him to stand on the board. He did.

Then their pa and their older brother, Oliver, would lift the board in the air, telling the young boys it was an airplane and they were taking off. The table board airplane was flying higher; in the sky now, far higher. Now it was time to parachute.

"Jump," their pa would say.

Lyle never did. He was too scared.

Kenny's turn was next. The table board airplane went into flight again, high in the sky.

"Jump," their pa said.

Kenny always jumped.

I walk downstairs into the hotel restaurant for breakfast. Special Agent Larry Carr is waiting. We sit at a table by the floor-to-ceiling windows that reveal the frigid chop of Puget Sound. There is heavy fog along the water, hiding the peaks of the Olympics and the tugboats and commuter ferries as they move in to dock.

Carr is the FBI agent assigned to the Cooper case. He's been on it only a few months, but he's already obsessed with the nagging mystery of it all and piecing together whatever snippets of actual data or facts are buried in the Bureau's Cooper file. For the last forty years it's been a morgue of dead-end leads, futile reports, and bureaucratic bilge. A new clue has to be in there somewhere.

Carr is tall and built and in shape. In high school, he was an All-American track star. His event was the pole vault. His detail in the Bureau is now with the Seattle field office's Bank Robbery Task Force. It's a decent assignment. After he retires, Carr could join a private security firm and parlay his expertise on how to protect banks from robberies into a second career.

I want to tell him about Kenny. I want Carr's opinion on him as a suspect. But now I'm paranoid. Carr wants to solve the case as much as I do. So why should I spoon-feed him all the details about Kenny that Skipp Porteous and Lyle have given me? Carr could scoop me. I could tell him about Kenny, hand over the military files and photo, and see it all on the evening news.

Instead, I ask Carr for access to the Bureau's files. Perhaps I can dig up a clue that has never before been made public and match it to Kenny.

Carr takes a stab at his huevos rancheros.

"Gonna need approval for that," he says.

Technically, the case is still open. Nobody has been caught. Carr wouldn't mind publicity on it, though. In fact, that's one of Carr's goals in the case. He's hopeful that a blizzard of write-ups on the hijacking could shake loose a few new leads.

He can't do much. The Bureau is devoting its resources to actual cases, not legends.

He asks me about my suspect.

I'm cagey. I defer, obfuscate, punt.

Carr isn't too concerned.

Why not?

Because he's isolated a top contender, he says.

Really?

The suspect is so good, Carr says, he's asked headquarters for permission to dig up the suspect's grave to collect DNA evidence.

There's DNA evidence?

One of the first things Carr did was send the physical evidence in the case to the Bureau's lab in Quantico, Virginia. The last time scientists analyzed the material collected on the hijacked plane, DNA analysis was not available.

I prod. This suspect of Carr's, might the fellow have a name?

Carr won't say. Confidential.

Well, what about the grave? Where is the grave located?

"Utah," he says.

Now it is time to cry. Utah? Kenny never spent any time in Utah. It's official: I have no story.

Then I remember. Utah? I've been reading up on the case. A prime suspect was from Utah.

April 7, 1972
Aboard United Airlines Flight 855,
Over Provo, Utah

He is flying under the name James Johnson. His ticket is one-way, to Los Angeles. He sits in the last row of the plane, in front of the lavatory, just like Dan Cooper. He has heavy tan makeup on his face, which makes him look swarthy. Spanish, a witness later says. The toupee on his head is dark and wet with sweat. He wears mirrored sunglasses and a blue and red sport jacket. Underneath the seat is a plaid suitcase. In his waistband is a pistol. Close by is a pineapple grenade and notes he typed out on his typewriter.

> *WE HAVE A GRENADE, THE PIN HAS BEEN PULLED. WE HAVE PISTOLS, THEY ARE LOADED. WE HAVE C-4 PLASTIC EXPLOSIVES.*

Despite a few unruly passengers Richard Floyd McCoy gets what he asks for: $500,000 in cash and four parachutes. Through his typewritten notes, the pilots reroute and now hover over McCoy's drop zone: Provo, Utah, his hometown.

The jet is empty. The passengers deplaned in San Francisco. In the rear of the cabin, McCoy lowers the aftstairs. The night is dark and clear.

He stuffs the ransom in a duffel bag. He clips the duffel bag to the D ring on the parachute's harness. He inches toward the aftstairs of the Boeing 727, grips the bag of cash with his knees, and falls feet first.

The rush of air feels like he's falling off a bank building. The cold air flattens the skin on his face.

He stems, arching his back so the air flattens against his chest. This slows him down. The duffel bag slips loose from his knees. It whips around, pulling him, twisting him, as he falls.

One thousand feet. Two thousand feet.

McCoy feels weak. No, it is his stomach. He is sick. He will vomit.

Simmer down, Richard, he tells himself. Simmer down.

He blacks out.

Three thousand feet. Four thousand feet.

The duffel is floating to his left. He comes to and sees it. He stems toward it.

In the sky he can see the giant lights of the search planes. He needs to pull the ripcord before he is too weak. He strains to grip the release handle. He pulls.

The canopy does not release. The handle is jammed.

Five thousand feet.

Richard thinks about his own funeral. He figures they will probably have it on a Tuesday.

Seven thousand feet.

He tries the ripcord again. With both hands. Pull.

The pilot chute pops. He is moving too fast for it to deploy. He's on top of the canopy, tied up in the shroud lines. The canopy is now underneath him. He falls away. The chute unfurls.

His vision is blurry. The headlights along the freeway appear in streaks. He sees a cow pasture.

Two hundred feet. One hundred feet.

He braces himself for landing. His knees buckle against the grass. He collapses on top of the duffel bag, resting on his $500,000 fortune. The white canopy of his parachute rustles in the wind over him.

I did it, he thinks. I really did it.

No time to celebrate. He gathers the canopy in his arms, grabs the duffel. He starts to run.

He runs through a wheat field. He runs along a road and when the flash of headlights finds him he jumps in a ditch. He waits, gets up, and runs. He finds a culvert. It's dry. McCoy stashes his parachute and his duffel bag filled with cash here. He'll come back for it later.

He runs. He runs until he sees the lights of the Hi-Spot Drive In.

It's around midnight. Through the windows, McCoy can see the employees are cleaning up. He gives his order to the counter girl.

Okay, she says. One large Coke, coming up.

McCoy looks outside. A teenager is getting into his car. McCoy steps outside. He asks for a ride.

"Five dollars will buy a lot of gas, man," he says.

The kid's name is Peter Zimmerman. He is eighteen. Need a ride, sure. Hop in.

Driving on the dark roads, McCoy and Zimmerman listen to the news on the radio. A plane has been hijacked over Provo, reports say. The hijacker parachuted out the back with a half a million, the biggest ransom any skyjacker has gotten away with.

Checkpoints are set up along the road. The sky is lit with red magnesium flares.

"How come they stay in the air for so long?" Zimmerman asks McCoy about the flares.

"They have little parachutes on them," McCoy says.

When McCoy comes home, his sister-in-law Denise is watching the news.

"Have you heard?" she says. "Some guy jumped over Provo with half a million dollars!"

"No, I haven't. Where's Karen?"

"Oh, she's out visiting somebody. . . . Van Ieperen called twice. He thinks you did it, Richard! Wants you to call him. Did you do it, Richard? You can tell me."

Robert Van Ieperen is a state trooper and McCoy's parachuting friend.

Richard knows he can trust Van Ieperen. The trooper would never turn him in.

Richard goes into the bathroom and runs the hot water in the tub.

He closes the door and takes off his clothes. He slips in the water and closes his eyes. He did it. He *really* did it.

✗

A few days later, Richard wakes up for National Guard duty. It is dawn. He is putting on his military uniform. He hears pounding on the front door. He races into the living room. He sees Stetsons. The feds are waiting for him.

"Richard Floyd McCoy, you are under arrest for the charge of air piracy. You have the right to remain silent."

In response to the rash of skyjackings, legislators in Washington have toughened the penalties for air piracy. The crime is a capital offense. McCoy now faces the death penalty. In Utah, the method of execution is a firing squad.

The agents cuff him and comb the house. They find a black parachute harness, a black crash helmet, a pistol, and $499,970 in cash in his closet, among other incriminating evidence.

In handcuffs, Richard pleads with the feds.

Let me change into a suit, he says. He does not want to embarrass the service, walking into a criminal court in his military uniform.

Agents push his head down into an unmarked car.

Neighbors are up, standing on their lawns. Reporters arrive on the scene.

"He was a real kind person," says Mr. Cluff, McCoy's neighbor. "Always friendly and always smiling. He would help push our car out of the snow."

"He was the type of fellow you could always say hi to and get a response," says Mr. Peterman, another neighbor.

"He does not seem to be the kind of a kid to hijack a plane," says Mr. Reynolds, who lives near the Cluffs and Petermans.

McCoy's wife, Karen, and their children are rushed to a neighbor's house. Blinds are drawn.

On the lawn of Richard's house, reporters linger. The home is empty. The reporters hear McCoy's telephone ring.

In Raleigh, Richard's father, Floyd, is convinced the arrest is a mistake.

"He's not that kind of boy," Floyd says.

August 26, 2007
Seattle, Washington

I am in the lobby of the Edgewater. I am talking to the concierge.

"You know where I might find a metal detector?"

I feel stupid saying it.

The look on the concierge's face is as blank as a sheet of paper.

"It's Sunday," he says, about my metal detector request. "The hardware stores are all closed."

Problem solved. What could I find with a metal detector anyway?

I unfurl the map in my rental car and search for Bonney Lake. It takes a while. Finally, I find the tiny dot.

I drive out of the city, past the port and endless stacks of red and green and blue shipping containers. The empty cars of freight trains rumble as seagulls caw and peck along the tracks.

Could Lyle be wrong about his older brother? The Kenny he described growing up on the farm in Minnesota seemed too kind a soul to hijack. Kenny kept his own flower bed of red zinnias and was good to his younger brother.

"Us kids were playing tag out by the garden," Lyle wrote me. "Kenny was almost impossible to catch because he was a tricky runner. I chased after him and he would almost let me catch him. Finally I gave up in anger and started crying. Kenny was surprised by this and came over to me and said, 'Why don't you try again, maybe you can catch me this time?' Sure enough, I went after him and I caught him that time."

18406 Old Sumner Buckley Highway. I must have passed the house four times. Then I realize: Kenny's old house isn't a house anymore. It's a shop.

PRICED RIGHT PRINT & SIGN, is the name out front.

I pull into the driveway. The shop is closed. I'm nervous. I don't know why.

I step out of the rental and onto the gravel. I am haunted by a strange, and weighty feeling. Am I being watched? My eyes dart around: along the road, into the windows of the houses across the street, into the trees up the hill out back.

I can't see anybody. Who is watching? Kenny?

I sneak up to a window. The lights in the Priced Right are off. I can't see anything inside. I imagine Kenny in here, wearing his overalls and blue conductor's cap. I imagine him singing after dinner the way Lyle told me he did, or stashing the ransom in the walls and under the floorboards.

There was also an old army locker that Kenny kept. When Lyle looked inside it after Kenny's death, he found a slip for Harrah's casino in Las Vegas. "Maybe it was a good place to launder money," Lyle wrote, or perhaps Kenny hid the ransom in the locker. "He kept it secure by a big padlock," Lyle said. "It would have been handy to take a few bills out now and then."

I press my nose onto the glass and peer into the dark chasm. Was this the kitchen? I remember a poster Lyle told me about, a poster Kenny hung in the kitchen. The poster read:

THERE ARE THREE KINDS OF PEOPLE.
Those who MAKE things happen.
Those who WATCH things happen.
And those who WONDER what happened.

I wonder myself: Which one was Kenny?

I get back in the car and drive up the hill to find old neighbors. One man is pulling out groceries from the trunk of his car.

I roll down my window. I ask him if he knew a Ken Christiansen.

He did.

Really?

"You know he had them boys living with him," the man says, lifting a bag onto his knee.

Boys? What kind of boys?

Runaways, he says.

Did he happen to know any of their names?

"The one that stayed with him the longest was Kenny."

Another Kenny?

"Kenny McWilliams," he says, and heads into his house.

Back in the Edgewater that night, I scour every online phonebook and directory. I call every Ken Kenny Kenneth McWilliams MacWilliams in the state of Washington. After midnight, I find him. Kenneth B. MacWilliams is living in Walla Walla, over the Cascades.

"He was an amusing character," MacWilliams tells me about Kenny. "He didn't speak much about the past."

MacWilliams met Kenny as a teenager, after he ran away from home. I ask him about Lyle's theory: that Kenny was the infamous hijacker D.B. Cooper.

"He could have been him," MacWilliams says. "D.B. Cooper could have been anybody if you really think about it . . . But I can't really see that happening."

Why not?

"You know, he didn't have any particular lifestyle. Everything was a little different. Different directions."

How would MacWilliams describe it?

"Odd," he says. "It was uncomfortable for me because I am not like that. I told my folks he was gay, but not everybody lived in that house at night."

※

So Kenny was gay? Was that why he was so secretive? Always escaping around the world? And was that what his deathbed confession ("*There is something you should know*") was really about?

And where does that leave my investigation into Kenny as D.B.? Are Kenny's sexual preferences—and perhaps his fear of coming out of the closet—relevant to the hijacking case?

It's absolutely critical, I decide. According to Dr. Hubbard, the sky-jacking expert, the vast majority of hijackers had effeminate manner-isms and homosexual urges. "For these men, to command a woman or even attempt it approaches the outer limits of imagination," Dr. Hubbard wrote.

I wonder what the eyewitnesses on the Northwest 305 flight think of Kenny. I have photos to show them. Some forty years later, will they recognize him?

I find Alice Hancock, the first-class stew, living outside of Minne-apolis. She answers the phone with a sweet voice, a cheerful personality. In retirement, she is studying Chinese. She remembers clear moments from the hijacking, how she attempted to lure young Tina away from the hijacker with playing cards, how copilot Bill Rataczak was freaking out in the cockpit and told her for some reason to remove her shoes.

Alice was a decent witness. She hadn't spent the same amount of time with the hijacker as Flo or Tina, but she had a look at him. I send her a photo of Kenny.

"The resemblance is definitely there," she says.

But?

Kenny is too bald.

"This fella had a head of hair," Alice says of Cooper.

Tina Mucklow is her own mystery. After the hijacking, she disappeared. In 2001, when agents working the Cooper case wanted to meet with her, they found her living under the name Tina Larson at the Carmel of Maria Regina, a convent outside of Eugene, Oregon. Tina had become a nun.

Tina had been a good witness. After the hijacking, she met with federal agents at least twice and delivered extensive interviews about the hijacker, his mood, his mannerisms.

"He was never cruel or nasty," Tina said.

For the last forty years she has been almost completely mum about the case. Her silence has spurred a number of conspiracy theories in Cooperland. Does she know something that she's hiding about the hijacker? Did he approach her and threaten her, telling her not to come forward? Did he do something terrible to her that prompted her to become a nun?

I find Tina living in Springfield, a town outside of Eugene. I call. I leave messages. I write. I imagine the aging stewardess sitting on her sofa in her living room listening to her answering machine, wondering if she should pick up after holding back whatever secrets she's been keeping all these years. I pray for her to pick up.

Please, Tina, please. I send her telepathic messages, mental beams aimed to direct her hands to her telephone receiver. Pick up, Tina.

Tina does not pick up. And then, after a year or so, she does.

Her voice is soft and cautious.

I find myself lowering my voice to mirror hers, desperate to connect with her. I tell her about my investigation. Would she be willing to look at a few photographs of my Kenny?

"No," she says. She doesn't want to talk about the case.

I ask her why.

Passenger safety. She doesn't want to "promote something that was not intended to be a good thing, and endanger anyone in the airline business." In essence, her worry is that a would-be hijacker could read my story about D.B. Cooper, get inspired, and hijack another plane, just like so many copycats did in the early 1970s.

But that was forty years ago! I plead with Tina for an interview. She agrees to a follow-up call.

Never going to talk to her again, I think. But she picks up.

"I've made a decision," she says.

I'm sending warm vibes through my fingers into the plastic receiver of my phone. I am ready to shop for plane tickets. I can be at her doorstep in Oregon in twenty-four hours—less, when you factor in the time change.

"I won't be part of the journey," she says.

It's not fair. Why?

"I don't think I have to explain the reason why I've chosen what I've chosen," she says.

I try to persuade her. She's part of history here. Her experience counts.

"I will honor the decision I've made," she says. "It's about my personal choice. . . . It's final for me."

I find stewardess Flo Schaffner in South Carolina. She is living here under a different name and prefers to keep it anonymous after what has happened to her. I fly into Columbia and walk out of the airport, and there she is, waving from behind the wheel of her car.

The air is hot and sticky. I push through it and get in the car. Flo looks different than she did on the front page of the *Minnesota Star* the day after the hijacking. Her hair is short and frosted. She wears a tank top, and her biceps are ripped. A workout fanatic, she teaches classes at her local gym. That's where she met Art Rish, her boyfriend. He's a cop. He is sitting in the front seat.

We drive to Lizard's Thicket, a restaurant near the airport.

It is Sunday morning and the booths at Lizard's are filled with a post-church rush of dusted-off suits, dresses, hats, girls playing tag in Mary Janes. The menu is Southern and deep fried.

Flo is also paranoid. Too many strange things have happened to her: agents knocking on her door, a pair of convicts approaching her on her wedding day. She feared for her life. She was the only witness to see the hijacker's eyes. She could testify against him in court, put him away for the rest of his life. The first thing he would do, she worried, would be find her and, gulp, eliminate the witness. She'd look under her car for bombs. Turn over the keys real slow.

I remove a few photos of Kenny. I place them on the table.

She reaches for the image of Kenny in his Northwest Orient uniform. She stares deep into the grain of black and white as if trying to reacquaint herself with that night. Her hands are trembling. She reaches for another photo. She lays the image flat on the sticky countertop. Her eyes zoom in on Kenny's face. She rubs it with her fingers as if she is touching up a charcoal drawing.

Well, is it him?

"The ears, the ears are right," she says. "Yes, thin lips. And the top lip, kind of like this, yes. . . . A wide forehead, yes."

Then the hair.

"Receding, yes, the two areas—yes, yes—sort of like this."

Flo is pushing down on the photo hard now, rubbing the image as if she is a medium and is now trying to summon the spirit of Kenny.

"There was more hair, though."

The eyes?

"About like that."

The eyebrows?

"About like that."

I want to give Flo space. I look up and around the room. Tables are getting cleared. The smell is heavy on lard, collards, Sunday-morning ham. Older men are hunched over their food, sipping sugary soda from straws. The hijacker would be about their age by now, mid to late eighties. I wonder if I could recognize Cooper now if I saw him in the back of a plane forty years ago. I doubt it.

"I think you might be on to something here," Flo says.

"Really?"

"But I . . . I can't say . . . 'Yea.'"

That's not what I want to hear.

What about the other suspects she's seen? How does Kenny compare?

Of all the suspects, Kenny is the closest match, Flo says. But she doesn't feel comfortable saying definitely, absolutely, without question, this is the guy. It doesn't mean no. It also doesn't mean yes.

I ask her about Tina's silence. Why does Flo think Tina won't talk about the case?

"She's hiding something," Flo says. But what? Flo doesn't know.

I don't either. Tina, what are you hiding?

I ask Flo about the hijacker's manner, his vibe. Was he alpha macho tough guy or soft and bashful? Did she think he could have been, as Ken Christiansen was, gay?

No, Flo doesn't think so. But how could she know for sure?

Plus, the case was bizarre. So many strange things happened after. She took a month off from work to clear the night from her mind; then a man started following her like a shadow. He boarded Northwest planes she was flying on. Why was he stalking her?

"I know the hijacker, from prison," the man said. "He wants to talk to you."

Flo pushed the man away, told him to leave her alone.

He resisted.

"I want to tell you, this guy is not just a hijacker," the man said. "He was in the Bay of Pigs. This guy works for the CIA."

June 29, 1972
Salt Lake City, Utah

Richard Floyd McCoy Jr. has no good closing arguments. In fact, he has no legitimate defense. Agents found $499,970 of the ransom in his closet. They matched handwriting samples. The question before jurors is not whether McCoy is guilty of air piracy. The question is whether he should be sentenced to death, or serve out forty-five years in federal prison. The official who may have the most control over how much prison time McCoy serves is Bernie Rhodes, chief probation officer. If jurors opt to spare McCoy's life, Rhodes will interview McCoy and prepare a sentencing report for the judge.

Throughout the trial, Rhodes has been observing McCoy's behavior in the courtroom. Rhodes notices McCoy is making funny faces at his daughter, Chante, and toddler, Rich, in the front row of the courtroom, making them laugh. One morning, before the judge and jurors and lawyers arrive, a pair of marshals escort McCoy into court and Chante sidles up to him. McCoy holds out his palm. Inside is a yellow spinning top. How did McCoy manage to get the toy in jail, Rhodes wonders, and smuggle it in for his daughter?

During closing arguments, the judge makes an announcement.

"Something that pleases this court and I'm sure has been weighing heavily on you people's minds," he says, "is whether or not you'd eventually have to give this fellow the death penalty. Well, the court's gonna help you solve that little problem right now. You can, as of now, dismiss that dilemma from your minds."

This morning in Washington, the Supreme Court declared the death penalty unconstitutional. McCoy's life has been spared.

In handcuffs, McCoy is escorted out of the courtroom. He walks past Rhodes, who will interview him in jail the next day. McCoy then passes a female journalist. McCoy can't miss her. Blond, tall, leggy. She wears red ladybug lipstick and matching red heels.

"Wish me luck, ma'am," McCoy says to the goddess.

She nods, stomps out her cigarette, and turns to Rhodes.

"Was it Hemingway?" she says. "Damn it! Or Steinbeck? Or who in the hell was it? Well, whoever it was that had the good sense to come up with it must have been thinking of our boy McCoy when he came up with the line: You show me a hero and I'll show you a tragedy."

The jury finds McCoy guilty in under two hours.

After the courtroom closes, the feds camp out in the law library. The agent who investigated McCoy's case, Jim Thiessen, lights a Winston and paces in his penny loafers. Russell Calame, who recently ran the Bureau field office in Salt Lake City, removes an initialed handkerchief and mops his brow. The agents discuss the case they failed to make. All along, they have been convinced McCoy is D.B. Cooper.

They've been able to match up physical evidence. During his investigation, Thiessen showed the photos of Cooper's black clip-on tie left in the rear of the Northwest 305 plane to Denise Burns, McCoy's sister-in-law, and Mildred Burns, his mother-in-law; both identified the tie and tie clasp as belonging to McCoy. Thiessen also showed the photos to Robert Van Ieperen, McCoy's state trooper friend. From Thiessen's report:

> ROBERT VAN IEPEREN *advised that* MCCOY *likes to wear conservative solid-colored clip-on ties similar to the tie recovered after the hijacking of a Northwest plane on November 24th, 1971.* VAN IEPEREN *stated he had been out socially with* MCCOY *and recalled that at a movie one night* MCCOY *wore a clip-on tie and removed the tie when he sat down to watch the movie.*

Thiessen paces, thinking about how to come up with enough evidence to charge McCoy with NORJAK.

Probation officer Bernie Rhodes walks in the room. Thiessen and Calame get an idea: Maybe Rhodes can get McCoy to confess to the Cooper hijacking.

Rhodes is familiar with the Cooper case. He wonders what proof the agents have.

"That area isn't as rough or forestlike as some people think," Calame says about the Cooper drop zone in southwest Washington. "He should have been just fine. He walks or hooks a ride into Portland, next day catches a plane, or bus or whatever, back to Vegas."

Las Vegas?

As part of McCoy's background investigation, Thiessen assembled McCoy's financial, telephone, school, National Guard, and auto records. On the morning of the hijacking, Thiessen found, McCoy used his Bank of America credit card to fill up the tank on his Volkswagen bug. The location, Thiessen found, wasn't Provo, Utah. It was Cedar City, which is several hours south and east of Provo, directly on the way to Las Vegas.

McCoy *was* in Las Vegas. That's fact. On Thanksgiving, a day after the Cooper hijacking, McCoy's home in Provo received a collect call from the lobby of the Tropicana Hotel. The time of the call was 10:41 p.m. Who else would have called McCoy's home from the lobby of the Tropicana other than McCoy?

McCoy was near the Tropicana, and on Thanksgiving, Thiessen found. The same day the collect call was made to McCoy's home, McCoy purchased 5.6 gallons of gasoline only two miles away from the Tropicana, at the Power Thrust Service Station. The Power Thrust, Thiessen found, is located alongside the airport.

The agents speculate. On the morning of November 24, the day Northwest 305 is hijacked, McCoy drives to Cedar City and then on to Las Vegas. Here, he boards a flight to Portland, where he then boards Northwest 305 as Dan Cooper. A genius setup.

After bailing out, McCoy gets back to Portland the next morning, flies back to Las Vegas, picks up his Volkswagen bug waiting for him in the airport parking lot, tops off his car with gas at the Power Thrust, calls Karen collect from the Tropicana, and drives home to Provo.

Rhodes is suspicious. He's read up on the Cooper case.

"How do you get around brown and blue eyes?" he says.

Cooper had brown eyes. McCoy's are blue.

"First of all, we're not sure they were brown," Calame says. "The stewardess could have been mistaken."

And the Raleigh filter-tip cigarettes?

The feds have researched the smokes. Raleigh is produced by Brown & Williamson and is the least popular of all the company's brands, representing only 1.5 percent of all brands sold. So Cooper must have a connection to them.

"If McCoy, a Mormon, smoked as part of his disguise," Calame says, "he would have needed to buy a pack of cigarettes in the Portland airport. What brand would he choose? Well, it's naturally going to be Raleigh, his hometown, his home brand, isn't it?"

The signatures of the hijackings were also similar. Both McCoy and Cooper sat in the last row of the plane, in front of the lavatory. Both used notes and one stewardess to relay information.

Rhodes has a question. If McCoy was Cooper and got away with $200,000, then why four months later would he risk the death sentence and hijack United 855 for $500,000?

"He lost it," Thiessen says. During the first jump. "He lost the damn money!"

"Got away from him," Calame says.

The jail in Salt Lake smells of stale coffee and cigarette butts. In an interview room, Richard McCoy waits for the questions. Probation officer Rhodes lights a Marlboro. He holds out his pack.

"Do you smoke? Do you smoke cigarettes?"

"Nope," McCoy says. "I don't use tobacco, but it doesn't bother me when you do."

"Do you gamble? Shoot dice? This sort of thing."

"No. I don't gamble. Don't have the money to shoot dice. Don't know how."

"Do you drink alcohol?"

"Nope. I've had liquor a few times in my life, but when you're ready to jot these things down for Judge Ritter, give him the truth: Richard Floyd McCoy Jr. doesn't drink, smoke, or gamble."

Rhodes reaches into his bag and removes the Bureau's sketch of D.B. Cooper. He places it on the table in front of McCoy.

"If you can," Rhodes says, "and I know this was a while back, but try to remember where you were last Thanksgiving, November twenty-fifth, and the day before, Wednesday, November twenty-fourth, 1971."

"Thanksgiving is still a holiday, isn't it, so naturally I would have been around the house. I didn't have school and I didn't have Guard. I was home. Why?"

"Cook or clean, or help Karen with anything she might remember?"

"Yes. I cooked, yes, and helped Karen with Thanksgiving dinner."

Rhodes doesn't waste time. He wants a confession.

"What I'd like you to tell me is how you can be in Provo cooking Thanksgiving dinner and make a collect call from the Tropicana Hotel-Casino in Las Vegas at 10:41 p.m. that same night?"

"And how do you know it was me who made the call? Could have been anybody."

"For the sake of argument, let's assume for a minute that you're right. You didn't make that call. Someone else made it, okay? Well, I've got an even better one for you. Explain, if you can, how someone driving your green Volkswagen bug, North Carolina license plate number SA 1334, purchased 5.6 gallons of gas just after eleven p.m. Thanksgiving night at the Power Thrust Service Station in Las Vegas, using your credit card—Bank Americard #4763160217773—which is yours, isn't it?—signed your name, Richard Floyd McCoy Jr., to that credit charge slip. How about it?"

McCoy is picking his teeth with a paper clip.

"How about it?" McCoy says. "You seem to have all the answers. You tell me."

"Why were you in Vegas during the Cooper thing?"

McCoy holds his hand in the air as if swearing on the Bible.

"How many times do I have to tell you? I helped Karen cook turkey dinner."

The next morning, Rhodes arrives at the jail for a follow-up interview. McCoy is crying. "I can't even comprehend forty-five years," he says. "Even if I got out in, say, thirty years. . . . Chante would be thirty-five years old; Rich, thirty-two. I don't think I'll put them through that. Or me either." He is contemplating suicide.

Again, Rhodes removes the Bureau's sketch of Cooper. He lights a cigarette and goes through the routine questions: financial statements, statement of offense. Six, seven hours pass. Rhodes packs up his things.

"Aren't you forgetting something?" McCoy says.

He is holding up the Bureau's sketch of Cooper.

"I don't know," Rhodes says. "Am I?"

"That's up to you. You wanted to talk bad enough yesterday about— you know, the *other thing*?"

"What *other thing*?"

"This thing. This guy here."

McCoy is flapping the Cooper sketch in the air like a Polaroid.

"Do you or don't you want to talk about this thing?"

"What other thing? Be more specific."

"*This* other thing."

"Are you absolutely sure you know what you've got there?"

"Yes. I know what it is, but I'm beginning to wonder if you do."

"You tell me then, what is it?"

"Let's just forget it," McCoy says. He flicks the sketch across the room. "I think you're having a harder time, for some reason, than I am."

At dawn the next morning, McCoy is wrapped in six feet of belly chain that is threaded through his belt loops, handcuffs, and leg irons. He is escorted by federal marshals into an unmarked car. In the backseat, he watches the sun as it rises over the Wasatch range and the soft light flashes against the smokestacks of the Kennecott Copper Corporation, into Parley's Canyon, past the Mormon temple.

Six hundred miles later, it is dark. The marshals stop in Brighton, Colorado, and escort McCoy into the county jail where he will spend the night. The Drunk Tank, it is called. The next morning, the marshals come to take him to federal prison. He is not there. McCoy has escaped.

November 23, 2007
Seattle, Washington

I'm back West again. Down the street, tourists descend on the ice beds of Pike Place Market to watch the mongers throw fish. The neon lights of diners and strip clubs like the Lucky Lady blink in the early darkness of the afternoon. It's not raining yet. The Vietnamese noodle house is loud and crowded.

Over a bowl of broth and beef and sprouts, Special Agent Larry Carr has news to report. The lab results are in. The physical evidence has come back from Quantico, and Bureau scientists have made a determination about the DNA evidence in the Cooper case.

What is the news?

There isn't any. The samples aren't reliable, Carr says.

He's bummed. His hope had been that the Bureau's forensic scientists would be able to detect a fleck of genetic material—a hair, say, or dandruff—to use as a sample. Once Carr had the genetic code of the hijacker in place, he could easily rule out (or rule in) suspects.

On the tie, Carr reports, the Bureau's lab technicians did find a faint trace of saliva. But the sample is too weak to extract a full DNA code. Now Carr cannot use DNA to identify the hijacker. So much for his plan to send a grave-digging crew to Utah.

This can't be. There must be some genetic matter in the case. What about the Raleigh filter-tip cigarettes agents found in the ashtray near the hijacker's seat? The filters of the smokes, I imagine, are probably soaked in saliva.

Gone, Carr says.

Gone? Where are they?

Not in the Seattle evidence room. The cigs were in Las Vegas, where agents had deposited them after searching the plane in Reno. They must have gotten lost, Carr says. Or most likely thrown out.

Thrown out? It doesn't make sense. How could agents toss arguably the most critical piece of evidence in one of their most infamous

unsolved cases? The rest of the evidence—the tie, the deployed parachute, the in-flight magazine—have all been preserved in evidence bag-
gies. So why not the eight Raleigh filter-tip cigarette butts?

We march up the hilly streets, away from the market. No longer in an
old bank near the piers, the Bureau field office is on the corner of 3rd
and Spring.

Carr removes his wallet, swipes his badge, presses his finger against
the pad. Now we're in. Holy of holies. Here we go.

Over the past few months, a letter-writting campaign—coupled with
Carr's desire to attract media attention to the Cooper case—has resulted
in an I-can't-believe-this-is-happening moment of unprecedented access
to the confidential Cooper files. For years the file has been gathering
dust in the basement archives of the field office building. Now, Carr has
selected the major case files for my perusal.

I follow Carr up the elevator and down the hall to another
finger-scan pad and—*voilà!*—we are on the floor. On the far wall is a gallery of mug shots. Agents pass and I solemnly nod—should I really be
in here?—and follow Carr to his desk. He collapses in his chair.

I sit across from him and wait. Over the walls I can hear other
agents talking about a case. I close my eyes and listen in. The agents are
talking about a spy case. I strain my ears to listen harder.

"Here," Carr says, "This is the meat and potatoes of it."

He drops the files in front of me. They are as thick as phone books.

I rub my hands together, blow on the fingertips. The cover is yellow
and waxy. The pages are brittle. I read the words on the first page as if
secrets are buried in the typeface.

THE HIJACK, it reads.

The dossier reads like a play. There's Flo Schaffner, telling the feds
about the bourbon and Seven-Up the hijacker ordered. And Alice Han-

cock, describing the hijacker's hair as wavy. And Tina Mucklow, relay-
ing the hijacker's motive verbatim.

"I don't have a grudge against your airline, miss," he said. "I just
have a grudge."

I just have a grudge? I read the line again. Is this Kenny? It doesn't sound
like him. According to Lyle, Kenny's grudge was not vague or univer-
sal. It was specific: Northwest. Is Lyle wrong about the motive? Or was
Kenny playing coy with Tina?

I dash off an e-mail to Lyle about the grudge line.

"It sounds very like what he would have said," Lyle writes back.
"Kenny was at a time in his life when he hit a low and was wondering
where his life was going. His siblings were having family life and he was
still alone. I think he was so lonely that it hurt."

I plow through the file, reading hundreds of pages over several
days. What I find is not evidence supporting Kenny. I find more Lyle
Christiansens. The file is littered with suspicious brothers, parents,
neighbors, business associates, scorned ex-lovers.

"You've meant so much to me this past year," one man writes in a
letter, which his ex-girlfriend apparently submitted to the Bureau for
analysis. "I'll always love you (which you have to hear) but always felt
that this is temporary and we would both move on." There are names
to go through, too many names. Maurice Chevelle. Dennis Panther.
John Gortel. Bobby J. Brummett. Robert P. Carter. Billy Dean Mc-
Connell. James R. Parker. Donald Earl Collins. Ed Adkins. Scott Kaye
Kingsworth.

February 12, 1980
Portland, Oregon

Cameron David Bishop. Richard J. Jaquish. Gordon Dale Erwin. John Emil List. Earl Gene Larson. Doyle Wayne Harvell. Frank Taus. Russell Lee Cooper. Fred Angelo Catalano. William Francis Johnston Jr. Dan O'Halloran. Joseph Gilpatrick . . .

At the Bureau field office in Portland, agent Ralph Himmelsbach is bombarded with leads. Himmelsbach can't understand how one man could parachute out of an airplane and vanish. It's as if D.B. Cooper never existed. Maybe he didn't exist. Maybe that was the clue. Perhaps Cooper faked his own death?

One tip of this sort comes in about a boater who went out on Lake Shasta and never came back. After a search, he was pronounced dead. Two years later, the same man is spotted pumping gas at a service station in Southern California. Going through records, agents find the man had serviced his car in Portland, and before the hijacking.

Agents locate the man in Los Angeles, go to the address. It's a porno bookstore. The man looks nothing like the Bureau sketch.

More names, more leads. Peter A. Parlo. Everett R. Coovert. Paul Alan Van Riessen. Garnett Hollish. Lawrence Allison Hobart. Robert Hampton Keely. William Johnson Mason. Joseph Royce Stagg. Anthony Lambert Cole. John Henry Marlin. John Galvan Douglas. Robert K. Bertsch. Ronald Ross Newman. Max Arnold Freeman . . .

There are others, arrested and questioned. Like the drunk man in Madras, Oregon, who was found sleeping on the street with $9,000 in cash in his pockets. Or the man who ordered coffee in a Fresno diner at 4:30 a.m. and tipped with a $50 bill. Or the steelworker who always wanted to be a paratrooper and never came back to work. Or the retired special agent living in a Washington boarding house.

D. F. Franklin confesses. Franklin is the notorious skyjacker, he tells police. But when they interview him about what he remembers about the hijacking, his details are all wrong. A phenomenon is emerging. In the Cooper case, citizens are turning themselves in!

Himmelsbach receives letters from psychics and patients in asylums. They knew Cooper personally, they claim. Some spoke directly to God.

One letter comes from an inventor. After years of research, he tells Himmelsbach, he has created a machine that finds missing people. A sniffer, he calls it.

Himmelsbach agrees to meet and check out the man's sniffer.

The inventor arrives at the field office carrying a black box covered in dials and gadgets.

The way the sniffer works, the inventor explains, is that it smells an object that once belonged to the person. Then, using the inventor's patented system, it computes a location.

The inventor asks Himmelsbach for an object that belongs to the hijacker.

Himmelsbach hands him a flashlight that belongs to his younger daughter.

The inventor rubs the flashlight along the black box. Nothing happens.

Professional treasure hunters emerge. Diving expert John Banks conducts his hunt for Cooper under the waters of Lake Merwin. To avoid publicity, Banks launches his custom-built submarine into the lake at night. Its high-power search beams illuminate the murky waters like a ballpark outfield.

On his first dive, Banks descends. He sees giant trunks of dead trees through the sub's observation portal. It is like maneuvering through an ancient forest. Diving deeper, he sees he is headed into the trunk of a massive tree. He braces himself for the crash.

The trees are so waterlogged, his sub snaps through trunks and branches like pretzels. At the bottom of the lake, he catches his breath. He monitors his equipment. Then he hears the sound.

Thump.

What was that?

Thump, thump.

He looks out the portal. The branches of dead trees he broke through are now crashing around him. *Thump thump thump . . .*

Banks spends months searching the ancient underwater forest. He finds nothing.

The case almost dies. The statute of limitations for air piracy is five years. Before the deadline date, agents from the Bureau and prosecutors from the Department of Justice debate whether they should file a "John Doe" indictment and charge the hijacker in absentia. Technically, this would make Dan Cooper a fugitive and extend the statute indefinitely. Internally, agents and prosecutors quarrel over what to do until the day of the anniversary. In Seattle, a prosecutor rushes to a grand jury to present the case. But Seattle doesn't have a grand jury sitting. Portland does.

Himmelsbach is the only witness. An indictment is returned in hours. The hunt is on for Dan Cooper, indefinitely. Himmelsbach wonders if the feds made a mistake in their calculations. Did Cooper land somewhere else and survive the jump? Could it be that the man they're after is a local, living in the area, hidden in plain sight?

Two weeks away from retirement, Himmelsbach is past the realization he may never catch that rotten sleazy bastard Cooper, may never take his elk. Then he gets a phone call.

"Money has been found," an FBI secretary tells him.

The agent pays little attention. He's been pranked dozens of times before. He asks the secretary to match the serial numbers of the found money to the list of Cooper bills.

She already did. They match.

The next morning, Himmelsbach waits for the finders of the money to appear. He is annoyed because they are forty-five minutes late.

Dwayne Ingram and his wife, Patricia, drove here all the way from Vancouver, Washington, where they live. They recently moved from rural Oklahoma. Dwayne has a job painting trailers and cars. Patricia stays home and takes care of their eight-year-old son, Brian.

Himmelsbach wants to see the money.

Patricia removes a plastic baggie. She hands it to the agent. Inside he can see three clumps of old bills. They are caked together, dark around the edges like burnt toast.

We were all on a picnic on Tena Bar, Dwayne Ingram says.

Tena Bar is a sand bar along the north shore of the Columbia River. It's where fishermen run lines for chinook and hippie kids go to swim, play drums, drink beer.

On the beach, Dwayne wanted to build a fire, so he asked his son Brian to clear space in the sand. Brian dropped to his knees, smoothed out a patch and knocked the first bundle over. Then he found two more. The Ingrams wanted to take the money to a bank and cash it out, but a friend noticed the bills were twenties.

"That's Cooper's money," he said.

The Ingrams asked about the reward. How much money will there be?

Himmelsbach needs to check the bills first, to see if they are real. They'll be easy to eliminate, he thinks, because the real ransom bills were issued in the years 1950, 1963, and 1969.

Himmelsbach picks up a packet of bills. He reads the series number.

"1963," it reads.

He writes down the serial number.

"55376548."

He leaves the room to fetch the booklet that contains the serial numbers of the bills the hijacker was given. He goes through all ten thousand serial numbers, hunting for a "55."

It is a long search. The ransom money was used. The serial numbers aren't in order. He looks for a 1963 bill combined with a "55." He finds one. He compares the remaining serial numbers. It's a match.

Where did little Brian Ingram find that money again?

Tena Bar, the Ingrams tell him. Along the Columbia.

Himmelsbach looks at a map. The location doesn't make sense. Tena Bar is roughly forty miles south of where the feds thought the hijacker bailed, and around five miles from the Northwest 305 flight path. How in the world did the money end up there? And where's the rest of it?

November 23, 2007
Seattle, Washington

"The real mystery is the money," Larry Carr tells me. "The mystery of the money is almost more interesting than the mystery of who Cooper was. If you can figure out the money, that leads you to Cooper. It's all about the money. The money is our only shot."

I ask Carr what his plan is now. Like the tie he sent to the Bureau lab in Quantico for a fresh forensic analysis, the money could be re-analyzed with modern techniques. Carr's problem, though, is that the lab is backed up. Scientists don't have time or resources to burn on cold cases.

So what's the strategy?

Carr's gone undercover, he says, in cyberspace. Under a fake name, he's joined the Drop Zone, an Internet forum run by amateur D.B. Cooper sleuths. One of the most inquisitive (and caustic) is Snowmman, who refuses to identify who he is or what he does for a living. The most user-friendly is Sluggo_Monster, a nuclear lab consultant from Alabama named Wayne Walker who built N467us.com, or "Sluggo's Northwest 305 Hijacking Research Site." There is also 377, Orange1, an assortment of parachutists, former parachutists, parachute experts, and scientists. One is Georger, a retired lab whiz and entrepreneur named Jerry Warner. He grew up in the Cooper search area, and remembers talking about the Cooper case every Thanksgiving dinner.

Carr's plan is to leak information about the case on the forum for the cyber gumshoes to devour. If his bosses at the Bureau aren't willing to spend resources on the Cooper Case, then maybe the Cooperites in cyberspace will help him. Carr's handle: Ckret. It won't be long before his cover is blown.

> *377: I get the distinct feeling that Ckret is giving us taxpayers a free ride on much of the Cooper investigation. . . . Am I right Ckret?*

*Ckret: You don't trust me? I am from the government and here to help.
How could you not trust an FBI agent . . . By the way, that book you
checked out is two days late and at the moment your cell phone is off.
Oh, and that web site you have minimized right now, I didn't know
people could do that, very strange.*

The cyber sleuths want to examine the money. Scientist Jerry Warner has a proposal. If the Bureau is too cash strapped for resources to
investigate the money, why not farm it out? Warner has all the equipment in his lab. Plus Warner knows other scientists with equipment as
advanced as anything the Bureau has in Quantico.

Other agents might scoff at the idea of bequeathing criminal evidence to civilians in order to investigate a criminal case. Not Carr.
Best-case scenario is they find something. If the Bureau holds on to it,
nothing happens. With Warner, Carr makes plans to have the evidence
examined outside the Bureau. But Warner is too old to conduct the
forensic examination himself. He'll need to take on a partner, and he
knows the scientist for the job: Tom Kaye.

The next day, I head south to attend the annual D.B. Cooper party at
the Ariel Tavern.

The Tavern is the only store in Ariel. It sits along the roadside, its
shingled blue siding and clap-tin roof battling gravity. Out front, plants
grow from a urinal. The entrance is covered in signs: THIS BUSINESS SUP-
PORTED BY TIMBER DOLLARS and UNATTENDED CHILDREN WILL BE SOLD AS
SLAVES.

Conventional wisdom is that the party's origins are pure, an event
based on admiration for the hijacker's guts, and the celebration has
taken on the feel of a séance. Each year, there is hope that if the partygoers dance hard enough and drink enough beer, the guest of honor—
D.B.—will walk through the front door.

"They always say the criminal comes back to his old haunts, and I think he'll come back," Germaine Tricola, the founder of Cooper Days, would say. In time, the Cooper party became part of the Cooper legend, and they've both worked to keep each other alive for the past four decades. President Jimmy Carter called in once.

Some years, before the bands played, hundreds of partygoers were offered search tours, parachute jumps, seaplane rides, a D.B. Cooper look-alike contest. Lunch and dinner were the same: buffalo stew served with slices of buttered white bread.

News clippings are spread along the walls. In the old photographs, loggers with mutton-chop sideburns sit around the store's woodstove. One man presses two beers against his head to simulate antennas. A band is jamming, playing the Cooper ballads.

> He said I beg your pardon ma'am a big bad bomb it's true,
> But I won't set if off if you don't put me in the mood.
> Just take me to Seattle and we'll put down for to land,
> And I'll sell you back your airplane for a cool two hundred grand.

I am not drunk. I should be. I should be cursing Ken Christiansen and his brother, Lyle, for sending the wacky letter to Nora Ephron. Is this the final scene of Lyle's *The Bashful Man in Seattle*? The gullible reporter who flies around the country hunting for the ghost of a purser.

I look around the room. The light in the tavern is soft and murky, like the glow of an old Coleman lantern. A parachute canopy hangs over picnic tables and twinkle lights are laced through old license plates and taxidermy. Near the cash register is Cooper gear: T-shirts, matchbooks, mugs. Inside a hot dog roaster, a lone frankfurter spins away. The band is on break. I'm on my second bowl of logger stew and chasing it down with a cold can of beer when I see them. They are standing at the tavern door.

The older man is shorter. His hands are buried in his pockets.

His friend is younger, taller, stout. He is holding a three-ring binder.

I introduce myself.

The shorter man is Ron Foreman. He's an airline mechanic.

The taller man is Cliff Kluge. He is a Delta pilot.

"The reason we're here, is my friend Ron has a story to tell," Kluge says.

Ron can't get the words out of his mouth.

"Yeah, you see, it's just one of those things that when I tell people, the first thing they do is just, well, freak out, and their mind closes up and they say, no way, you're crazy."

"You have to have an open mind," Kluge says.

"Nobody takes us seriously, not even the FBI! We went to them, we got a lawyer. They didn't even call us back!"

We sit down. Kluge opens the three-ring binder. He points.

The photo is of a man standing in front of the propeller of an old Piper Super Cub airplane. The man has light sandy hair. He is thin and lean.

Kluge thumbs through the pages. He points again.

This photo is of a woman. She is middle-aged. Light hair. Dark horn-rim glasses. She is standing in front of an old Cessna 140. Her pose is similar to the man in the previous picture. Behind her are tall trees. I squint. I can see she is holding a cigarette in her right hand.

"Okay?" Kluge says.

Okay what?

"That's D.B. Cooper!" Ron says.

I don't get it. Which one?

"They both are," Kluge says.

I look at the binder. I read the first page.

"Timeline of our friendship with Barbara Dayton," it says.

THE CURSE

Jo,

You're seeing Jesus Christ in the toast.

I'm just selling it on Ebay.

Who's more fucked up? The person seeing the image in the toast, or the one selling it on Ebay?

—snowmman, posting on the Drop Zone, November 4, 2008

The envelope is sent by courier. Seattle to Phoenix, Phoenix to Tucson. The envelope is then driven across the desert to the border town where scientist Tom Kaye keeps his ranch and laboratory. When the package is close, his phone rings. It's them. The feds.

"Hey, Tom," the agent says. "We got your bills here. You wanna come get 'em?"

Tom wonders where the agents are.

"We're across the street from La Casita restaurant in the mall."

La Casita? In the mall?

Tom is disappointed. The feds are holding crucial evidence to the infamous case of D.B. Cooper and they want him to pick it up like it's a drive-through taco? And how do they know he is for real?

"Don't you want to come by and see the lab first?"

The moment is surreal. How could Tom have gotten so lucky? The scientist's career has been a rollercoaster of ups and downs. His unanticipated success as a paintball entrepreneur has fizzled out. At one point, Tom had seventeen employees and grossed $5 million a year as the president of AirGun Designs—until customers complained that his guns were jamming on them. Then his competitors started making semi-automatic weapons, and Tom decided to retire early.

He chooses not to work for anyone else. He doesn't have a Ph.D. or college degree, and his résumé (pizza delivery man, high school security guard) doesn't exactly make him easily employable. But among the world's brainiest astronomers, paleontologists, geologists, and physicists, Kaye is known as a problem-solving genius, a geeky renegade who can outthink the thinkers.

"I'm basically just a body that carries my head around," he tells people.

He's achieved some remarkable feats. In 2005, Kaye and a few collaborators used a spectrograph, which breaks down light into rainbows, and discovered a distant planet named Tau Boötis. After a few tries, he managed to get the findings published. Tom also co-authored several scientific papers with titles such as "Mass Extinction Enigmas in Context with Gamma Ray Bursts" in journals like *Society of Photo-Optical Instrumentation Engineers*. He studied rings on old trees, the finger bones of a T. Rex. With his microscopes, he peers into matter so small and so old that nobody has even seen it before, a peep show into a secret universe.

"Living on the edge," he calls it.

Tom's scientific interests are so varied he's developed an eclectic collection of friends, many of whom he meets on dinosaur digs or on nerdy Internet forums. That's where he met Jerry Warner, a.k.a. Georger, and learned of Warner's obsession with the Cooper case. Tom was in high school when the hijacker jumped and he remembers the story in the news. Now that Jerry Warner has cut a deal with the FBI to have them look at the Cooper bills, Tom is anxious to get to work in his lab. His job is to handle the money that Brian Ingram found, analyze it, and figure out how it landed on Tena Bar.

Tom doesn't expect to solve the case with science. Without a decent DNA sample to test, how can he? He can debunk a few myths, and write a paper about it for a science periodical. Maybe even a mainstream one like *Science*.

The car barrels down the dirt road, spitting up red dust. It passes the yucca plants and mesquite trees and cactus that dot Tom's ranch. It passes a steel dome that is part of an astronomy lab Tom has been building for the past eight years, and one of his telescopes, which Tom made from a septic tank, oil drum, bike chain, lazy Susan, and fan belt. This makeshift contraption (all operated by computer) sits across from the Geek Barn, a graveyard of old parts from Tom's inventions and failed businesses. Over the years, they've included: a doggy-proof latch for dog cages; a machine that makes a gizmo to mix paint; an air compressor that sprays paint on objects like gumballs; several recreational objects built from fiberglass, like hang gliders, water skis, canoes.

The industrial robot age, in the early eighties, should have been his moment. To learn about advanced computer systems, Tom crashed a robot convention like an undercover agent. Pretending to be a buyer, he asked salespeople how the robots worked and recorded their answers with a hidden tape recorder. He transcribed the conversations and built his own industrial robot in his mother's basement. But before his company went public, his investors put all their money in handheld breathalyzers.

In a way, cracking open the Cooper case, if only a smidge, would be a kind of redemption for Tom. To understand the case he would need to understand the facts and the players, and he'd been up late on his computer, reading the endless posts on the Drop Zone. The Cooper community was similar to the dinosaur diggers he works with: lots of infighting and questing for glory. One Cooper hunter, he learned, had made a name for himself in the woods in southwest Washington, searching for the hijacker's bones and his missing cash. This hunter, a former military survival expert named Jerry Thomas, was so convinced that Cooper's parachute came down in the woods he was searching, he'd been looking there for the last twenty-two years.

The car is a crummy brown Toyota. The agents get out.

"What, no SUV?" Tom says.

"Well, no."

The agents hand him the envelope and some forms. Tom signs here, there. He gives the agents a tour. He walks through the living room, past his dinosaur bone collection, down the steps and into the lab. Microscopes and machines are mounted on work benches under fluorescent lights. The cold floors are spotless. In jars and plastic jewel boxes are samples for different tests he is conducting. Soon the agents lose interest. He cuts the tour short, follows them out the door, and retreats back into the lab. He places the envelope on a workbench. He unfastens the hinge. He peers inside.

That's weird, Tom thinks: Why is the money so black? He gazes at the dark film coating the flaking old bills. He stares and studies. He places a sample on a slide, slips it under his microscope, adjusts the focus. The money is glowing. The color is a rainbow of incandescence, a shine Tom once saw on a beetle wing. He snips off another sample of the money and places it into the chamber of his electron microscope.

This machine is bigger than a golf cart. It does not operate on magnification power, like a microscope in a science class. It uses a particle beam and magnifies the Cooper bills a million times. What Tom sees on the screen looks like a scene on the moon. The shapes are tubular and grainy. They represent the emptiness of all matter. Tom runs what he sees through a spectrograph. He hopes for an accident. That's what will yield a clue he can work with: an abundance of an element, something strange, a question he can pick at, obsess over, then answer. He looks at the elements on a computer monitor. He sees a spike.

That's weird, he thinks again. Why are the Cooper bills covered in silver?

August 1988
Washougal, Washington

Jerry Thomas, retired drill sergeant, first class, Vietnam vet, wakes up in his pup tent. It is dawn. He peers out the flaps of the tent. The spears of the imperial trees—hemlock, silver fir, Sitka spruce—tower high above him. On the trunks are chanterelles, and in the bushes are berries, his food out here. In the military, Jerry was an instructor in survival training at Fort Greely, Alaska, and he led troops out into the frozen darkness and slept in ice caves. So, it's no great challenge to spend a month or so in the forests around the Washougal River, in southern Washington state. There are Hill people, though, so he carries his gun and keeps it loaded.

The certificates he keeps confirm where he has been, what he has learned. At Fort Greely: "WINTER OPERATIONS IN NORTHERN AREA, INSTRUCTOR QUALIFICATION COURSE." At Fort Benning, Georgia: "TACTICS COMMITTEE, COMPANY A, INSTRUCTOR TRAINING." At Fort Jackson, South Carolina: "LEADERSHIP AND MANAGEMENT COURSE." As a first class sergeant, Jerry took the Instructor's Creed: "I AM A PROFESSIONAL SOLDIER. PRIDE IN MY COUNTRY, MY FLAG AND THE UNIFORM I WEAR."

Time to get a fire going. Once the logs have taken, he puts a grate on top of the embers. The grate was once a shelf in an old refrigerator Jerry found on a hike. Which was not unusual. Jerry wanders through the forest every day, and he always finds the darnedest things: car seats, Indian arrows, rusted-out cars, wagon wheels, even a golf ball once. He can't figure that one out—maybe a bird dropped it. The wagon wheels, he knows, are from the old settlers who came here to mine gold.

Time for breakfast. Hippie glop again. Hippie glop is canned corned beef hash from the food bank, and anything else edible that Jerry can cook in his skillet.

He eats out of the pan alone, then gets his feet moving through the woods. The brambles and mossy vines are so thick it's easier to wade through the river. It is lined with slippery rocks and boulders. Often his feet catch in the crevices and he falls.

Jerry does not get cold. A combat injury from Vietnam ruined his nervous system. He lost sensation in many areas.

"I don't have a heart," Jerry tells people. "I got what you call a thumpin' gizzard."

He is in the woods because he needs to be. He suffers from post-traumatic stress disorder. He is drinking. He can't be around other people.

He has flashbacks. He can see himself as a private, in training, a year too young to enroll. He remembers the locker rooms and group showers and the shame of being naked in front of the other men in training. Now he is in Vietnam, up near the DMZ, creeping through the jungle. He hears the voices of Vietcong in the trees. The enemy is close. Too close. Retreat! Jerry tries to move. He can't. His feet are stuck, frozen with fear. He bends over. He pukes.

Switch. He is in his bed in the trailer outside of Wilsonville, Oregon, where he grew up. He is fifteen. There's a hand on his shoulder, the grip so firm it hurts. He opens his eyes and there's his father, whiskey on his breath.

"Come on out to the truck, son." Jerry follows his dad out to the pickup. It's dark, but he can see what's in the back of the truck: an elk doe. His father has shot it.

His father holds out a piece of flesh.

"Run your finger across that."

Jerry does as his father says.

"See how slick and smooth that is?"

Jerry nods.

"That's elk pussy," his father says. "That's what pussy is like, son."

Switch. Jerry is back in Vietnam. He is inching through the jungle canopy, careful not to step on any mines and BOOM! He opens his eyes and he's on a stretcher and other soldiers are scurrying him through the jungle. He opens his eyes again and he's in the medic tent. He looks at his body and he knows he is dead because he can't feel anything and he can see what is on his chest and when he sees the doctor he is screaming, "Doc, there are fucking body parts all over my fucking body," and the doctor tells him not to worry because the body parts aren't his. They're from his buddy who was next to him when the mine went off.

Switch. He is in the barracks at Fort Polk, Louisiana. He is the drill sergeant. He wakes up. Another gunshot is fired in the latrine, another suicide.

Switch. He is between marriages, trying to take care of his daughter. She is thirteen and embarrassed. "Dad," she says, "we need to talk." Okay, he says. Let's talk. "You know that thing, you know, that girls do? That thing that's supposed to happen . . . ?" She's doubled over with cramps, her eyes pleading, but he isn't getting it.

Switch. He is in the hospital and the detective wants to ask him questions about how the gun went off and the bullet struck his son in the face. How dare the detective suggest he tried to kill his own son?

Switch. Jerry is back in the woods in Washougal. Through the trees, he sees a dark hole in a rock. It is the Last Chance Mine.

He crawls inside. On the walls around him he can see inscriptions.

1906. Kilroy was here.

He moves down, deeper into the chasm. On the ground are pools of water. And there it is, by his wet feet.

The bag is old. The bag is made from canvas.

Could it be? Could Jerry have found D.B. Cooper's lost money bag?

Jerry calls the FBI. If anyone could confirm the bag he found had belonged to Cooper, it is the feds.

The lead agent in the case, Ralph Himmelsbach, has retired, but lives in the area, Jerry is told by the clerk who takes his call.

Jerry is curious if the feds know how to contact Himmelsbach.

The phonebook, the clerk says. Himmelsbach is listed.

Jerry looks up the number and calls. He tells Himmelsbach about the canvas bag he found.

Where did he find the bag, Himmelsbach asks.

Near the Washougal river, Jerry tells him. Lying on the floor of the Last Chance Mine.

Describe the bag.

Well, it's canvas, has a leather strap and a metal eyelet.

Nope, can't be. The canvas bag of money Cooper was given was all white—no leather straps, no eyelets. But Jerry was looking in the right place, Himmelsbach says, and shares his opinion that after studying the case longer than any agent he has come to believe Cooper parachuted into the Washougal area, and his bones were probably located at the river's edge.

The Washougal. Jerry knew he was onto something. He goes back in the woods. He follows Himmelsbach's directions, searching up and down the Washougal river bed. He does this every season, checking caves, old mines, under ferns. He rigs a six-foot stick with a hook so he can poke around in the bush and prod up into tree branches. Jerry does this for so many years he becomes part of the Cooper legend himself. When reporters call looking for information on the woods, Himmelsbach refers them to Jerry. He's the Woods Guy.

"I know there is something out here," Jerry tells one reporter. "There has to be."

Date Unknown, 1978
Thun Airport Field, Puyallup, Washington

She has blond hair, shoulder length. She is wearing shorts and sandals. Her toenails are painted red. She has a wrench in her hands and she is working on her plane and a '62 Dodge at the same time, transferring parts from each.

Her Cessna is the ugliest plane Ron Foreman has ever seen. The color scheme goes together like gruel: the engine cowler is brown, the wings are blue and yellow striped. Entire patches of paint are missing. Parked next to the plane, her '62 Dodge looks even worse. Foreman peers under the hood. He sees a block of wood where the oil dipstick was. He looks at the dashboard: It's been retrofitted with aviation-like turn signals.

She has created a kind of car-plane. She siphons high-octane jet fuel from the Cessna to fill the gas tank in the Dodge. Drives faster that way, she says.

Ron Foreman introduces himself. He's an airplane mechanic.

She's Barbara Dayton, and the plane is for sale.

"You interested?" she says.

He is. Not in her plane, but in her abilities as a mechanic. Later, Ron watches her remove a propeller with a ten-inch Crescent wrench. How can she be so strong? And when they finally fly together, he can't understand why her crummy Cessna flies five miles faster than his and all the other taildragger pilots at Thun?

As a pilot, Barb is reckless. She flies with her radio off. She buzzes so many treetops the branches get stuck in her wheels. She says strange and ominous things about flying and death. He's never met a pilot so emotionally connected to the experience of being in the air. She tells Pat Foreman, Ron's wife, "Sometimes I feel like getting into the plane and flying out over the water until I run out of fuel."

She is a loner. When the Foremans arrive at the airfield, they can see her under the wing of her Cessna and, later, her Aeronca Champ. When they leave, Barb is still there. Even on holidays. Even in the rain. Come have lunch? Come over for dinner?

No thanks, Barb says.

The Foremans are relentless in their friendliness. They push. Come on. One meal.

Barb has no choice. One Sunday night, after flying, she comes to their house and eats with them. Next Sunday, she returns. She tells them about her life.

She prospected for gold near the family ranch in the Mother Lode; nearly died of starvation in the Yukon with the Crazy Indian; rode with the Hells Angels; was nearly shot to death as a deserter in the Merchant Marines for abandoning ships and living with the Māori warriors. She's now a librarian, in the palatial Suzzallo Library in Seattle, on the University of Washington campus. She knows karate. She's a black belt.

The Foremans don't believe her.

To prove it, she gets into a crouch and leaps around the living room performing her martial arts moves. Then she hits the ground and starts to do one-armed push-ups.

One weekend, the Foremans visit Barb in Seattle. Her building is a rooming house of sorts. The stairs are narrow and rickety. Barb's room is number thirteen.

Thirteen is her lucky number, she says.

She opens the door and shows them around.

"I furnished the place for less than twenty dollars," she says.

They sit on orange plastic chairs. Her television is tiny, with a six-inch screen. Inside her fridge is a half a head of cabbage and a bottle of grape juice. Along her windowsill is an old coil that was plucked from a Model-A car. Ron sees wires running from it.

An alarm system, Barb says. The wires running are attached to a 6-volt. Anybody who comes through her window will get zapped.

"Where's your bedroom?" Ron asks.

"You're in it," Barb says.

Another night, Barb is over again for Sunday night dinner.

"I have something to tell you about my past," she says. "You'll probably never want to see me in your house again. The last person I told about this tried to kill me."

"Don't tell me you were a prostitute!" Ron says.

"No. I wish it were as simple as that."

"Give me a hint. Does it have anything to do with money?"

"In a way. At one time I had all the money I could want, but I just blew it."

"I know. You killed someone."

"No, that's not it, though I could have if things kept going the way they were."

"Did you do something illegal?"

"Well, no, what I'm about to tell you about wasn't illegal."

"You were in a mental hospital."

"No, that's not it."

Barb looks at Pat.

"I think your wife knows now," Barb says.

It takes a few minutes for Pat to figure it out. Ron and Pat retreat into their bedroom. Pat tells Ron that Barb was once a man. Ron feels angry, betrayed. He befriended Barb because he was so impressed that a woman could possess such extraordinary mechanical skills. The sting lingers for a few days, but he likes Barb and likes to fly with her so much. Eventually, he gets over it.

D.B. Cooper comes up for the first time one afternoon at Sanderson, a small airport near Thun. It's close to Thanksgiving, Cooper anniversary stories are in the papers, and every pilot at the lunch table has a theory about the missing hijacker.

Ron thinks Cooper is an idiot. Why jump over Ariel? No way to make it out alive.

Barb defends Cooper's intelligence. She sounds angry, offended almost.

Ron jokes with her.

"I know," he says. "Barb is the real D.B. Cooper!"

Later that day, Barb pulls Ron aside.

"Don't ever say that in public again," she says, about calling her Cooper. "Not even as a joke."

A few months later, over Sunday night dinner, the topic of the hijacker returns.

"The FBI doesn't know what they're talking about," Barb says, and goes on to discuss the case in detail. Cooper's actual drop zone, she says, is nowhere near where the FBI was searching.

The Foremans are skeptical. How does Barb know so much about the case?

"Okay," Barb says. "Ron guessed it at Sanderson. I am D.B. Cooper."

They don't believe her. How could they?

"You can't tell anyone," Barb says. "I get claustrophobic. I couldn't survive in prison."

August 2000
Pace, Florida

McNeil. Ohio State. San Quentin. Soledad. Canon City. What convict did Jo marry? She flips through the *Soldier of Fortune* that Duane left in his safety deposit box. Was he trying to tell her something by leaving this magazine for her? Are the clues in here? She scans the personal ads again. NIGHT VISION BINOCULARS, one reads. GORGEOUS ASIAN WOMEN. More listings. WHO KILLED KENNEDY?

She remembers a few names of the friends Duane had, people he introduced her to in Atlanta and New Orleans where they went for parties. She met Tommy Gunn once in Mobile, Alabama. She looks up his name, finds it in the directory. After the call, she trembles when she remembers what he told her.

"If you want to see your grandchildren, burn everything. Duane knew people in high places."

What people? What places? How high?

Jo calls the FBI again. They don't call back.

She is hysterical. What has the FBI found in Duane's past? Why aren't they calling back? What are they hiding?

With a dial-up connection on her computer, she painstakingly punches out more e-mails.

"Please help me," she writes to the Missouri Department of Corrections. "I am a 64 yr old widow who just wants to piece together her husbands life. . . . My husband told me his name was Dan Cooper . . . so be assured the FBI thinks I'm a loo loo."

She studies the commutation paper she found in the ostrich-skin wallet again. She looks at the date. March 1968. She realizes that March 1968 is one month before Duane's prison mate James Earl Ray was suspected of assassinating Martin Luther King.

What was going on inside Jefferson City when Duane and James Earl Ray were there? Had James Earl accepted some kind of deal to escape from Jefferson City? If he did, would Duane's ex-wife Mary

Jane know about it? Did Duane have some part in the killing of Martin Luther King? Or did John C. Collins?

Jo scans her mind for the names and faces of the men Duane introduced her to. How else can she figure out who Duane was and who John C. Collins is?

She remembers the one-legged man, who drove them to dinner in Denver and said he once worked for Howard Hughes. She remembers the man with cupid lips and a diamond horseshoe finger ring at the Red Rooster, a bar in southern Colorado. They met at the bar so early in the morning. Why?

More memories. Why did Duane's boss Ed Hurran—or was it Hurrand? Or Horan?—not want Jo to take his picture? Or founder of American Life Insurance Bernie Rapoport—"Kissy Kissy," as they called him? Did these men think she was annoying? Or were they hiding another piece of her dead husband's secret life?

She sees a photograph of "Macho," or Bernard Barker, who was involved in Watergate. The Nixon Plumber looks familiar. Did she meet Macho at a private party in New Orleans? She thinks so. Can she be sure the photo is of him? No. And what about the man wearing the blue jacket in Salt Lake City? Duane asked her to take his picture. Why?

Another memory. Members of Duane's family told her a story. When Bobby Kennedy was campaigning for president, in 1968, Duane took a job working as a bellhop at the Muehlebach Hotel, in Kansas City. On the campaign trail, Bobby Kennedy and his entourage checked in. When Kennedy left the hotel for the day to campaign, Duane snuck into the candidate's hotel room looking for a memento to steal. In Kennedy's room he allegedly found a tie and swiped it.

Was it possible the tie Duane left on the plane was the same tie Kennedy wore? Was that another clue, revenge perhaps for Kennedy's blundering at the Bay of Pigs? Was it even possible that Bobby Kennedy would wear a clip-on tie?

That can't make sense, Jo thinks. And then it does. On the campaign trail in 1968, folks were always pulling at Robert Kennedy's body, his hands, and probably his tie. Perhaps he wore a clip-on to avoid being choked?

Or maybe it wasn't Kennedy who wore the clip-on tie? Perhaps Duane snuck in to the room, got nervous, and grabbed the skinny Towncraft that belonged to one of Kennedy's security guards?

That also made sense. When Bobby Kennedy was shot at the Ambassador Hotel in Los Angeles, he grabbed the tie of one guard, and it came off. Kennedy's guards did wear clip-ons.

Once again, Jo goes through Duane's files. One letter she finds is from the Government Employees Benefit Association, a company based in Georgia. The letter claims Duane worked for Government Employees between November 1973 and December 1977. She looks up the company. Government Employees, she finds, is the leading provider of insurance to the CIA. Was Duane really selling insurance to CIA agents? Or was that his cover? And if Duane was a rogue operative working with the CIA, was the Cooper mission a "company job"? Or maybe it was former CIA agents, or mercenaries, the folks who read *Soldier of Fortune,* who contracted out the mission. If so, why?

The conspiracy theorists believe Cooper's hijacking was a black operation, staged during a moment in the news cycle when Americans would be home and watching television (Thanksgiving). It was designed to pressure legislators to pass more stringent safety laws on airplanes and in airports, and to push airlines to pay for metal detectors to deter hijackings. That makes sense to Jo. The Nixon era is chock full of black bag jobs and covert ops. But if the Cooper hijacking was an inside job, who called it? And how was Duane chosen to be the jumper?

✕

July 26, 1972
Brighton, Colorado

The sheriff reads the names for morning arraignments from a list.

"Benjamin Namepee?"

Richard Floyd McCoy looks around the drunk tank. A few inmates are still sleeping off their hangovers. No hands go up.

"Benjamin Namepee?"

McCoy raises his hand. He walks out of the cell and proceeds to the courthouse. He keels over, cringing in pain. He's sick, he tells the sheriff. Needs to use the bathroom, fast. He holds out his wrists. The sheriff uncuffs him. He runs.

Later that afternoon, the marshals find McCoy a few blocks from the courthouse. They place him back in handcuffs and belly chain and finish the drive east to Lewisburg.

The federal penitentiary at Lewisburg is a massive prison in rural Pennsylvania that was built during the Great Depression. McCoy is housed in the prison's maximum security wing, Dog Block. His job is in the prison's dental laboratory. He makes fake teeth for inmates.

Working with the plaster, McCoy begins to think about another escape. Didn't John Dillinger use a fake gun to escape from jail? And if Dillinger could whittle a phony gun from a piece of wood, why couldn't McCoy make his own pistol out of the plaster he works with in the dental lab?

He needs a sculptor. Through inmates, McCoy makes contact with Melvin Walker, who made the Bureau's Most Wanted List. The feds call him the Flying Bank Robber.

Walker has ice-cold eyes, a menacing Fu Manchu mustache, jail-house tattoos crawling up his arms, and a résumé of epic escapes.

On a transfer to Marion, then the most secure prison in the nation,

Walker made a handcuff key from a refill cartridge of a pen. He hid the key in his sock, handcuffed the marshals to a maple tree, stole their badges, credit cards, guns, car, then disappeared.

On the lam for months, Walker was eventually caught and transferred back to Marion. The fences were fourteen feet high, topped with swirling rolls of razor wire.

Using two pairs of bar spreaders, Walker pried open his window. He shimmied down the prison wall with a rope made from his bed sheet, clutching a wool blanket. Fired at by guards with high-powered rifles, Walker jumped the prison fence, using the wool blanket to shield himself against the razor wire. He ran for most of the night. The next morning, prison guard dogs discovered him sleeping in a tree.

Now in Lewisburg, Walker is biding time, writing poetry, waiting for his next escape.

> *If I'm destined to be in your prison,*
> *Then bury me deep underground*
> *Just the sight of a light, for a man like me*
> *And I know I am freedom bound.*

In his cell, McCoy flips through magazines, looking for images of guns. He cuts one out. Through other inmates, he sends the image to Walker. McCoy's next shipment is a block of wax he pilfers from the prison dental lab. Walker sculpts the wax into a replica of a .45 caliber pistol. He sends the replica back to McCoy, who writes to the judge who oversaw his trial in Salt Lake. He begs for a reduced sentence. His letters are not returned. McCoy writes to the judge again.

> *It has been nearly six months since I wrote to you. I know*
> *you are quite busy and I don't want to impose on you, but*
> *there are important personal considerations which require*

solutions in the near future. Knowing the final outcome of my case could very well influence some of the decisions that need to be made.

Like escaping from Lewisburg.

March 1, 2008
Catheys Valley, California

The sun is blinding. I squint through the windshield. I see endless rows of almond trees that line the farms of the Central Valley. We are driving toward Merced. As a young man, Bobby Dayton drove the same route. I imagine him pulling over in his beat-up truck, asking for work. With his fair hair and blue eyes, Bobby would have burned in the sun. Or maybe he tanned dark. Bobby was a quarter Indian.

That fits. On the plane, witnesses described the hijacker as dark, swarthy.

"He says he was Kickapoo, and when my grandfather went to check it he says Winnebago, so I don't know really what tribe we are," Rena Ruddell says.

Rena is Bobby's daughter and closest living relative. Her brother, Dennis, died years ago. Shortly after he returned from Vietnam, police found him in a friend's bathtub. The bathtub was filled with milk, and a needle was stuck in his arm. A heroin overdose, the coroner said.

Now in her fifties, Rena has picked me up from the airport in Modesto, where she teaches elementary school. We are en route to Catheys Valley to see the old Dayton ranch and visit with Barb's relatives.

Rena is a believer. At first, when Ron and Pat Foreman contacted her and told her they thought her father was D.B. Cooper, Rena doubted it. But that's changed. The more Rena thought about it—Barb's love for airplanes, her hatred for the airlines, her lust for The Score, her suicidal tendencies—the more it all made sense.

"You had to know him," Rena says. "He just didn't care if he lived or died."

Listening to Rena talk about her father, I think of Dr. Hubbard, as if the psychiatrist had left me clues to uncovering Cooper's identity.

Failure after failure gradually aroused an intense hostility that was slowly transferred from himself to society in an attempt to defend him-self against a rising desire to commit suicide.

. . . After years of inadequate and misguided effort, these men had steadily depleted their sense of self-worth, until in a last desperate moment they plunged into this symbolic action in which they saw themselves more or less permanently as men who had done one fine thing.

Yep. This was Bobby. Or, Barb.

The hills of the Mother Lode are marked with the mouths of old mining claims and the tombstones of bank robbers. In clearings, oak trees stand alone and the spindly branches cast shadows that look like witches' fingers. The road is now dirt and we follow a creek. In the creek a man has his jeans rolled up and is showing a boy how to use a sluice box, working the water that runs over the rocks and through the dirt for flakes of gold.

The Dayton ranch exists only in memory. The house and barn are gone. All that's left are a few stones of a chimney Elmer built. Rena and I walk the grounds. She wonders if her father buried the ransom money here. Across the stream, I can see an old mine that must have been active in the 1860s. Did Barbara hide the ransom in there?

A car barrels down the dirt road, pulls over. I see a white cowboy hat. It's Sharon Power, Rena's aunt. She was married to Bill Dayton, Bobby's brother. Sharon is also the sister of Dixie, Bobby's first wife. Sharon spent years on the ranch with the Dayton family. She learned to ride horses here. She walks around the property in her stiff dungarees and cowboy boots, pointing to where she and Bill and Bobby stabled Toots, Sugar, and Buck, their horses. She points to a patch of grass that was once a kitchen where Bobby's mother, Bernice, made her hominy grits and tamale pie.

Sharon does not doubt that Bobby Dayton turned into Dan Cooper.

"He just had that kind of mind," she tells me.

Sharon is a poet. She wrote a few verses to explain her theories.

> *A lonely man sat in the night*
> *The spirit within, was just not right.*
> *The bomb he held was violently loaded.*
> *A move of his finger and it would be exploded.*
> *Stilts in his shoes raised him from short to tall.*
> *He had always hated being somewhat small.*
> *The unfamiliar tie was bothersome.*
> *Becoming edgy it troubled him some.*
> *He shot out in the turbulent air*
> *In a free fall, if he died he didn't care.*
> *In small pieces he burned the chute*
> *And note by note he burned all the loot.*
> *This was his hidden treasure*
> *No one would find it, not ever.*
> *He changed into women's clothes*
> *Put on makeup and powdered his nose.*
> *It would be a long walk to the road to catch a bus*
> *SHE would find amusement in all of the fuss.*

Sharon's daughter, Billie Dayton, lives nearby. Billie was close with Bobby too. Bobby was her uncle. When the hijacking occurred, Billie remembered her father hearing the news and saying, "That's Bobby."

Billie Dayton is a believer too. Her uncle Bobby was always trying to prove he could do something others could not. He was also suicidal over his sex change operation and depressed over his failure to obtain a commercial pilot's license. Bobby was a man with a grudge.

After the operation, Billie's father didn't speak or visit with Barb until she got sick. She'd moved out of Seattle and into a trailer in the desert near Carson City, Nevada. She was broke, gambling all her money and social security checks away in slot machines.

When Bill and Billie arrived to visit, Barb was in the hospital.

Bill and Billie suspected she might have some of the Cooper bills. They searched her trailer for them, but nothing turned up.

Then a curious thing happened. In the hospital, Barb began to make strange gestures. Bill and Billie thought she finally wanted to confess to the hijacking. But Barb's condition had deteriorated. She could no longer talk. Then she was gone.

"I have no doubt in my mind Bobby was D.B. Cooper," Billie says. "I know it."

August 2000
Pace, Florida

Jo Weber does not leave her house. She has too much work decoding the clues Duane left her. Her friends stop calling. Her daughters are embarrassed by her obsession with the Cooper case. But how can Jo let it go? She has to find a piece of evidence to prove Duane is Cooper. She has to prove it because she needs to show everyone who doubts her that she isn't making up this story—that she isn't a loo-loo.

She calls the FBI again. They don't call back. What have they found? What are they hiding from her?

After the story about Duane is published in *U.S. News & World Report,* Jo gets calls from all over the country. One of them is from Bob Knoss.

Knoss knew Duane, he claims. He met Duane through Richard Floyd McCoy Jr. They were training for the hijacking together.

What? Can't be true. How could two Cooper suspects (Weber, McCoy) be involved in the Cooper hijacking?

Bob Knoss is a picture-framer who once lived in Bloomington, Minnesota. He had forgotten about Duane until the *U.S. News & World Report* story was published in July of 2000. Knoss had recently broken his back. He was marooned on his sofa, taking painkillers. Watching television, Knoss saw Duane's face. That's the dude, he thought to himself.

The memory Knoss claimed to have meshed together into a wacky comedy, a story about a gung-ho aspiring covert agent (McCoy), who in order to impress his rogue bosses recruited a charming crook from prison (Duane Weber). Together they conspired to hijack a Northwest plane, to accomplish the dual purposes of getting rich together and capturing the attention of legislators in Washington to increase airport security.

Knoss knew about it because he was involved, he says. His story is complicated. Knoss was a draft dodger who got caught. Instead of going to prison, he volunteered to help McCoy on the Cooper hijacking.

Knoss was McCoy's witness, he tells Jo. In case McCoy got arrested, Knoss was to testify that McCoy was operating on behalf of interests friendly to the government.

And how did McCoy and Duane get involved?

McCoy got Duane out of prison, Knoss says. Only Knoss never knew Duane as Duane, Knoss tells Jo. He knew Duane by his nickname, Coop. And his alias, Dan Cooper.

Jo does not believe Bob Knoss's story. How can she? But she does check it out.

One late night on the phone, she asks Mary Jane if she and Duane ever lived in Bloomington.

"No," Mary Jane tells her. "We never lived in Bloomington, just stayed there for a few weeks."

So it was true. Or possibly true. Duane had been in Bloomington, Minnesota. Bob Knoss could have known Duane. If that part of Knoss's story is true, what about the rest?

She reads every book and article written on the case. She calls all the major witnesses. She flies to Washington to see if she can retrace her steps, to see if she can remember where Duane took her, that road near the town of Orchards where Duane said, "That's where D.B. Cooper walked out of the woods."

A few memories come back to her. Especially down near the Columbia. She passes the Red Lion Inn. She's been to the hotel before. Duane pulled the car over. She went to use the ladies' room. When she came back to the car, Duane was gone. She circled the lobby. She checked the car again. Where did Duane go? Finally, she found him down near the river's edge.

"What you looking at, Duane?" she asked.

"The bag," he said.

Jo strained her eyes and scanned the river. She saw a paper bag. She didn't know what was in it. Duane was using it for trash, she thought.

She scolded him for tossing trash into the river.

"You don't do that!" she said. "You don't litter like that!"

Now, after learning about the case, and about the Cooper bills Brian Ingram found on Tena Bar down the river, Jo wonders about that bag. Maybe it wasn't filled with trash like she thought. Maybe Duane was throwing away the Cooper bills. The year was 1978. Or 1979. She can't remember. She tells this story often. Few believe her. What if Jo is making up the entire story?

March 4, 2008
Woodburn, Oregon

I pull into the parking lot of an Arby's south of Portland. I am here to meet Ron and Pat Foreman and Ron's pilot friend Cliff Kluge. Our mission: find the rest of Cooper's missing ransom.

We have a guide of sorts. In the late 1970s, when Barb Dayton confessed to being the skyjacker, the Foremans took notes. Our plan is to follow the notes, as if they are clues Barb left for us to use, like a treasure map.

"A white house," the first note reads. "The front faces the south. There is an old tractor kitty-corner to the house. The pecan orchard is longer than it is wide and runs east and west. The money is hid in one of the irrigation cisterns."

There is more. "Cistern at end, so not used."

We drive down the freeway, retracing the flight path, until we get to turn into Woodburn.

"Woodburn," according to the Foremans' notes, "is exactly 38 miles south of Columbia River."

The notes describe how Barb pulled the job. On the night of the hijacking, she rode a bus from Woodburn to Portland. Foreman note: "Bus not as conspicuous." Her motive: "Bitterness against FAA & airlines. Too many rules against the average pilot. Everything for the airlines." The bomb: "Two five-pound charges with detonator in zippered brown briefcase. Battery switch in pocket. Detonator was a staple remover with wires soldered to it."

The staple remover, I think, is a revealing detail. After the hijacking, Tina Mucklow reported seeing a "a little clip at the end" of the wire of the hijacker's briefcase bomb. Was the "clip" Tina saw really Barb's staple remover?

I see grassy fields of the Willamette farms and labyrinths of trees in the orchards.

In the passenger seat, Ron Foreman looks at the sky to get his bearings. As pilots, he and Barb flew over the flight path of the hijacked plane and the farms around which we are now meandering. Ron also knows where Barb says she jumped. According to his notes, her visual cue from the sky was "Aurora State Airport." On the map, Aurora State Airport is a few miles south of Portland. In the night sky, Barb would have been able to see the lights of Vancouver, then Portland, then Aurora.

Note: "Jump was made from 10,000 feet with a 9,000 foot free fall. Speed of 727 was 220 mph. Wind was at 30 mph from the southwest."

It's true. How could Barb know such arcane details as wind speed and wind direction, and be right about them? According to the Bureau files, meteorologists reported the wind speed between Portland and Salem, Oregon, to be between 20 and 30 knots—so, on average, exactly 30 miles per hour on the night of the hijacking. And the wind direction varied between south and southwest. Was this coincidence? Or was Barb really Cooper?

In researching Barb's past, Ron and Pat Foreman found other evidence they believe links Barb to the hijacking. They went through Barb's medical records, and notes from doctors were revealing. In one interview before the surgery, Bobby Dayton told doctors about his hobbies. From the records:

> He has also been a skydiver, but lost interest in that because he found it boring.

Boring?! How could jumping out of a plane, Ron Foreman wondered, ever get boring?

The medical records also contained notes from follow-up visits. Eight days before the hijacking, on November 16, 1971, doctors noted that Barb was depressed. She was considering suicide again. Two weeks after the hijacking, on December 8, 1971, her mood had changed.

> [Patient] doing well. Not depressed. . . . Is on welfare but strangely un-worried despite inability to get work. Welfare expires in three months.

"Strangely unworried" about money? Why? Because she now had a $200,000 ransom, a ransom she hid in a cistern, a cistern that is some-where around Woodburn, where we are now driving.

I see a white farmhouse out the window. Is the front facing south? It is. We follow the road along the trees to check the direction of the field. It looks just like Barb said: longer than it is wide. Now, where are the cisterns?

We drive farther, circling the orchard, past a trailer park. In the far-thest corner, we park, get out, and there it is, over the fence: a cistern. It is just as Barb has described.

We look down the alleys of trees and check the orchard for big dogs and farmers with guns. This is private property. Should we go?

Ron Foreman stays with Pat in the car. Cliff and I hop the fence. I hear the distant buzz of a tractor. I look around the orchard. Far off, I see a plaid shirt. Who is that? Better hurry.

I close my eyes and cross my toes and pray, Oh Lord do I pray, that when we get the cistern open, there will be, just as Barb left it, the remaining portion of D.B. Cooper's missing ransom. I want it bad. I want it now.

Screeching, scraping. Cliff and I are breaking sweat to pry the heavy metal cover off the cistern. Finally we get the thing off.

A hole in the ground is now open, a tunnel to our treasure.

I get down—chest first. I stick my head into the pit. I look. There is no mistaking what I see. Absolutely nothing.

Back in the car, we look for another white house that faces south, a pecan orchard longer than it is wide, running east to west. We see a farmer and pull over to ask him about white houses. He gets off his tractor and tells us there are a lot of white houses around here. I ask him what he is growing.

"Hazelnuts," he says.

The trees on his orchard look like all the rest we have seen and that doesn't jibe. According to the Foremans' notes, Barb landed in a pecan orchard. Another note they kept disturbs me too. Barb, according to them, claimed to have kept eighty bundles of $2,500 apiece in the cistern. That was wrong. The bills came in a hundred bundles of $2,000 apiece. Did the Foremans hear Barb wrong? Or had Barb made the detail up?

I wonder about Barb and her wrong color eyes (blue), her short height (five eight), her tale about hiding a change of clothes (and the ransom) in the cistern. If she hid the ransom, how did the Cooper bills get in the sand miles away at Tena Bar?

Chasing Barb Dayton, I have found another Ken Christiansen. I can't prove she was Cooper. I can't prove she wasn't.

I call Larry Carr in Seattle. I am planning another visit to look at more files. I wonder if he has any news.

He does.

A parachute has been found, he tells me.

A parachute?

An old parachute, Carr says. And military.

Military!

White canopy, Carr says. And conical shaped.

Holy shit. Must be Cooper's NB6, I think. Where was the chute found?

Amboy, Carr says.

I don't need a map. I know where Amboy is. Amboy is just south of Ariel, across Lake Merwin, in Clark County. Amboy is D.B. Cooper country, directly in the drop zone.

The story is innocent enough. In Amboy, a man had been using a back hoe in his backyard. His children were playing in the dirt. In the dirt they found the white fabric of the parachute. Suspecting it was Cooper's, they called the FBI.

Carr mentions the discovery to a local television reporter, who runs with the story. The wires jump on the news, and so do the national papers, including the *New York Times*.

The discovery of the white conical parachute in Amboy (which turned out to be a bust) sends shockwaves through Cooperland. In Alabama, cyber sleuth Sluggo_Monster (aka nuclear lab consultant Wayne Walker) reconfigures the preferences on his Internet search browsers to collect the avalanche of news stories following the Amboy parachute find. One story he snags is published in *AvioNews,* an Italian periodical that covers the aeronautics industry.

The story is written in Italian. It's difficult to follow. But scrolling through a garbled translation of the text, Walker makes his own discovery: The author of the *AvioNews* piece has picked up on the mystery of the hijacker's name.

"Dan Cooper," the Italian story states, "was the name of a toon created by Albert Weinberg, from Belgium, during the 50s."

Dan Cooper a toon? A cartoon?

"He was a Canadian airman, involved in many adventures regarding spying's cases and science fictions."

Walker runs more searches on the Web. He digs up images of old comics. Dan Cooper, Walker finds, is not just an "airman." He is a combat pilot. Cooper flies fighter jets and test planes for the Royal Canadian Air Force. Walker can't understand the words he reads. The comic is written in French. It has never been translated into English. But the images are clear.

Dan Cooper is a Canadian version of GI Joe. He has a square chin, rippling biceps, clear blue eyes, a crew cut. He skyrockets out of the earth's orbit to battle men in spacesuits with metal hooks for arms, aliens, and enemy frogmen. He runs (*Pang!*) and dives (*Plouf!*) and is chased (*Halte!*) and takes off again in his jet (*Tchiiiiiiiouw!*). Dan Cooper is an aerial acrobat, and his save-the-day missions all seem to end the same way: floating down in a conical parachute, just like the hijacker Dan Cooper did with the NB6 on November 24, 1971.

The comic is not a coincidence, Walker thinks. I agree. There is a connection between the French-Canadian comic book hero Dan Cooper and the hijacker who used his name. There has to be. But what is it?

His creator, I hope, will know.

✕

I find comic book artist Albert Weinberg in Corseaux, a town on Lake Geneva, in Switzerland. I imagine his château as vast and ornate, with doors that lead from his studio to a veranda that looks out onto water that ripples with the wake of a passing speedboat.

Weinberg was not trained as an artist. Growing up in Belgium, he dropped out of law school and was hired as an illustrator for Hergé, creator of Tintin, the legendary French comic that follows the adventures of a boy reporter. After *Tintin* became its own magazine in the '50s, Hergé asked Weinberg to come up with his own character and strip.

Weinberg needed a backdrop, a universe for his character to explore. He chose the sky. He wanted the air filled with jets, parachutes, drones, spaceships. Weinberg had family in French Canada, and he imagined his hero as a Royal Canadian Air Force pilot.

Weinberg is old now, almost ninety. I want to see him. I want to sit on the veranda and watch the speed boat go by, ask about the character he created, and the hijacker he must have inspired.

I call him in Switzerland. The voice on the end of the line is smooth and deep and kind, a grandfather speaking in a slow and pleasing French. Battling the language barrier, I ask for a visit. Best to meet in person. That way, I can sit across from the old comic book artist in his rocking chair, a shawl over his shoulders, and he can lay out the secret to this case for me.

Impossible to meet in person, he says.

Why?

He will be on holiday, he says.

So perhaps when he returns?

Impossible, he says. Holiday will be several months.

I settle for a phone call with a translator.

"It's a bit of a mystery for me as well," Weinberg says about the case when I call again. In the early 1970s, when the identity of the hijacker was first reported as "Dan Cooper," Weinberg says he received phone calls from his contacts in the Royal Canadian Air Force notifying him.

"I don't remember exactly the date," Weinberg says, "but it rather amused me because I said to myself, Look here, it's probably a former pilot or a reader. And francophone, Canadian francophone. But we were never able to uncover more of this story."

I ask Weinberg about the name. Was there any symbolism? Where did he come up with Dan Cooper?

"The phone book. I picked two hundred names in Quebec and went to my family and I said, 'Which ones do you like?' . . . Eventually the name Dan Cooper was chosen."

And what about Dan Cooper? How would he define his character?

"I think the main quality of my character is that he is very, very sensitive," Weinberg says. "Even though he was a military pilot, he always held a high regard for human life. It would have been difficult for me to make Dan Cooper proudly shooting on another plane."

August 10, 1974
Lewisburg, Pennsylvania

Richard Floyd McCoy's letters to the judge are introspective. He writes about Vietnam. He explains why he was shipped home with a shrapnel wound and the Purple Heart.

> *Maybe you're wondering whether I was capable of harming any-*
> *one. . . . During my first tour of duty in Vietnam, I was wounded. The*
> *only reason, Your Honor, is that I was unable to kill a man up close.*

McCoy's letters are not answered. His motion to reduce his forty-year prison sentence is denied. McCoy and Walker discuss terms. Prison escapes are negotiations.

"If you shoot it out, I'll shoot it out with you," Walker says. "But only if I can see we can make it. If I can't, my hands go over my head."

"Not me," McCoy says. "I'd rather die a thousand deaths before I spend one more day in Lewisburg."

They wait until deep summer, until the cornstalks outside the prison fence have grown high enough for them to run through. From the wire report:

> *Lewisburg, PA—Four armed convicts, including a Mormon Sunday*
> *school teacher involved in a bizarre 1972 hijacking, crashed a com-*
> *mandeered garbage truck through a gate at a federal penitentiary Sat-*
> *urday and disappeared into the central Pennsylvania mountains.*

They drive east and south and over the Mason-Dixon Line, down to North Carolina. McCoy has family there. Along the way, the convicts shave each other's heads. In North Carolina, they make news again.

> *New Bern, N.C.—Authorities say four men who robbed a Pollocks-*
> *ville, N.C., bank were convicts who escaped from the federal prison at*
> *Lewisburg, Pa., last Saturday.*

There is more.

The bandits then switched to another car with Ohio tags. It was subsequently spotted by police helicopter on an unpaved logging road in the Great Dover Swamp. Officers aboard the helicopter exchanged fire with the fugitives as they abandoned the vehicle, police said.

McCoy and Walker press on to Gatlinburg, Tennessee. They hole up at a Howard Johnson's motel. One afternoon, they watch *Butch Cassidy and the Sundance Kid* as they count their score from another robbery. Thirty thousand . . . fifty thousand . . . seventy-six thousand. At night, they go out for dinner and steal license plates from cars and look for people who look like them, so they can steal their identification. But what is the point?

The Howard Johnson's is its own prison. What have they done it all for? They decide to live big, splurge. Fuck it. McCoy buys his daughter an Arabian horse for her birthday and rents a horse farm in Tuskegee, Alabama. He and Walker rent an apartment in Virginia Beach, furnish it lavishly, and stockpile it with a small cache of weapons.

McCoy plans another airplane hijacking, to make an even bigger score. He and Walker start running to get in shape.

One fall night, making the drive from Tuskegee back to Virginia Beach, McCoy gets a strange feeling. He is talking about God, the Mormon church, the stillness of the ocean.

"Tell me again," McCoy says, "what's the name of those evergreens along the front of the house?"

"Arborvitae," Walker says. Means "tree of life."

"Arborvitae. Arborvitae," McCoy says, forcing himself to remember the name.

McCoy pulls onto Great Neck Road. He does not want to enter the house. What if somebody has given them up?

"It's your turn," Walker says.

McCoy pulls over the car. He places a pistol in his waistband. He jogs toward the house, strolls up the front walk. He turns the key.

The orange glow of streetlights floods the window in the front room. He hears the crackle of a radio in the other room. It is blaring voices. He reaches for his gun. He hears a scream.

"FBI! . . . Close the door. Be quiet."

Gun sparks fly in the dark. It sounds like cannonballs have gone off.

"I'm killed," McCoy says.

He stumbles. He falls back through the front door, onto the porch, into the Arborvitae bushes.

"Somebody run!" an agent says. "Get some bath towels! Before this man bleeds to death."

"Fuck him," another agent says. "That son of a bitch just tried to kill me."

The agents hover over McCoy's body. It is too late for a D.B. Cooper confession. The coroner is called.

February 28, 2009
Battleground, Washington

I pull into the parking lot of the Best Western in southern Washington.
It's my fifth trip to the state—no, my sixth. I can't remember. I can't
remember what I am looking for. The ghost of a closeted airline purser
who lived with young boys and looked exactly like an FBI sketch that
may not have looked like the hijacker at all? Or a gold-obsessed trans-
gender librarian-pilot who had a grudge against the airlines? Or am I
after a fanatic of Dan Cooper the comic book hero? Or should I stop
looking and wait for scientist Tom Kaye to break open the case with his
microscopic scientific thinking?

I am here to document Kaye's fieldwork. I am not alone. Tom has
assembled a team that has traveled across the country to help him
analyze the money. The technical brain will be Alan Stone, a metallurgist from Chicago whom Tom knows from the dinosaur world. Another
dinosaur buddy is Carol Abraczinskas. She is a scientific illustrator from
the University of Chicago. She's here to help in the field and draw pictures for Tom's planned scientific paper. Also with us is the little boy
who found the money, Brian Ingram, who is not so little anymore. Tom
flew Brian in from Mena, Arkansas, and offered to pay for his trip. Brian
knew the area; after all, he found the money there. He is also press bait.
The story of the boy-turned-man who returns to the spot that changed
his life, Tom hopes, will entice reporters to cover his fieldwork.

The last member of the team is a last-minute addition: Jerry Thomas.
For help navigating the woods in the Washougal area, Jerry is a natural
choice. He's been looking in the area for Cooper's body and ransom
for the past twenty-two years.

Tom is ready to get started. Tall and lanky, he wears simple blue
jeans, a blue sweatshirt, and black sneakers that are worn out from
walking across Montana hunting for T. rex teeth. He is hungry because
he gets hungry when he is anxious. Tom buries his head in the rear of
a rental minivan. It's stuffed with science equipment: test tubes, note-
books, sample jars, and a fishing rod to which he's affixed a bundle

of cash to test its buoyancy. The equipment and tests, he hopes, will confirm his "explosive" hypothesis—which he revealed to me, under the provision that I not reveal it until now. So, here it is.

×

Think of the plaque on your teeth. It forms, over time, from bacteria that grow and collect. Well, the silver on the Cooper bills that he saw under his microscope formed in a similar way, Tom hypothesizes.

His first step was to call Alan Stone ("my metal guy"), who looks exactly how you would imagine a metallurgist to look: spectacles, mustache, fanny pack. He runs Aston Labs, a metals research firm in Chicago. When Tom discovered silver on the bills in his lab in Arizona, he sent the images to Stone for his opinion.

Yes, definitely silver, Stone confirmed. But how did it get there?

Together, the scientists gazed at Tena Bar on Google Earth. The sand on the beach where Brian Ingram found the Cooper bills, they saw, was not white and powdery. It was black.

After studying the properties of silver, Tom and Alan learned that microscopic traces of silver can seep out of sand. And when silver comes into contact with a porous and natural element—like the linen that money is made from—a chemical event takes place. "Bacterial ooze," as Tom puts it, would seep out of the sand and form on the bills and protect them from the elements. This ooze, like a plaque, would explain all that black stuff he first saw.

But the Silver-in-the-Sand theory, if true, is limited. Other questions remain. How long had the money been at Tena Bar to develop the microscopic plaque? And perhaps more important, how did the money get there in the first place?

Tom thinks the feds goofed. Tom is not the first Cooper hunter to suspect that the real drop zone was not where the feds were looking.

After reviewing data about the flight path, amateur sleuth Wayne Walker (Sluggo_Monster) found the error on a timeline that charted

Northwest 305's position. A licensed pilot, Walker found minutes 8:01, 8:02, 8:03, and 8:05 all accounted for. So where was minute 8:04?

The Missing Minute, as Walker's catch came to be called, suggests that Cooper had to have landed, at the very least, three miles farther south than what agents first thought. Using the Bureau's old data and modern mapping techniques, Walker composed a digitally enhanced drop zone. Walker now believes Cooper landed thirty miles south of Ariel, around the town of Orchards, roughly fifteen miles from the Columbia River.

Tom envisions a different scenario. Teetering over the night sky on the aftstairs of Flight 305, the hijacker sees the glow of city lights from Portland. He jumps. Not being able to steer the NB6 a great deal, he floats down toward the Columbia River and lands in it. He floats downriver toward Tena Bar and loses the money. Or loses some of the money. Tom does not know how. Perhaps the hijacker died of hypothermia in the Columbia and got washed out into the Pacific as the wakes of freighter boats pushed the ransom money to shore. Or perhaps the hijacker sank to the bottom of the Columbia and then got shredded in the giant blade of a passing cargo freighter, which cut up the money bag and sent two hundred packets of ransom bills floating through the water.

Tom is not the first to arrive at this conclusion. A number of Cooper hunters spent years analyzing the case and came to believe the hijacker landed in the Columbia. One retired federal agent even went through the hassle of having the riverbed raked. But until now, nobody has been able to prove it. Tom feels he is on the verge.

"Hey, Tom?"

"Yes, Jerry."

Jerry Thomas has stepped out of his massive pickup truck. He drove five hours over the Cascades from Baker City, where he now lives, to be with us. He clutches a vintage-looking suitcase that is powder blue.

Jerry looks different than I thought he would. I expected a hiker type with a long beard, a ponytail, dressed in microfleece made from tennis balls and late-edition hiking boots. But Jerry's cheeks are clean shaven. He wears dark trousers, an untucked button-up that drapes over his belly. On his feet are Wal-Mart sneakers that Velcro shut; they are the only shoes Jerry can wear because of his swollen feet, one of many postcombat ailments. Jerry is a few years older than Tom, and there is silver hair under a baseball cap that says THE WALL, a memento from one of his many trips to the Vietnam War memorial. His eyes are his most noticeable feature: dark, unyielding. Drill-sergeant eyes.

"I know you're an archaeologist, Tom," Jerry says, "so I brought back a coin for you I found up in the woods."

Jerry hands Tom the coin. It is sheathed in plastic.

The coin is a test. Jerry is skeptical of Tom. He wants to find out how serious a scientist Tom is. Jerry knows there is no conceivable way in the universe a coin like this one could be found in the Washougal area. It's an Asian piece, hundreds of years old and from Jerry's coin collection. So how will Tom react? Will he respond in a glib way, look at the coin briefly and say, Oh, wow, Jerry, that's really neat? Or will he see the markings on the coin and, in a sincere and astute way, call Jerry's bluff?

Tom inspects the coin. He hands the coin back.

"I appreciate that, Jerry," he says, "but I'm a paleontologist. The difference is that archaeologists deal with uncovering the history of people that goes back hundreds of thousands of years, and paleontologists study everything before that. We like to say, 'We don't have to deal with people's problems.' "

Jerry moves on. He scans Carol Abraczinskas with the drill-sergeant eyes. Carol: late thirties, bookish glasses, North Face jacket.

Jerry moves on to Brian Ingram, scans the little boy who found the Cooper treasure. Brian is thirty-eight now. It's hard to imagine—in

Cooper lore, Brian is forever a young boy in the newspaper pictures. Photographers captured him on his knees in the sand on Tena Bar, showing agents where he found the money. He had bowl-cut hair, a toothy grin. He's achieved what all boys dream of: finding buried treasure.

As a grown man, Brian remains strangely youthful, as if his life peaked when he was eight and he has been trapped in that moment ever since. The toothy grin is the same, only now Brian is a bit overweight, has a goatee, and wears a jockey cap that covers thinning hair.

Brian has been in the news recently, having auctioned off several Cooper bills.

"Shame you had to sell those bills," Jerry says. Alimony can be a bitch and he knows all about it.

Brian has to think. Did Jerry use the word "alimony"? How does Jerry know the real reason Brian auctioned off those bills?

In the lobby of the Best Western the front-desk girl peers into the screen of her phone, the silver shine of her nose ring illuminated by its glow, waiting for the next text message to appear. The guests who rent rooms here are truckers hauling freight, high school kids on prom night.

It is late, almost midnight. We are in our War Room, which doubles as the Best Western's complimentary breakfast room. Tom is at the head of the table, Jerry at the other. The plastic silos of cereal are behind us.

I look out the window. A freight train rumbles by.

"Fuck the word 'oscillations,' " Tom says.

Our conversation is about when the hijacker jumped, and the language the Northwest pilots used around the time the cabin pressure gauge began to spiral out of control. The lack of clear data bothers Tom. As a scientist, he needs exact measurements and exact terms. What does some of the vague language in the flight transcriptions mean?

"The whole story is the 'pressure bump,' " Tom says. "Are 'oscillations' and 'pressure bump' the same thing?"

He picks up two salt shakers and a pepper shaker. He points to a crack in the table.

"Okay," he says. "The crack right here is the flight path."

He holds up the salt shaker.

"Salt number one," he says, "is where Cooper took off in Seattle. Salt two," he says, "is where the FBI thinks he bailed."

And pepper?

"Pepper," he says, "is where Brian found the money."

✗

Brian remembers it—or, he remembers moments. He remembers Tipper, the old fisherman who had a gray beard so long he could tuck it into his pants. Tipper showed Brian how his fishing rod worked, how the bell at the end of the rod rang when a Chinook tugged his line. Brian remembers George, the family dog, and his smelly breath. George was part timber wolf; he was a watchdog for a gas station until the Ingrams won him in a card game. George would trap Brian under his legs and lick his face and not let him go.

He remembers his father wanting to cook up hot dogs. He remembers getting down on his knees and clearing out the sand and smoothing it out with his arm like a broom, and then his arm touched the corner of the first packet of bills.

He wonders how he remembers these things. He was only eight.

There is another version of the story. After Brian's discovery was reported in the news, members of his family came forward. Brian didn't find the money, his aunt Crystal said. It was Denise, Brian's five-year-old cousin. Crystal Ingram went to the FBI shortly after Brian's parents did. She was entitled to a reward too, she said.

Himmelsbach questioned her. What evidence did she have that it was her Denise who found the Cooper bills?

Crystal produced four additional Cooper bills.

Asked about the four additional bills, Brian's parents said Crystal was out for the reward and made the story up. Himmelsbach came to believe that it was Brian who actually found the money, but how could the agent really know? And how could Brian?

⚔

My motel phone is ringing. I look out the window. It is dawn, the next morning. Who is calling? Who knows I am here?

I roll over, pick up. Hello.

It's Jerry. He's talking fast, as if he's been up all night. He says he wants to get out of the hotel and get up to the Washougal area and get our feet moving through the woods up there and to hell with the sand tests at Tena Bar and water samples that Tom has planned for us this morning because really, what's the point of that?

He's ready to go, whenever I am. Am I ready?

I want to go back to sleep.

Jerry starts to complain about Tom, how he is so controlling.

"Everyone needs to have a few beers," Jerry says. "Get the keys out of their butts."

⚔

I drive with Jerry to breakfast. I'm in the backseat of his pickup and he's got his foot on the gas, cranking his rig, blazing past the Radio Shack and Mexican strip mall taco joints and empty Main Street storefronts.

Somewhere in the backseat is a 9-millimeter pistol Jerry claims he keeps when he camps out near the Washougal River. I look on the floor. I spot the biggest package of economy-size frankfurters I have ever seen, a case of Dr. Pepper, and the small powder blue suitcase. What's in there?

Brian is in the front seat. He has his headphones on. Jerry is talking to him. Brian takes off the headphones.

"I'm going to blast something into their minds," Jerry says. "I've been holding it long enough. I have to tell it to him straight."

"No need to be crooked," Brian says.

Jerry smacks his hand on the steering wheel. The louder he talks, the faster he drives.

"Murphy's Law," he says. "That's what nobody has talked about. MUUURRR-PHEEZZZ Law. What can go wrong?"

He's interested in the errors of the case, what mistakes the hijacker made. On every mission, at least something goes wrong.

"Nobody has talked about that," Jerry says. "I haven't heard any talk about that."

He complains about Tom.

"He's too damn controlling," Jerry says again. "I've spent twenty-two years out there. Today I'm going to bring it up. I'm not going to let him get away that easy. We're asking the wrong questions to get the right answers."

"Jerry," Brian says, "can I ask you a question?"

"Sure, Brian. You go ahead. You ask me anything you want."

"Jerry, tell me how it feels . . . I mean, seriously, tell me how it really feels . . . to know that for the last twenty-two years you've been up in those woods looking in the wrong place."

Jerry believes Cooper landed in the Washougal. But Tom is on his way to proving Cooper landed in the Columbia, several miles away. If Tom can prove his theory, he will also be proving that Jerry's quest has been off. Way off. In a way, Tom's science is threatening the identity and reputation Jerry has built up looking for Cooper along the Washougal all these years. Tom's science is also threatening the theory Ralph Himmelsbach had espoused, a theory that Jerry has devoutly followed, and one that's triggered an almost paternal relationship Jerry has formed with Himmelsbach.

These are high and personal stakes, and the battle brewing between Tom and Jerry is becoming a fight between logic and intuition. As a scientist, Tom is looking for data to prove his case. As a former soldier, Jerry is using the raw instincts of a hunter to challenge Tom's methods.

In his pickup, Jerry pushes the gas. He's getting upset.

"If they don't like it, fuck 'em," Jerry says. "Can't take a jab, shit."

After breakfast, I ride with Tom, metallurgist Alan Stone, and Carol to Tena Bar. Tom's minivan was special ordered to come with power outlets. His laptop is plugged in and propped up. Tom watches the computer screen and follows our movements via satellite. One eye is on the road, the other on the virtual road on the laptop. Tom is anxious to get there on time because a local television station will meet us at Tena Bar, and a documentary crew from *National Geographic*.

Tom looks in the rearview mirror. He fixes his hair into place.

"For those of us who haven't been on TV much, you take pictures of us and we'll take pictures of you," he says.

Noticeably missing from Tom's team is Jerry Warner (Georger), who had referred him to Larry Carr at the FBI. Before the trip, there was a falling-out. Tom's issue was confidentiality. After his discovery of silver on the bills, he e-mailed a copy of his microscopic scan to Warner, who posted it on the Drop Zone website. Tom felt the leak was a violation of trust. According to Tom, that's why Warner chose not to come.

Warner's story is different. He says he lost confidence in Tom's judgment and scientific methods. He felt Tom was more concerned with attracting attention to himself and his role in the D.B. Cooper investigation than with executing his assignment.

"We were asked to analyze the money and we agreed to analyze the money–that's it, not mug in front of any cameras," Warner will tell me later.

I look out the van window. I see wetlands and geese. Tom tracks our position on his laptop.

"We're getting into the holy land here," he says.

Tena Bar is private property. The land belongs to the Fazio family, who run a sand and livestock business along the Columbia River.

We pull into the driveway.

Tacked to the welcome sign at the Fazio Brothers Ranch is the scalp of a bull. Behind the sign are the scruffy hides and angular joints of cattle grazing in pens.

We pass an old house. A man in jeans and no shirt comes to the door. He waves us on.

I smell manure. Fazio Brothers backhoes and Fazio Brothers dump trucks are parked along the cattle pens. Strapped to one truck, a carcass hangs by the hooves. Ranch hands hack away at the muscle.

"Okay, folks," Tom says. "We are in situ." That's science talk. It means we're in the field. He parks the car in front of the sign.

TENA BAR–MEMBERS ONLY.

Brian gets out of Jerry's truck. Slowly, he snakes down the path and through the gate, careful not to snag himself on a rusted nail. He sees the old fishing shack that belonged to Tipper, and he remembers the stinky breath of his dog, George, who sprinted off down the beach on the day they first arrived here.

Brian wishes he'd never found the money, after what it did to his family. The Cooper Curse, as the Ingrams call it, started a few minutes after Brian's parents, Dwayne and Patricia, turned in the old money to the feds.

Your lives will change. Those were Ralph Himmelsbach's words.

Their lives did change.

They did not get rich. In the Bureau office in Portland, moments after they turned in the evidence, Himmelsbach went to check on the rewards they were entitled to. Unfortunately, the rewards had all expired. The Ingrams did not take the news well.

The Ingrams also didn't like getting attention from federal agents, one of whom followed Patricia into the bathroom. The Ingrams were not seeking publicity, but federal agents decided to hold a press conference to announce the find. Within hours, Dwayne and Patricia and Brian Ingram were national figures.

The Ingrams were more interested in the Cooper bills. As collectibles, they could be worth a lot of money, far more than any reward.

Himmelsbach did not give them back. The feds had to keep the money as evidence. The lab at Quantico would be testing it for fingerprints.

The Ingrams sued the FBI to get the bills back. After six years in court, the judge in the case finally awarded them half of what they found, much of which is in fragments.

The media attention was poison. First, Brian's father got a strange call. He asked who the caller was.

"Nan," she said. "Nan and Tap. Dwayne, we're your grandparents."

Dwayne didn't know he had grandparents. He didn't even know who his own father was.

Nan and Tap invited Dwayne and his family to San Francisco, where they lived in a nice house. Technically, they were not his grandparents—they were his stepfather's parents—but they had cared for Dwayne when he was a baby. Dwayne took a trip to visit them, but once his stepbrothers found out that Dwayne had gone to see their parents, they told him to never talk to Nan and Tap again.

Later, Brian and his mother were out of town, visiting friends in California, when Dwayne came home to find their house in Vancouver was on fire. Everything the Ingrams owned, all the clothes and furniture that Patricia had found for her family in church basements was destroyed. Dwayne and Pat had come to Vancouver looking for good schools, clean air, and a good place to raise Brian, better than the Oklahoma hillbilly towns where they were from. Now, that dream had burned to the ground.

Inspecting the fire, cops showed up.

"You Dwayne Ingram?" one said.

He nodded.

The cops cuffed him on the spot.

Later, in the station house, Dwayne learned that he and Patricia were late on a car payment. When they left Oklahoma and moved to Vancouver, they forgot to notify the bank, and a warrant was issued for Dwayne's arrest. In Oklahoma, officers saw his name on television after the Cooper money had been found and recognized it from the warrant list. Dwayne had been arrested for stealing his own car.

That night, television stations ran the news. In California, Patricia saw one headline: BOY SENDS FATHER TO PRISON.

The Ingrams moved out of Vancouver.

"I told you that money was cursed," Patricia would tell Dwayne.

Brian enrolled in a new school, which was unfortunate. After finding the Cooper ransom, he had been instantly popular in his class in Vancouver. Dwayne started drinking heavily and doing drugs, not coming home. Brian doesn't think it's fair to blame his father's addictions on the unfortunate turns of fate that followed the discovery of the Cooper bills. The drama didn't help any, though.

$\maltese$

"Can I ask you a question?"

That's Jerry.

"I'm not getting under everyone's skin too bad, am I?" he says.

I lie. Of course he isn't.

"Well, I've been trying."

The sky is a white board. The fog is rolling in. The Columbia is too wide to swim across, but narrow enough to see smoke curling out from chimneys on the far bank.

Brian sloshes around in the sand. He doesn't know where he found the money. He was too young, just can't remember.

It starts to rain. I ask Jerry where his coat is.

"I don't wear coats," he says. "I can't feel anything."

Brian looks into the water. He sees specks of gold in the sand.

"Pyrite," Jerry says.

"Isn't that fool's gold?" Brian says.

Tom walks down the path wearing white gloves. He holds orange flags to mark locations, glass jars to collect samples. He clutches the fishing rod baited with a packet of dollar bills. He watches the water. He is disappointed. His Silver-in-the-Sand theory depends on a strong muscular wake—something that could push the Cooper bills from the river bottom onto the beach. The wake here couldn't push a paper boat onto Tena Bar. It is too weak.

Tom walks down to the wet sand with the fishing pole. He casts his packet of bills into the river. Under the water, the bills in the packet fan out like the fins of an exotic fish.

He calls out to Carol to make a note. "Money does not float."

Jerry is bored. He tosses a piece of driftwood into the water. He watches the wood float into the current and down the river. Then it stops. The wood hovers in the water, a natural trap.

"This is where they found that money," Jerry booms.

Tom rushes over.

Brian looks down the beach to get his bearings.

"Is this the place, Brian?"

Brian isn't sure. It feels right.

Tom stomps away. Feelings don't count. Feelings don't get published.

"We have to get back to basics here," Tom says.

✗

We caravan into the hills. Now it's time to collect samples from the Washougal River. We pass the motels where Jerry would spend a few dollars to take a shower after spending months looking for Cooper in the woods. Jerry talks about family, old memories. He gets sentimental. Before our trip, Jerry called his mother. He got her answering machine.

Is this a mistake? Have I got this on right? You have reached Doris Thomas. If you leave a message, I'll call you back. If you don't, don't worry about it. I know you called.

Then Jerry went to her grave, cleaned up the site, put flowers there. His mother died years ago. He keeps paying her cell phone bill so he can hear her voice whenever he wants. His way of keeping her alive.

My cell phone is ringing. It's Tom. He's run out of gas.

"Oh, I ought to jap slap his ass," Jerry says. "If I had my way I would just leave him right there."

Jerry slaps his wheel.

"I mean, *man!*"

That such a brilliant self-taught scientist like Tom does not possess enough common sense to check his own gas tank is all the evidence Jerry needs: Tom will never solve the Cooper case.

✻

I ride with Tom to the Washougal. We follow Jerry's pickup as it climbs up back roads, past hilly farms.

Tom sees houses lined up next to one another. He sees American flags on the lawn.

"Where are these *woods*?" he says. "This looks like suburban Pittsburgh! You have to fend off the dogs on chains!"

Jerry pulls over. He gets out of his truck. He walks over to Tom's van, cranes his neck in the window.

Tom is hunched over his laptop. His GPS monitoring system is not functioning. The satellite signal is too weak where we are.

"Where am I?" Tom says. "Where am I, Jerry, in the scheme of things?"

"Little Washougal. Want to get higher?"

"How do we get there? Show me how to get higher."

"Well, the farther up we go, the higher up we get."

We unload the equipment—test tubes, stopwatch, fishing pole, and money packets. We follow Jerry down a dirt path under a small bridge. We are at the bank of a creek. The afternoon sun breaks through the tree branches. The running water glistens gold.

Tom reaches into his pocket. He pulls out a stack of money: twenty $1 bills. Attached is a laminated note.

REWARD IF FOUND!

This label is part of an investigation of the 1971 DB Cooper hijacking. . . . You may keep the attached money and we will give you an extra 100 dollars if you call in the location.

He chucks the bills in the water. This packet of bills is perhaps the ultimate test that will confirm or destroy Jerry's theory. If the bills are found far downriver or somewhere along the Columbia, then the Washougal is a likely possibility for Cooper's true drop zone. If Jerry comes back here a month later and finds Tom's packet of bills under a rock downstream, it will suggest his theory is bunk.

We drive higher. Jerry pulls over on an old logging road.

"You got black sands all up in through there, Tom," Jerry says.

He points.

"And this entire area right here is covered in wait-a-minute vines," he says.

And what are wait-a-minute vines?

"Vines that when you see them, you go, I better wait a minute."

Tom walks to the water's edge. The Washougal current is stronger here. Tom is surprised. Maybe it was possible for the Washougal to carry the Cooper bills down to Tena Bar. Maybe Jerry is onto something.

The forest around us drips with lime green moss and shadows. The colors are emerald and parrot greens. The moss coats the tree branches.

Jerry is looking into the water downstream.

"Hey, Tom, would a periwinkle help you?"

"What's a periwinkle?"

"It's like a cocoon with a worm in it."

"Can't think of how that would be useful offhand, Jerry."

Jerry comes over and opens his chapped hand. He shows him the periwinkle.

Tom calls over Carol.

"Note that there are snails in the water," he says. "Many snails. Thanks, Jerry."

It is dusk. It is time for dinner. Jerry is behind the wheel of his monster pickup. Brian is in the front seat, I'm in the back with all the hot dogs. I rummage around. Where is that 9-millimeter pistol Jerry was talking about?

"Brian, I'd like to ask you a favor," Jerry says.

"Okay, Jerry," Brian says.

"My daughter works over here at the Shucks in town."

"Okay. Shucks?"

"Yeah, Shucks."

"Okay."

"Well, what I wanted to ask you was, would you meet her? She would love it. I mean, it would really mean a lot to her."

To Jerry, Brian and the Ingram family are Cooper royalty, historic figures in the case. True celebs.

"No problem, Jerry," Brian says. "I'd love to meet your daughter."

"Now, it's a bit . . . complicated."

"What do you mean?"

"Well, I haven't spoken to her in almost two years."

Brian stares straight ahead into the windshield.

"I don't know if she'll talk to me, but I know with you here, I know she will. I don't know if she'll tell me hello or to go fuck myself—even that would be something. At least that's talking."

It is a long ride into town.

"Jerry, I don't want to offend you or anything, but this is kind of weird," Brian says. He wants to know what Jerry did to his daughter. Why isn't she talking to him?

"Now be honest," Brian says.

Drugs, Jerry says. Her husband got arrested for growing pot and spent time in jail. Jerry's daughter suspected he was the one who turned her husband in to the police.

"Did you turn him in?"

"No, no I didn't," Jerry says.

He rants on about his daughter, how she isn't doing things the right way.

"I'm not scared of her," Jerry says.

"Can you tell me something about her? This way I can say Jerry's told me about what you like to do. This way I have something to talk to her about."

"Her name is Deanna. But she goes by Charlene. Her mother named her Deanna. I named her Charlene. I love her. I named her."

I call Tom in the van behind us. I tell him to pull over. We are going to meet Jerry's daughter in a place called Shucks, whatever that is.

Shucks is an auto-parts retailer. Brian, Jerry, and I get out of Jerry's truck and follow him in.

A line has formed at the cash register. I open the door for Jerry.

I turn. I see her.

Charlene has long black hair and a long face. She has hearing aids in both ears. She wears no makeup. She is missing part of a tooth and when she sees us her hand goes up to cover it.

"Hi, honey," Jerry says.

Charlene does not speak, cannot speak.

A customer steps into line. She rings him up and grits her teeth and tries not to look at Jerry.

"I'm at work. I can't talk to you."

Jerry speaks to her in a slow and careful tone, as if she is pointing a gun at him.

"Honey, I'd like to introduce you to someone," he says. "Honey, this is Brian Ingram."

Charlene inspects Brian: Male, thirty-eight, cargo pants, goatee.

"Honey, this is the boy that found the money."

Charlene takes another look.

"You're the boy who found that money?"

Brian flashes the same toothy grin he had as a boy.

"Yes, ma'am."

"Yeah, honey. We're on a team with a bunch of scientists and it's really been interesting. Just fantastic," Jerry says.

She looks at her father and the words *I hate you I hate you I fucking hate you* twinkle in her dark eyes.

"I'm at work, I can't talk at work," she says.

"Okay, then," Jerry says. He storms off, leaving Brian and me standing in the store.

Charlene looks at us. Her chest is quivering. Her eyes tear. I think she is going to scream.

✗

"Nothing you can do," Jerry says, pulling himself up into his truck.

I ask him how he feels. Is he happy he was able to see Charlene?

"No. I am not happy. You saw it. She was in a cold sweat. Sweat on the nose. And I saw that man behind her. You saw how he was fidgeting. She was high."

I didn't notice this.

"You see, she called me about a year ago needing money to pay her electricity bill. And I called her husband and he said he didn't need the money. So you see it's like, *Who is lying here?* And the next thing I know, click."

In Jerry's passenger window, Tom appears. A croissant is dangling from his mouth. He's gnawing on it, the anxiety fueling his appetite again.

"We're just getting ourselves together to meet your daughter," Tom says.

Jerry is ready to drive off. Tom is confused.

"I guess she's not coming out to play with us," he says.

The bar at the Chinese restaurant is lined with hunters in camouflage. Inside the dining room, we eye the laminated menus.

"We learned something today," Tom says.

The Washougal is not as powerful a river as he thought. There is almost no chance it could have carried the Cooper ransom to Tena Bar. Jerry's theory is a virtual impossibility.

Jerry protests. The Washougal is plenty powerful, he says. Especially when there are heavy rains and it floods. The river we saw was not the river the Washougal can be.

"Jerry, you and I were never blood brothers in any generation," Tom says.

Jerry does not speak.

"You got the woods down, Jerry. It's the people part," Tom says.

Jerry peers out from the menu, gives Tom a stare down.

The talk turns to eating food that is bad for you, like what we ordered, and people we all know who have heart problems.

Jerry has heart problems, he says.

"Knowing Jerry, he would have a heart attack in the middle of the woods, and nobody would be around to help him," Tom says.

He's laughing. We're all laughing.

"And he'd keel over and die in the woods . . . and he'd become D.B. Cooper! His ultimate dream would be fulfilled!"

Jerry smirks. He knows he is looking in the right place. When the meal is over he looks at his fortune cookie.

"YOU WILL OBTAIN YOUR GOAL IF YOU MAINTAIN YOUR COURSE," it says.

On the way back to the hotel, we pass Shucks again. I see Charlene. She is outside, taking a smoke break.

"Go talk to her, Jerry," Brian says.

I push him, too. The last encounter was a disaster.

Jerry puts the truck in park. He follows Charlene back inside. I run back over to Tom's van to tell him what is happening.

Tom makes a John Wayne voice. He's goofing around.

"Hell, bitch, you better come on out," Tom says.

"Tom, that's not funny," Carol says.

My cell phone is ringing. It's Jerry.

"She wants to meet the team," he says.

The store is empty. Almost closing time.

We all go inside. Tom reaches over to shake Charlene's hand.

"I'm sure your dad didn't want us to tell you this but he was . . . he was crying, literally, in tears at dinner," Tom says.

Charlene is not moved.

"He's not who you think he is," she says. "He's a lying, manipulating . . . You don't know what he's done. He's threatened me."

Jerry is standing tall, his back stiff, as if lining up for roll call.

"He wants to be famous," Charlene says. "He wants to be a hero."

Tom asks Charlene if she likes the woods as much as Jerry.

Charlene closes her mouth and shakes her head no no no.

"I was grounded to the woods," she says. "When I was fourteen, for using hairspray."

"It was the watch," Jerry says.

"I almost blew up the entire forest. I was trying to use kerosene for the lantern and my dad insisted I do it the redneck way, by siphoning the gas out of the truck. I couldn't see and I had a candle and . . ."

A terror creeps over her face.

"The whole truck was on fire," she says. "I tried to put it out with a cup. I thought I'd get spanked for that one."

Charlene looks at us as if we have arrived from another planet to save her.

"The caves," she says with a shiver. "I still have the scars."

The next morning, I follow Jerry out to his pickup. He places the powder blue suitcase in the back. We are driving to Seattle to examine the physical evidence in the case. Jerry isn't coming. He is scared of cities and has to get home. His wife Shelly's horse died last night. He needs to dig the grave. He'll have to rent a backhoe.

"It was a big old horse," he says.

I think about the way Charlene looked at him, what she said. *He's a lying, manipulating* . . .

Jerry claims to have been trekking into the woods for the past twenty-two years to hunt for Cooper's money, but how can we prove he was there all the times he says he was? And if he is making some of it up, why? What is he really looking for?

He hops into his rig. He turns the keys over. I ask when he's coming back into the woods.

"Summer," he says. "The trees change, everything changes."

Brian and I drive to Seattle in my rental. A few miles up the highway, I ask him about Jerry. Is it possible he's making it all up?

Brian can't say. But it is strange how much Jerry knows about the case. Like what?

Like the reason Brian sold his Cooper bills. Jerry used the word *alimony*. How did he know Brian needed to sell the Cooper bills to pay his first wife?

Brian met her in high school, at a roller skating rink. She was shy, religious. He'd push himself on her.

Not until we're married, she would say.

He has memories of how things went wrong, like the time she visited when she was in college and he had enrolled in the Army. He was training to become a medic, and they had been away from each other for so long. Finally, they were together and alone in his barrack at Fort Benning and he was touching her and she was touching him back, and when they embraced he told her, though not very convincingly, "We don't have to do this."

Or the time after the wedding, after Kara was born, when he was installing electrical and sewer components for mobile homes around Oklahoma. One night, he was at a friend's trailer for dinner, had too many beers and got a little drunk, heard something he didn't want to hear, pushed over the table, nearly got into a fight and disappeared.

For months, he was missing. He'd driven into Oklahoma City and pulled over at another friend's house. He knew there would be crank there. He liked crystal meth best. Hillbilly crack. It was the cheapest to buy and lasted the longest. There was cocaine in the house, too, and if someone offered it to him, he would cut it up and snort it. Or drop acid. One night he took thirteen tabs. He was so high he wanted to get naked and ride the moon. Or kill himself. He was on a bender. He was awake for twenty-three days once. It was an eerie and ugly existence, living with other addicts as they moved in and out of the house, peering down at the street, paranoid, thinking the cars that were passing by were undercover cops.

His parents couldn't find him. His wife didn't know where he was.

Some nights he was home. He'd escape from the drug house and drive his car to a spot behind his home that was just far enough so his wife couldn't see him if she stepped out the door, but close enough so when the lights were on in the living room he could the silhouettes of her and the baby girl as they moved around. He did not have the courage—to sober up, to tell them what had been bothering him, what sent him on the drug binge. Six months passed before he finally knocked on the door.

Where had he been? His wife thought he had deserted them. The girl was crying. She had filed for divorce, she told him, and he never came home again.

Brian can talk about it now, because he's proud about the way he was able to stomach the pain of drug addiction, to beat it, to work again. He's been on the lines in front of a sewing machine. He's worked in the freezing cold to build pipelines. His specialty now is roofing. He's also built a mausoleum to Cooper, collecting every artifact he can find that's related to the hijacking: T-shirts, toys, matchbooks. He hopes the hijacker is never caught. He enjoys the speculation. It's also better for his investment. The longer the case goes unsolved, the more his bills might be worth.

The interstate to Seattle is a blinking mess of indoor water parks, Chinese buffets, Indian casinos, and porn shops that border the military bases. I ask Brian to recall every detail he can think of about the day he found the money.

He remembers the faces. Tipper, the old fisherman; George, his dog with the smelly breath; and the feeling of the sand against his forearm.

But as he got older, Brian says, he wondered about these memories. How much of what he knew was really what he knew? Were his memories his own? Or was his mind imbued with the stories of those around him? How much can one remember at eight?

He wondered about his parents. Did they lie to him? Was his doubt natural? Was he the boy who became famous around the world for actually finding buried treasure? Or was he a fraud?

He didn't think so. But how could he be sure?

Before he sold the Cooper bills, Brian approached his parents. He asked his mom, Patricia, if he really found the money. He did, she told him. His father told him the same.

Still, Brian was unsure. When his grandmother got sick, Brian went to Florida to visit her in the hospital. His cousin Denise was there at the hospital, too. It was Denise's mother, Crystal, who had always claimed Denise was the one who found the Cooper money. Brian hadn't seen Denise in years.

Brian remembered how close he and Denise had been as kids. They watched movies together on the couch. They built a fort underneath the sheet on his bed.

Brian felt that part of his recovery from drug addiction and other turmoil in his life was to be honest with himself and those around him. He was willing to accept the fact that he wasn't the boy who found the money, if that was true.

In the hospital, Brian pulled Denise aside. He asked her what happened. Was he the one who found the money in the sand? Or was she?

Denise didn't want to talk about it.

"We both know what happened, Brian," she said.

But he really doesn't.

✕

In Seattle, the evidence is waiting for us in the Bureau field office. Special Agent Carr has spread out more files, photos, the parachute canopy, the clip-on tie.

Tom places a loupe on his eye. He examines the reserve parachute first. The canopy is watermelon pink. Tom inspects each incision. He counts the number of cut shroud lines.

That's strange, he thinks. Five shroud lines are cut. According to the Bureau file, agents first discovered that only three shroud lines had been cut during the hijacking. Who cut the other two? Did Bureau agents snip them as souvenirs?

The clip-on tie is next for inspection. Tom uses sticky tape and presses it against the polyester fabric to collect pollen samples. Despite its age, the pollen he finds could tell him where the tie has been.

He studies the fabric under his loupe. He rolls his eyes upward and inspects the clip of the clip-on tie. The hook is painted white. It is stripped in spots.

Nothing here.

He scans the fat part of the tie. Under the loupe, Tom's eye combs the polyester fields of microscopic fibers. How incredible it would be to stumble upon a flake of dandruff! A hair follicle!

Tom thinks of the dandruff and hair on his own computer keyboard back on his ranch in Arizona. He is always amazed at how much of it finds its way into the keys and how annoying it is to clean it all out. How does so much gunk get in there? As he thinks about this, he moves on from the fat part of the tie to the fake knot of the tie. Then he gets the idea.

The feds missed it! In the lab at Quantico, Bureau scientists looked for forensic matter *on* the tie. Where they didn't look is where a good DNA sample may have been hiding all these years. *In* the tie.

A brief argument ensues. Metallurgist Alan Stone isn't sure they should do this. If they break open the knot of the tie to extract samples, Tom and the Team could be criminally liable, right? Isn't this tampering with evidence? Stone can't go to jail. He has a wife. He'd have to hire a lawyer. At the very least, Tom and the Team need to protect themselves: get approvals, sign forms. They can't rush into this.

I offer the position, unsolicited, that Tom and the Team move now and fast and quietly. Our window is small. An approval could take weeks.

I'm getting pushy. We aren't coming back here, folks. Open up the sucker. Get the damn sample. And let's get out of here.

Larry Carr agrees. As official Cooper case agent, he's been stymied by the Bureau's watch-your-ass-at-all-times attitude. Besides, Carr already received permission to have the Cooper money delivered to Tom for analysis. Isn't allowing Tom to open up the tie (and potentially destroying it) the same thing?

It isn't. At least not technically. But it's a good enough rationale for Carr, which is good enough for Tom, which is good enough for Carol. Alan folds. The scientists go to work.

✕ .

"Is there a light here somewhere?" Tom says.

"Turn that projector on," Alan says.

"Don't talk as much if you can."

"Don't open it up too much."

"*WE GOT GUNK.*"

"Wait, wait, Tom," Carol says. "There, I got a light. Seriously. Where do you want it?"

"*WE GOT GUNK.*"

"Whoa."

"There's some hair."

"Hold on. I don't have the focal . . . oh yeah, I see."

"Oh yeah, there's some hair in there."

"I don't think we got the hair we saw."

"Pull it apart."

"You see the hair?"

"Nope."

"Ah yeah."

"And some dandruff flakes."

"Hold it, shine it in there."

"*I SEE GUNK!* The tie is loaded!"

"So that ties it all together."

"Look at this cheap tie."

"I can photograph into that."

"That's good. One more."

"I got a gazillion megapixels."

"Hold it right there."

"Oh yeah. We be the bad D.B. Cooper investigators. Yeah, baby, yeah. Show me the money."

"It's in the Columbia."

"How do they look?"

"There's obviously stuff in there. *Mmmmmm.*"

"You got the hair?"

"There's a hair in there."

"At least one. Now we got some horsepower. *Yeah, baby, yeah.* We be the bad D.B. Cooper investigators. . . ."

Later that night we sit on the bed in Tom's motel room. We toast each other as if an imaginary bottle of champagne has been uncorked to honor the Team's improbable coup. In a few hours, Tom was able to do what the FBI couldn't: find evidence that could reveal the genetic makeup of the hijacker. If the gunk Tom collected is good enough (and Tom believes it is), the DNA can be grown and identified and run through millions of gene libraries. A match could be imminent.

"I don't want to get carried away, guys," Tom says, "but we might actually solve this thing."

September 15, 2009
New York, New York

Jimmy's Corner is a dive bar in midtown that is as narrow as a subway car, and the walls are crowded with boxing photographs. The back area is a stockroom of sorts. Skipp Porteous and I sit here to discuss the case. More than two years have passed since Porteous told me about the envelope he delivered to Nora Ephron for Lyle Christiansen. Now, more than ever, the Manhattan PI is convinced Kenny Christiansen is D.B. Cooper.

"I'd say with ninety-five percent certainty it's him," Porteous says.

I have doubts.

Himmelsbach *was* right. Kenny was too short. In the Bureau's Cooper file, I found an interview with Tina Mucklow in which agents had asked the stewardess her height. "Five eight," she replied. And the hijacker, she added, was taller than she was.

Ken Christiansen also did not have enough hair. While the sketch showed a balding man, the hijacker was described by at least two witnesses (paint man Robert Gregory and first-class stew Alice Hancock) as having wavy hair. "Marcelled," Gregory had said. In 1971, Ken Christiansen had thin straight hair.

Kenny looked like the Bing Crosby sketch, but so did a lot of people. Besides, it isn't clear if Dan Cooper resembled the Bing Crosby sketch. Or the next composite. Or the next one. There were multiple sketches, all different.

Kenny's motive was also weak. Despite being a loner, Kenny, according to Lyle, seemed to carry a balanced if not sunny outlook on life, a naive Midwestern optimism. I can't see him in the back of the plane, holding the wire with a clip on the end and telling Tina, "They're not going to take me alive."

Porteous disagrees. And he has proof. It's a photograph that Lyle found after Kenny's death.

I look at the photo. Kenny is wearing a black raincoat. In his left hand, he holds a briefcase. In his right hand, he holds a white canvas sack.

Now, Porteous asks, why would Kenny wear the same outfit as the hijacker, and carry what looked like a replica of the briefcase bomb and a cloth bank bag? Analyzing the photo closely, Porteous also noticed a Christmas wreath on the door. He asked Lyle when the photo was taken.

"1971," Lyle told him.

If the Christmas wreath was up, that means the image must have been taken just after the hijacking. So who took the picture?

Kenny did. It was taken on a self-timer, Lyle told Porteous.

So why would Kenny take this extremely weird picture of himself that seems to connect him to the hijacking? Or was it all just another coincidence?

The answer, Porteous says, is in a tree. Or was in a tree. Porteous spoke with Dan Rattenbury, owner of the Priced Right print shop. Before he purchased the property from the former owners, Rattenbury told Porteous a young boy had once found $2,000 in $20 bills buried inside the crack of a tree in Kenny's backyard.

So Lyle was right! Kenny did bury the money in the backyard! Fuck. I knew I should have rented that metal detector.

I ask Porteous for more information. Were the bills in packets? Or loose? Were there any rubber bands? Did Porteous find the boy who found them?

"I can't tell you," he says.

Can't tell me? Why not?

"I'm writing my own book," he says.

"In the older models, I feel like a bird because I can feel every little gust on the wing," Barb Dayton says. She is talking about flying to a reporter from the University of Washington newspaper. Ron and Pat Foreman found the clip, which confirms Barb's claustrophobia, her general hatred of the airlines, and her fear of commercial planes.

"I don't like being under someone else's control," she says. "In my plane I feel like I'm totally inside the sky, totally free."

I liked Barb as a suspect. She had the grudge that Kenny didn't. As an electrician, she knew how to rig a bomb. She knew dynamite from working in the logging camps. She was suicidal. A civilian pilot, she knew the air routes across the Pacific Northwest. She knew how to parachute. She even found it "boring."

She was also a chain-smoker who didn't have money, who would have smoked coupon cigs like Raleighs. I could see her in Dan Cooper's out-of-date clothes: the russet suit with the wide lapels, the skinny clip-on tie. It all could have come from the Goodwill bin where she shopped for clothes after her sex-change operation. As a woman, she also had access to makeup. She could powder her face bronze. Or she could be herself: part Native American. Most of all, Barb was cocky. I could see her reading about hijacker Paul Cini ten days before Thanksgiving Eve and saying to herself—just as she told her doctors about her father—"I can do anything he can do." And do it better.

Skyjackers, I learned, were not creators. They were imitators. After interviewing dozens of skyjackers, Hubbard found that the crimes were last-minute rush jobs, conceived to cure a feeling of emotional despair.

"All of the forces in life converge in one moment in which there is an impulsive act," Hubbard wrote.

Yes, Barb Dayton was D.B. Cooper. She had it all!

Except the hair (blond), the height (five eight), and the right color eyes (blue). And what was her connection to the French-Canadian comic book character Dan Cooper? And if Barb got away with the hijacking, why did Brian Ingram find the Cooper bills at Tena Bar? Did Barb plant them there? Was it Barb who tossed them off the bridge upriver from Tena Bar and not Duane Weber?

Richard Floyd McCoy Jr. is a phantom. It's as if any evidence of him has been scrubbed from history. Sure, there are legal files from his case. I spend weeks poring over them. I reread the official statements for his military medals that were submitted as evidence in his trial.

> *With the position of the compound marked by a flare and the firefight marked by tracer rounds, McCoy began a series of firing passes, launching rockets directly into the Vietcong positions until all his ammunition was expended.*

Did this really happen? Was the enemy "completely routed," or was this fiction? Are medal honors always this detailed? Or are McCoy's military records fake?

The facts in McCoy's case file are curious. Why did he travel to Las Vegas during the Cooper hijacking? Who did make the collect call to his home from the Tropicana hotel?

Karen McCoy must know a lot. Was McCoy Cooper? Did McCoy have a hand in the Cooper case? Did she and McCoy ever live in Bloomington, Minnesota, and happen to know a picture-framer named Bob Knoss?

After a few months of digging, I find her attorney in Salt Lake City. He won't tell me where Karen lives, how to reach her. She doesn't want to talk about the Cooper case, or about her dead husband, he says. I write letters. No response. Karen, what are you hiding?

I find Floyd, McCoy's father, in the obituary section of the *Charlotte News & Observer*. The obituary is brief and lists all of McCoy's family members except McCoy. Why did the family choose to leave out Floyd's first and only son?

I find Russell, McCoy's brother, living in North Carolina. I leave messages. No reply.

I need to talk to Karen. Or Chante. Or Richard Jr., his son. They must know something.

I can't find them. I hire a private investigator. He gets the numbers. I call each one. I leave messages. I leave more messages.

✗

I fly to Minnesota in a snowstorm. The story Bob Knoss told Jo Weber about a conspiracy and McCoy handling Duane Weber had sounded absurd. But what about the Cooper case so far hasn't been absurd?

Besides, Knoss has references. After the *U.S. News* story on Duane Weber was printed in 2000, he contacted Don Nichols, a prominent lawyer in Minneapolis. Knoss worried he might be criminally liable. He claims he witnessed McCoy engineer the hijacking.

Nichols was at first puzzled by Knoss's story. The hijacking was in 1971. Why didn't Knoss come forward sooner?

Knoss couldn't remember. His memory was blocked.

Blocked? Nichols asked how that could be.

He'd been hypnotized, Knoss said. By the military. At least he thinks it was the military. He can't be sure.

Knoss's recall started after his accident on the beach. A wave crashed over him, broke his back. Knoss could barely walk. It was the heavy painkillers, he thinks, that unlocked the memories of the hijacking that he had been ordered to forget.

Lawyer Nichols was suspicious. Was Knoss making this all up? Then again, how could anyone spin a yarn so fanciful?

They met in the lawyer's office. Knoss told his story again.

"He presents well," Nichols tells me.

Knoss's second reference is R. A. Randall, a former public defender who became a judge on the second-highest court in Minnesota.

I meet Randall at a Perkins outside Minneapolis for breakfast. He is wearing a camouflage hunting cap and sweatshirt. His fingers are covered in turquoise rings, mementos from Indian reservations.

I ask the retired judge whether he thinks Bob Knoss is telling the truth about witnessing the planning of the hijacking.

"If there were two men in Minnesota that I would expect not to fabricate or lie, they would be Homer and Bob Knoss," Randall says.

Randall grew up with the Knoss family. Bob's father, Homer,

repaired old clocks. Homer taught his son the trade. They both had mechanical minds, like engineers, not storytellers.

"If Bob Knoss says, 'I tried to dodge the draft,' I'd bet lunch he tried to dodge the draft," Randall says. "If Bob Knoss says, 'I got hypnotized,' I'd bet dinner he was hypnotized. The question is, what happens to the mind when you get hypnotized?"

The sun is coming in bright off the snow in the parking lot and through the window.

"I believe he perceived it. The question is, what did he perceive? The question is, are we dealing with a case of the seven blind sisters, where, you know, one grabs the head and one grabs the neck and one grabs the dick and they think they have got their hands on a snake but really they are holding on to an elephant built like a wall of mud?"

Randall takes a slug of coffee.

"The question is, is Bob Knoss after the last digit of pi?"

Bob Knoss lives in Anoka, an exurb forty miles north of Minneapolis. After a few turns, I see a narrow, wooded driveway covered in snow. My rental careens on the ice and just misses the trees as I make my way down the slippery driveway.

I see a sign out front. PICTURE FRAMING, it says.

Knoss squeezes out the front door. He is big like a linebacker and wide like a billboard. Across his chest is a football jersey. "Hawaii 00," it reads. His eyeglasses are off center and smudged. A bushy goatee hangs from his chin in the style of old pharaohs.

Knoss can't remember exactly where he was hypnotized. We drive around, pull into a few strip plazas. He thinks it was in here, a make-shift office amid pizza parlors and surgical supply stores.

We finally give up. Knoss can't remember. That was part of his hypnosis. He was told to forget everything.

Our next stop is Aqua Court Apartments, in Bloomington.

On the way he grooms over the story once again, careful to separate what he witnessed ("Now that's fact") and what he has extrapolated ("Now that's me trying to piece things together"). He insists everything he tells me is true and that he'd take a lie detector test to prove it.

I ask him why he cares at all.

He has a grudge, against the government, he says, for subjecting him to hypnosis in the late 1960s. He was placed in a small room, he says. The doctor showed him a sparkly crystal and there was a metronome, and just like in the movies the doctor snapped his fingers and—poof!—Knoss was under the spell.

The hypnosis poisoned his mind and he wants payback for his nightmares. D.B. Cooper ruined his life, he says. He thought he would go to prison for what he witnessed in the late 1960s.

In Bloomington we pull into the back parking lot of Aqua Court. "Coop," or Duane Weber, lived in the 9120 building with his wife, Knoss says. He can't remember her name. Knoss lived in 9150 with his wife, Cheri. They were the caretakers at Aqua Court. Knoss mowed the lawns, cleaned the filters on the swimming pool. Rent was $105 a month. He points to a snowy patch of grass between 9120 and 9150.

"That's where they practiced," he says. "The parachute—it was white—was unfolded on the grass."

There was another figure involved, an employee of Northwest Orient airlines, Knoss says. He told them what to ask for, how the pilots would react. Mr. Northwest was interested in airplane safety. Airplanes were getting hijacked on a regular basis and pilots were getting killed and airline bosses were not doing anything about it, only joining together to break the unions.

It was true. The high-profile nature of the Cooper case and others did in fact prompt legislators and administrators to install magnetometers in airports. But were McCoy and Weber behind it together? Couldn't be. What was in it for Weber? With McCoy's help, Duane Weber was released from prison, Knoss says. Duane wanted to keep his freedom. A professional thief, he also wanted to keep the ransom money. His jump, his reward. Then, according to Knoss, Duane Weber lost the ransom on the first jump—so McCoy decided to try pulling the job himself on United Airlines Flight 855.

How could I trust Knoss? The whopper he was telling could not be accurate. But what if it was? Or part of it was? How could I afford not to listen?

Knoss has files back at the house. Do I want to review them?

Sure.

The snow is picking up. Heavy flakes. The rental slides on the highway back to Anoka and down the driveway to Knoss's home.

I follow Knoss through the front door, and he shuffles up the stairs. The house is a wreck. Boxes are everywhere, closets are stuffed with old toys, more boxes, framing equipment, cases of V8. The dining room is buried under papers, antiques, tchotchkes.

I use the bathroom. The cabinet over the sink is open, and the shelves are lined with empty pill bottles. I try the spigot to wash my hands. It doesn't work.

What happened to Bob Knoss?

I walk into the living room. It is a graveyard of old clocks and bronze statuettes, a small army of figurine soldiers that stand guard on the shag carpet. The soldiers are designed to protect the clocks, he says.

"That one's Don Juan. That's Don Cesar."

He is sitting at his computer, trying to find the documents on his hard drive. He spins around in his chair to explain the business of repairing old clocks. As he talks, the screen saver on the computer screen behind him flashes on.

I see breasts. Huge breasts. Colossal jugs. The screen changes. Now it's a thong buried in the crevice of an oiled-up butt. Now it's a vagina. Now another vagina.

I look around Knoss's computer station. I see a copy of *Domination*

Nation, a porn movie that features women taking over the world. Richard McCoy played a role in *Domination Nation* under a different name, Knoss claims.

Wait now. How could McCoy play a role in a porn film if he was shot dead by FBI agents back in 1974?

All a hoax, Knoss claims. McCoy never died in the shootout. His death was faked.

I want to get out of here. Fast. But I have more questions. I wonder what Knoss thinks about Albert Weinberg's comic *Les Aventures de Dan Cooper*. What possible connection could a career con like Duane Weber and a war hero turned porn star like McCoy have with a French cartoon?

The puzzle of the French comic book is easy to explain, Knoss says. McCoy was an avid comic book collector. Some of his friends were comic book artists. McCoy gave Duane Weber the name Dan Cooper to use as an alias. McCoy must have been a fan of the strip.

Can any of this be true?

I go to the libraries in Bloomington and Minneapolis. I scan old phone books for the names *McCoy* and *Weber* and *Dan Cooper*. I search for other aliases. I search the microfiche at the Minnesota Historical Society for stories in the local *Bloomington Sun* that Knoss claimed were printed in the summer of 1968 or 1969 about Duane's wife getting arrested for stealing checks. I can't find anything in the old newsprint. Have I missed it? Are my eyes so tired that I glazed over the magic words that would place Duane Weber and Richard McCoy in the same town before the hijacking, and prove that Knoss is telling the truth about his hypnosis after he dodged the draft?

I look again in the Minnesota microfiche. Nothing. I have the rolls sent to New York. I go to the public library. I look one more time. I can't find anything.

Is Knoss lying? If so, why? Have the painkillers created these whoppers? Or are his facts off?

Late one night, I find myself scanning the film credits of *Domina-*

tion Nation. What am I doing? It is simply not possible for McCoy to be in the porno movie. He was shot dead by FBI agents seventeen years before *Domination Nation* was produced. But here I am, looking anyway. And right there, in the credits of the post-apocalyptic porn—in which "women rule and men live like wild animals," according to one write-up—I find the name: Tommy Gunn.

Wasn't that Duane Weber's friend? Didn't Jo Weber claim to meet Gunn once in Mobile, Alabama? Didn't he tell her that *Duane knew people in high places*? Is Gunn McCoy? Is McCoy still alive?

"Believing in Bob Knoss is like believing in the tooth fairy," Jo Weber tells me. "I only found one truth in ten years of talking to that man. He must have known Duane." But how?

I fly into Pensacola, Florida. It's taken over two years of phone calls—most of them late at night, all of them long—to secure an interview with Jo Weber. In Cooperland, Jo is widely considered a madwoman. She has talked to every Cooper hunter, witness, agent. Her posts to the Drop Zone are endless, miles of text and rants in ALL CAPITAL LETTERS or new **bolded clues** that *make no SENSE!* as her streams of thought go on. I don't know who I am going to find: the widow of Dan Cooper, or another Bob Knoss.

She lives outside of Pensacola. It's an hour's drive across the panhandle. As I pass churches and doughnut shops and parking lot barbecue pits, I think of Jo's rule. She made it clear before I left: no pictures. Jo does not want people to know what she looks like. She rarely leaves her house. Has her obsession with the case turned her haggard? Or is she so paranoid that she doesn't want any of Duane's spooky associates to know what she looks like?

I pull into the driveway.

She is in the garage, smoking a Doral. She wears lipstick and blush.

Her white hair is swept up into a bun. Her shirt is a pattern of pink and purple plaid, the sleeves rolled up as if she's been gardening. She is not haggard. She is an attractive woman. She seems strangely . . . normal. Maybe Jo Weber isn't such a loo-loo after all?

"Oh, it's ruined my life," she says about the case as we go inside. She cracks open a Diet Dr. Pepper and takes me on the tour.

Her home is immaculate. The carpets are groomed and dirt free. The sheets of the beds are made and taut. Kitchen counters spotless.

She shows me her bedroom. Also spotless. On the bureau is a picture of her third husband. She married him after Duane. He died several years ago.

"Hi, Jim," she says and waves to the photo.

Her files are in order. The binders are stored in suitcases she keeps in the trunk of her car. Jo doesn't leave her home without taking Duane's files with her. How could she? What if there was a fire? What if she was robbed? These files are all she has to show for her fifteen-year odyssey exposing her ex-husband's secret past.

We set up in the kitchen. She removes her evidence from a box. She shows me the *Soldier of Fortune* magazine she found in his safety deposit box. I touch it. It's real. She shows me the ostrich skin wallet that was recovered in Duane's van, along with the fake licenses, Navy ID. It's all real. I read the gobbledygook of newsprint hidden away in the billfold: "Bombproof and crowded with oxygen . . . terrace, volcallure at casa Cugat, Abbe Wants Cugie Gets."

All of it is here, just like she said. I want to hear her taped phone conversations with Mary Jane Ross, who was married to Duane at the time of the hijacking. I want to hear Mary Jane's alleged confession that she lived with James Earl Ray's wife while Duane was in prison.

I'd read up on Ray. I couldn't find evidence of him marrying until he was back in prison, for shooting Martin Luther King. Jo goes into her safe, produces the cassettes and a recorder. She presses play. The conversation is the same as she has said.

Within the binders, Jo has printed out volumes of old e-mails, messages in which she has desperately tried to enlist the help of others on her hunt. In some messages, she refers to topics he might have said or somebody might have told her, like "Operation Mongoose," the covert CIA attempt to assassinate Castro. But too many years have passed. She can't remember who told her about Operation Mongoose. She has talked to too many people, sent too many e-mails. It's all part of a trap she's built for herself. She can't prove Duane was Cooper. She can't prove he wasn't.

Duane Weber has been vetted. The Bureau has checked out his background, some physical evidence such as hairs from a razor Jo sent in. They have ruled him out. Using the partial DNA strain found on the tie, Carr says he was also able to rule Duane out.

Jo is unfazed. If the DNA sample on the tie is incomplete, how could the Bureau trust it? Besides, how do the feds know the traces of saliva on the tie are Duane's? What if he borrowed the tie before the hijacking? What if he stole it? What if an agent drooled on it?

She can't scrub the lyrics from her mind: *"If you don't know me by now,/ You will never never never know me . . ."*

Was this another clue Duane had left her?

"Perhaps [Duane] sang that song to me for a reason," Jo says. "Damn him for ever telling me anything. Damn him! Why couldn't he have just kept his damn secret?"

Jo Weber has enemies.

> *Orange1:* "Plenty of people *were* listening to Jo's story . . . until it became clear that what there wasn't so much a 'story' as a hodge podge of unverified statements, suppositions, grasping at straws and wild theories."

> *georger:* "Jo, the mistake you make is thinking YOU are important. The rest of the world is laughing or trying to avoid

you, trying to work around you, or without you. You are living a lie here. The emotional part of your brain is running the rational part of your brain."

nigel99: "When the threads started your story was really interesting . . . over the last few months a very different picture has emerged and I strongly believe that you have been hoodwinked . . . I feel very sorry for you as I think you are probably an innocent old lady . . ."

Sluggo_Monster: "Yes Jo . . . Whatever you say Jo. It's obvious that you 'Just Don't Get It.' Oh yeah . . . for everybody else: Did you know the FBI lied to Jo? I hadn't heard that!"

snowmman: "Oh and one more thing. Jo: you're a nut case."

Jo's biggest enemy in Cooperland is Cooper hunter Jerry Thomas.

JerryThomas: "Jo your still here shocking. I don't Know why But it is cool that you are. Your funny in a ignorante way But still ypour post and fiction, Is refreshing. Have fun Kiddo. I'm sure everyone on this forum enjoys your fiction stories . . . One more thing leave this forum. Jerry"

Jerry's cyber assaults bring Jo to tears. "That man is evil," she tells me one night, crying. "He's like the interrogators they use in Iraq."

Why can't she ignore him?

"You can call me anything you want, but you can't call me a liar," she says.

Jerry is unapologetic. The Drop Zone, which he recently discovered, is a place for a serious exchange of information. It should be presented accordingly. Jo has taken over the case with her hysterics, he and many others feel. She's simply getting in the way.

So is Tom Kaye, Jerry thinks. After our field trip, they had a few conversations about Tom's findings and the paper Tom was planning to write. Jerry expressed interest in being a bylined contributor on his paper. Tom told Jerry he was not "part of the Team," meaning his team of science buddies: Alan and Carol.

Jerry was offended.

"What does he mean I wasn't part of the Team? Not part of the Team! He invited me!"

Three months after the trip, Jerry returned to the Washougal area to see how far the river had moved the packet of bills Tom had thrown in. Jerry walked down the path under the small bridge like we had done and followed the current as it moved. He scanned the water, looking for the money bundle with: REWARD IF FOUND!

Jerry found it. Didn't take long. It had traveled only about a hundred yards downstream. It was trapped in a pool of water, under a boulder. Tom was right. The Washougal was too weak to move the money to the Columbia. It would have taken a biblical flood to get the bills there.

Jerry is unfazed. Once the seasons change, he'll be back and get his feet moving through the woods. If he can find the time.

His daughter, Charlene, is now living with him. After our trip, she split up with her husband and lost custody of her children. She slept on park benches and on the street for a few weeks. She was spending any money she had on drugs. She decided to walk the I-5 bridge that spans the Columbia River and commit suicide.

On the bridge, she called Jerry.

"Either help me or come to my funeral," she said.

She later moved into a trailer on his land.

"It's hard," she tells me. "I'm not a bad person. He won't let me do anything. Like the other night I want to go dancing. He tells me, 'A mother your age should not be outside dancing.' But it's like, there are people fifty and sixty years old at that bar."

Charlene overdosed a few months later. She had hitchhiked into town to go to a bar. When Jerry arrived at the hospital, the doctor told him that Charlene had died at least twice before she was resuscitated.

After checking out of the hospital, Charlene moved into town to look for a job. I ask her why she thinks her father has spent so long looking for Cooper.

"At first it was the money, he wasn't doing too good then," she says. "Now I think it's the publicity. He's a bragga-muffin."

"The Curse, the goddamn Curse," Tom Kaye says when we meet six months after the trip at his ranch. He's in his basement lab. He is shaking his head.

"I've become one of *them*," he says. "What separates me from Jo Weber?"

His forensic investigation has backfired. The implosion started when he returned from Seattle and had a conversation with another metallurgist about the high amount of silver in the Cooper bills.

The metallurgist was not surprised. In the 1980s, the FBI used silver nitrates to locate fingerprints on criminal evidence. Tom raced to Wal-Mart to get a nitrate test. He came home and tested the bills.

"They were loaded," he says.

It was a gut-wrenching blunder. How did he manage to make such an epic mistake? He spent six months and thousands of dollars to discover the Bureau's own fingerprint dusting solution.

"It was like finding a treasure map to the Lost Dutchman's Mine, and digging and digging and there's nothing there but dirt," he says. "I don't want to be part of that story. I want a success story."

The pollen tests were revealing. Once Tom analyzed the sticky tape he'd used on the tie, he did not find traces of pine. The lack of pine pollen suggests the tie did not come from the Pacific Northwest. Relying on the expertise of a pollen expert in Belgium, Tom was able to ascertain the species of flower the pollen had come from: impatiens.

"The problem is, there's about a thousand different varieties of impatiens," Tom says. "It happens to be one of the most common flowers."

In his lab, he pops a slide in a microscope to show me a grain of pollen. The slide is of a flower from outside his old house in Chicago. He brings the sample into focus. He discovers another problem. The pollen from his house flower looks similar to the pollen he saw on the Cooper bills. Was the expert in Belgium wrong? Could he be sure the pollen on the tie was actually impatiens? Even if he could, what would that prove? The pollen is another bust.

And what about the gunk he found in the tie?

"Just gunk," he says.

What about the hair he found in the tie knot?

"Wool."

Wool?

"It came from a sheep."

And the dandruff?

"Plastic, or white paint from the clip of the clip-on tie."

Analyzing the evidence, he was able to make one conclusion. Cooper did survive the jump, he thinks. Under the microscope, Tom noticed the money had been bound for so long, the ink of serial numbers on the bills had bled into each other. When he looked at them further, he found that they lined up precisely behind each other in the stack.

Tom did not expect this. When he used his fishing rod to cast a packet of bills into the Columbia River, what happened was clear: The bills fanned out in the water, like the fins of an exotic fish. So if the Cooper bills had floated loosely in the water, when they dried and stuck together, the serial numbers would not be in perfect alignment. They would be slightly off.

Which means what exactly?

"The money did not float down the river," Tom says.

So how did it get to Tena Bar?

"Nonnatural means," he says.

Which means?

"People . . . If there's one story the money tells us, it's that."

He does have more information. A new lead, he says. He found it by accident, under his microscope. I can see he is getting excited just talking about it. The lead, he says, "could end the case once and for all."

I push him. Is he telling me the truth? What kind of forensic matter could Tom have discovered that would be such a case closer?

He won't tell me.

I push harder. He won't budge. He and the Team are thinking of writing their own book.

"Either it's the biggest and best thing to happen to us, or the biggest and worst," he says. "The stakes are so high, success or failure, the balance is on a knife edge."

I call around Cooperland. Tom did find something under his microscope. The forensic matter was in the fibers of the Cooper tie. It is titanium sponge.

Among the elements, titanium sponge is rare. Its primary use is in very fast airplanes. Titanium is extremely resistant to heat. So, engineers crafted planes such as the SR-71 and prototypes for the Boeing Supersonic Transport from titanium.

In light of the timing of the hijacking, the discovery of titanium sponge is curious. In the fall of 1971, Boeing canceled its Supersonic Transport program and laid off the program's workers. Was it conceivable that a Boeing worker handled the titanium sponge while working on the Supersonic Transport, got particles of titanium sponge on his tie, then boarded Northwest 305 in a grudge-fueled moment after getting canned? More enticing is that extremely few companies processed titanium sponge for Boeing. The leading company is Timet, based out of Dallas. Was Dan Cooper a Timet employee?

Once I learn about Tom's discovery of titanium sponge, I ask him about it. He refers me to his lawyer.

"This is business now," he says. "Once it's business, the guns come out."

✗

I call a few experts on titanium sponge. While Timet handled the bulk of titanium sponge, other companies handled it, too, they say. Titanium was also used on submarines as well as airplanes. A lot of people could have handled titanium sponge prior to the hijacking.

Titanium sponge was also prevalent in household items, especially white paint, experts say.

White paint? Tom told me the dandruff he thought he found had turned out to be flecks of white paint off the clip of the clip-on tie. Was this the source of the titanium sponge? Did Tom waste his first investigation on the FBI's silver-heavy fingerprint solution, and his second investigation on flecks of white paint? Is Tom chasing himself around the case in circles? Am I?

Later, I get a call from Jerry Warner (aka Georger). He's upset, needs to talk. In his own lab, Jerry Warner has made a new discovery on the Cooper bills, he says.

What is it?

"Silver."

Silver again?

"There are other forms of silver *in* the fiber threads of the money," he says. "Completely separate and distinct from the silver nitrate issue. Okay? And these little beauties are sitting there in patterns—oh, it is a sight to behold! It's absolutely nature at its best!"

I need a minute to get this straight. Basically, there is natural silver in the Cooper bills, and it was there the entire time, masked by the silver nitrate that was contained in the FBI fingerprint solution that Tom found and ruined his hypothesis.

Warner is cackling with laughter. "It is absolutely hilarious. We finally proved there was silver! From a lab standpoint, this is really funny."

Can he describe what the natural silver looks like under the microscope?

"Like little doughnuts. . . . And these little buggers are just being held in there by those cotton fibers like babies in a bassinet."

So what does it all mean for the case? Does the natural silver suggest the money has been at Tena Bar the entire time?

"Not the whole time. I have reasons to believe it maybe came down in different stages," Warner says.

But from where?

"We're pursuing that," Warner says. He claims to have interviewed scores of former agents and air traffic officials. Warner's theory on the flight path is that Northwest 305 came west of the flight path, and close to Tena Bar.

"Whatever you do, I beg you, do not talk to Jerry Thomas about this information," Warner says. "If the flight path points west, the Washougal, as you know, is out for good. Once he got wind of where we were going, he was not happy."

I ask Warner why he thinks Thomas is trying to defend the Washougal theory so fiercely. Is it because he doesn't want to look foolish after somebody proves he has been looking for Cooper for the last twenty-two years in the wrong place?

"It's Himmelsbach," Warner says. "He wants to protect Ralph Himmelsbach, who really put out the idea that Cooper died in the woods. If Cooper landed west of the flight path, well, then, heck, of course he could survive the jump."

⚡

I call Himmelsbach. I ask him about his relationship with Jerry. They are close. "His father wasn't very nice to him, so I try and be as helpful as I can," Himmelsbach says. He still believes Cooper perished in the woods and landed in the Washougal River basin. "I haven't seen a lick of evidence to suggest otherwise," Himmelsbach says.

⚡

I fly to Arkansas. I want to meet and interview Brian's parents, Dwayne and Patricia. I want to know if they are telling the truth about what happened on Tena Bar. Did Brian find the money or not?

I land at Fort Smith and drive through the Ouchita mountains. An endless brigade of motorcycle riders passes me into Mena, near the Oklahoma border. It has been ravaged by a tornado. Debris lines the streets. Families are homeless.

The Ingram house is on the outskirts of town. Dwayne does not live here anymore. He lives in a trailer in Texas and works as an industrial painter. Water towers are his specialty. Before he paints each one, he climbs to the top of the tower and does a headstand.

He's also been drinking himself to death. It's not healthy to have him around the house. On a recent visit, Brian had to tackle him and wrestle a gun out of his hands.

Dwayne has a long white beard that reaches down to his belly button, and hippielike bracelets around his skinny wrists. He rolls a cigarette and we go outside to talk about the case.

Dwayne wants to figure out what the case means. He is not religious like Brian, but what was God trying to tell him when Brian found the money? What was the test? Why would he lose out on the ransom, get arrested, win a chance to have grandparents, lose that, lose the money, win it back in court? What was the deeper message in all that went wrong?

Back in the house, over a tank of goldfish, I see portraits of the Ingram family on the wall, before the money was found. I wonder how they might be different if they hadn't gone on that picnic on Tena Bar.

"What good is fame without the fortune?" Dwayne says.

"They treated us like criminals," Patricia says. She sits in a wingbacked chair and Dwayne sits in another across from her. Once again, they repeat the story of how Brian found the three packets of bills at Tena Bar, all the media attention they received after Dwayne's arrest, and their court victory getting the bills back.

"I always wanted to meet Connie Chung, but not like that," Dwayne says.

Dwayne is about to cry. He talks about Nan and Tap and how comforting it was to think about having a family again. He wonders if Brian found the buried treasure so that Dwayne could somehow find his real father. If Nan and Tap saw him in the news, then maybe his own father would too. But would Dwayne's own father even recognize him? He rolls another cigarette.

"The Cooper Curse," he says.

"Oh, it exists," Special Agent Larry Carr says of the Curse. He's no longer the agent on the case. In Cooperland, Carr is considered something of a hero for pushing the case forward. The discovery, on American soil, of the French comic book is largely a result of the media splash he made when he leaked that a parachute (albeit the wrong one) had been found. Carr also released data that exposed another fed bungle: the Missing Minute, which puts the hijacker over a not-as-wooded area. As significant as these discoveries have been, Carr's bosses at the Bureau couldn't have been too happy. Bureau culture frowns upon media attention for case agents. Whatever happened, Carr was reassigned to the most tedious detail in the field office: surveillance. Since, he's relocated to Washington, D.C.

Am I losing my bearings here? I want to talk to the other journalist who came close to unearthing Cooper. His name is Karl Fleming. Before he got involved in the case, Fleming had started his own newspaper, married a cute brunette—she was twenty-two, he was forty-four—and his life seemed to be peaking. He placed a classified ad in local newspapers in the Pacific Northwest, attempting to lure the hijacker into an interview. The two men who responded were later charged with fraud and sentenced to prison after Fleming promised them immunity and then turned them in in the hopes of not getting arrested himself.

I find Fleming living in Los Angeles. I leave more than a dozen messages for him and his wife, Anne Taylor Fleming, now a writer who also contributes to the *The Newshour with Jim Lehrer*. No response.

Why not even a courtesy call to say no thanks? Is Fleming ducking me? Is Anne Taylor? Why?

Fleming has written a memoir, I learn, published in 2005. I get it. I open the first page and read his dedication.

To All the Reporters Who Did the Right Thing

I find the chapter on the Cooper case. "A Fall from Grace," it's called. I want to find out what happened to Fleming after the Cooper story collapsed on him. I find this passage.

> *I slid into a dark depression, spending hours prone on the sofa in my little office, unable to function, often in tears, begging for night so that I could sleep. I often thought of suicide and considered how to go about it. I didn't like heights and a gun would be too messy. A pill overdose would do it.*

His wife and her father forced him into a car. They drove him to a mental health facility. Orderlies strapped him to a gurney.

> *As I lay there with a partially free hand I tried to stuff the corner of a sheet down my throat to kill myself.*

Institutionalized, Fleming was given heavy doses of antidepressants. He spent a significant amount of time in therapy. None of it worked. He began electroshock treatments.

I didn't have a choice and I was too far down to be scared. Finally,
slowly, I began to get better, began to see the sun shine again.

On a lark, I call Fleming again.

He picks up. Of course, he'd be happy to meet and talk about Cooper.

"You know, to this day, I still believe I had the right man," he says.

I fly to Los Angeles. I call to confirm the date and time. I call again. I leave several messages. I finally reach him several days later. He can't talk about D.B. Cooper. His wife's orders.

"Sorry to have led you down the primrose path," he says.

I check out another lead. Another confession. Bryant "Jack" Coffelt was a confidence man who spent much of his life in prison. A charmer, he was known to stuff wads of hundred-dollar bills in the roof of his Cadillac. He later worked in Washington as the chauffeur to the last descendant of Abraham Lincoln. The Lincoln heir had a reputation "as a dirty old man," according to one account, and with Coffelt at the family estate they organized "modern-day Roman orgies." Years later, Coffelt confessed to the Cooper crime, and witnesses claimed that after the skyjacking he mysteriously walked with a limp.

Socially, Coffelt was said to be close to a number of Washington elite, including J. Edgar Hoover, and was suspected by many to be working as an informant. Coffelt would conceal evidence in the most unsuspecting places. He once stuffed a note from his lawyer with the message "Burn This Letter!" inside a cookbook.

I had seen Coffelt's name in the Bureau file. According to the FBI, Coffelt had a lock-tight alibi. I spent a few weeks checking him out. I couldn't find much that jibed. At the time of the hijacking, the feds found, Coffelt was in a mental institution in the state of Illinois. Coffelt was a dead end.

I get more leads. A son tells me his father, a former air-traffic controller, once confessed to him in the family basement. Former Northwest employees tell me a lone-wolf employee who matched the hijacker's description disappeared after the crime, prompting widespread suspicions. Another private detective and lawyer tells me about Wolfgang Gossett, a former Air Force man and gambler turned priest who, among other things, helped the FBI investigate cults.

Another lead. I must have overlooked it. Buried in a book is another Cooper confessor who, after a stint in the Paratroops, enrolled at Rutgers and joined the varsity track team. He was, according to a witness, "a steady third-place finisher."

I drive to Rutgers. I camp out in the basement of the massive library on campus, flipping through old yearbooks. I scan the faces of the track runners, jumpers, pole vaulters, looking for my steady third-place finisher. I have to squint to see the details of the boyish faces in the team photos. I crack open another yearbook, and another. Focus now. If the clue to the Cooper mystery is here, I can't afford to miss it.

I return to the library the next day, and the next. I select suspicious names and faces from the Rutgers varsity track team from years '45, '46, '47, '48, and '49. I pull the individual student files, searching for a clue, a morsel of data that would correspond to something I had read in the FBI file, a link.

I request more folders. I go through all. The link should be here. It isn't.

There is no path. There is no story. What have I done? What have I found? Proof that the Cooper Curse has gotten me too?

I reread the story I wrote about Ken Christiansen in *New York* that was published three years ago. Maybe there is a clue in here I missed? A follow-up I've forgotten? I scroll down to the section where the readers can write in to discuss the piece. There is one comment.

The whole deal was a Spec Ops "black" bag job. My proof is that I
was actually in prison in Walla Walla until the week in question, then
let out on a "furlough" . . . Go figure.

The post is a crank, right? But how can I leave it alone? I go to the
magazine's tech department, where they trace the e-mail address of the
poster. I send him a note. He replies:

The facts are that DB was a "bag" job, because I participated in
it. . . . I had a barn, a vehicle, a "catch" team and a local driver, if
and when we picked up the jumper.

He was a professional mercenary, involved in the Bay of Pigs
invasion, the capture of Che Guevara in Bolivia, other high-profile
covert assignments.

"Same folks all the way into Watergate," the poster writes about his
colleagues. "Well, actually all the way into the White House."

He wants anonymity. I agree. From now on I'll call him Jake. Some
topics Jake and I discuss are so sensitive he demands we have "one-pad"
conversations. I don't know what the term means.

"One pad" is individual message cryptography, used only once between
sender and receiver. It is a very simple system, but almost unbreakable.
I understand that some dark groups have some code crackers, but it
takes a while.

At Jake's instruction, I set up an e-mail account in the Philippines.
His rules: I type a draft e-mail, he responds in the draft. The draft is
deleted. The message is never sent.

I learn about Jake. He was introduced to the mercenary world in a
logging camp in Alaska, where he had run away as a troubled boy. His
contact was an ex-Marine who he claims had his fingernails ripped off
during an interrogation by North Koreans.

Jake's specialty was transportation. "I can get a team safely from one place to another and back better than anyone on the planet. I was useless as tits on an Orchard boar on projects that did not require those particular kinds of capabilities."

In the fall of 1971, Jake was serving time in Walla Walla state prison for forgery, though the backstory is complicated. A few months before November 24, he claims, he was approached in prison.

"The folks that contacted me were 'suits.' Names didn't matter, but who they referenced for creds was a guy that I did some work for in Valle Verde in Bolivia in '67. That guy's resource team was out of Virginia . . . organized, managed and controlled by the same folks that contracted out operations to Air America in Camp Pong, Cambodia, and the GT up around Khan Falls."

Jake was offered a deal, he says: In exchange for his help in the hijacking, Jake would get parole.

He agreed. He left Walla Walla prison the day before the hijacking–November 23, 1971, he says–and was given his orders in the field.

> *Mine was to acquire a target (a male, no description provided), contacting me through a specific one pad code (that I can't and won't provide), transport target to a specific location, stop and evaluate target's condition, providing medical and other assistance as necessary, then transport target to a transfer point in East Portland.*

On the night of the hijacking, Jake was with his catch team, waiting for the one pad from the jumper.

> *My grid [or pickup area] was from Cedar Creek off the Cowlitz River, east to Yale Bridge Road, south on the Amboy Road to Yacolt and east to the old Amboy road that went to La Center. My actual extract point was the old Bucomb Hallow camp boat ramp at Lake Merwin.*

I check the location. It is in the heart of the flight path.

Jake and his catch team waited all night for the hijacker to respond, he says. The one-pad message never came. After his Thanksgiving fur-lough, Jake returned to Walla Walla, and his parole came through.

> *DB Cooper was a media event, staged to coincide with the expansion and funding of the secret war in South America. Financial, and Or-ganizational legislation was moving through the Congress, and a big splashy case of Air Piracy on the national media would help the legis-lative process get laws passed that dealt with Transportation Security, among many other things.*

If Jake was really a military-trained mercenary, I wonder if he can illuminate the mysterious items Jo Weber found after Duane Weber's death.

I send him a photo of the San Marino Sanitarium that Jo found in Duane's ostrich-skin wallet. Does Jake know what it means?

"The photo is easy," Jake writes back. "San Marino was the closest R&R facility to Edwards [Air Force Base] for contractors who were in route or recovering and couldn't be sent to a regular hospital or VA facility . . . very good medical OR staff and equipment. It was a go-to 'off the books.' If your guy [Weber] stayed there, guaranteed it was an Ops cover."

I press him for the identity of the hijacker.

"I have no idea who the jumper was, didn't ask and wasn't told," Jake writes. "I can guarantee you he was the most nondescript, un-assuming ex-military contractor they could muster. He wasn't opera-tionally very bright, or he wouldn't have taken the gig. . . . Did he get handled into the jump? Without a doubt."

I ask him about the gobbledygook message of newsprint that Jo also found in Duane's wallet. Does he know what "bombproof and crowded with oxygen" means?

He does. It is code.

"The first sentence is a one-pad cipher," he says.

And what about "terrace, volcallure at casa Cugat, Abbe Wants Cugie Gets"?

"The second sentence references the House of Cugat, which on first glance seems to refer to an actual casa de familia 'safe house' on the outskirts of Havanna [*sic*], as you may already know."

I don't. But what's Cugie?

" 'Cugie' is the cutout's actual name . . . that was an actual person, not a company. . . . So the last sentence seems to be a validation signature."

And what about John C. Collins? Ever hear the name?

"I have heard it, that's about it, don't know if he was the same one . . . some serious people thought he was a legit asset, and brought him to my attention. That's a long time ago and I never heard anything about him until you brought it up."

How can I be sure what he is telling me is true?

Check the prison records in Walla Walla, Jake says. In the paperwork from his prison sentence, there must be evidence of his "furlough" before the hijacking.

Using Jake's real name and Social Security number, I file a Freedom of Information Act request with the Department of Corrections in the state of Washington. The file I receive is over a hundred pages long. I see his mug shot. Jake has long sideburns. A sharp nose. An intimidating gaze. I check the facts.

It is true. As a boy, Jake was a runaway. And he did work at a logging camp in Alaska. His timing was also accurate. In the fall of 1971, Jake was in the state prison at Walla Walla. And just like he said, the charges were three counts of forgery. And it's true: Jake received a "furlough" in November 1971, during Thanksgiving weekend.

I leaf through more pages. Eventually, I find the furlough forms.

The documents are not clear. I find one file that claims Jake was approved for a furlough on November 23, 1971, the day before the hijacking. Another document claims he left the prison on November 24, 1971, the day *of* the hijacking. And yet another claims he left Walla Walla on November 25, the day *after* the hijacking. Which one was it?

I confront Jake about these discrepancies. Is the file off? Or is he using his Thanksgiving furlough to feed me another bullshit D.B. Cooper story?

"I am incredibly surprised there is any record at all," he says.

I check my saved phone messages.

"Geoff, it's Jo. I *need* to talk to you."

"Geoffrey Gray, this is Jo Weber. I . . . I don't know what's going on. I had some strange communications this week. A man sent me five pictures and of course I recognized two and two others possibly but they could be anybody."

"Geoff, Jo. I had a long conversation with a man yesterday. When you asked me if Duane could have been an informant, I always thought he was a Mafia informant for another organization, that he wasn't CIA, but one of those offbeat kind of groups . . . I didn't know what to believe but when he started talking about a priest, it hit me."

"Geoff! They stole it! They came in the damn house! They took everything!"

"Geoff, ignore my other call. I've been revealing so much I've become totally, totally paranoid. I have to get on a plane. I have to find Tina. I have to bury this thing once and for all."

I put down the phone on the kitchen counter. It is winter. I am now living in a cabin. It is located on the top of a mountain in the northern Catskills, upstate New York. I moved here to be alone and focus on the case. I haven't paid any bills. I have been living out of the same pair of sweatpants since I arrived. I went to the store on Monday for groceries and I don't know what day it is now and it doesn't matter because Cooper sleuths do not stop the hunt for weekends.

I am reading conspiracy theory books about the 1960s and 1970s, the Bay of Pigs, the assassinations of Martin Luther King, Robert Kennedy, John F. Kennedy. I am rereading e-mails Jake sent me.

There are a lot of other stories out there that aren't as dangerous as this one.

I go over the facts again. What is true? What am I projecting? I scan the documents from the FBI case files. They are dog-eared and coffee-stained.

I find it! I had overlooked it, all this time.

The SR-71. The spyplane. It was the fastest, highest, most advanced surveillance vessel the government had built. So why was a CIA spyplane looking for Cooper? Maybe Cooper was a spook after all. Maybe that's how he knew about the Boeing 727's aftstairs—built for the CIA's black ops subcontractor, Air America.

I call the Pentagon. The media liaison has no idea how to answer my question. I don't even know if I'm asking a question. I'm ranting about covert ops. He hangs up on me, just like the feds first hung up on Jo Weber when she called in her tip.

I'm running out of sources. I need ex-Boeing engineers, ex-CIA operatives, SR-71 experts. I write in desperation to the operator of an on-line museum dedicated to the spy plane. I ask if it would be unusual for the Blackbird to be used by law enforcement to hunt for a missing hijacker.

"VERY unusual . . . and a poor and highly expensive use of this national asset," the curator of the site writes back. "The Pentagon, and in some cases much higher authority, provided approval for these missions." Much higher authority? How much higher?

I think of Duane L. Weber. I look at more photos that Jo sends me. Weber had a full head of hair. And it was wavy, almost marcelled, like witness Robert Gregory had said. I think of the one-legged man. The man with the cupid lips. The man with the horseshoe-shaped diamond ring. Kissy-Kissy. Reading about the Bay of Pigs and mercs, I see that the characters in the books all wind up the same way: dead.

I lock my cabin windows. I place a few washed-out tomato cans in the doorways—my own homemade alarm system. I think about hiding a steak knife under my mattress. If the Cooper hijacking was an inside job, and I know about it, whoever was behind it ("the suits," as Jake call them) will surely come after me too, right?

In bed one night, I hear footsteps outside my window crunching in the snow.

Who knows I am here? I sneak down the stairs, careful not to make any noise. I don't turn the lights on in the cabin—that way I can see them out there, and they can't see me.

I put on my boots. I walk outside. The moon lights up the snow as bright as a living room. I circle the house. I look in the snow for footprints. I see them. They are my own.

The next night, a blast of light fills my bedroom window.

I look at the clock. It's after 4:00 a.m. I hear an engine revving. A big engine. I spring out of bed. Where is the steak knife? I run into the bathroom and look out the window.

A massive pickup is in the driveway. It is moving toward the cabin. What the fuck is going on? Who is driving the pickup? The handlers of John C. Collins? Richard Floyd McCoy Jr. back from the grave? Or maybe it's Jake, who has traced our clandestine e-mail exchange in the Philippines? Or maybe Jake's handlers? The suits? Kissy-Kissy?

I am ready to fight. I won't be taken alive. I go downstairs for the steak knife.

I change my mind. Better I hide. Where should I go? Under the bed, in the closet, in the attic? I feel like a coward. Why can't I be brave like Dan Cooper the comic book hero? Why can't I stand up and face *them*, whoever they are? And isn't that what Cooper, whoever he was, is all about? *To stand on their own feet, to be men, to face their God.* . . . Am I seeing my own face in the Cooper sketch?

Out the bathroom window I watch the pickup. It eases down the drive and disappears. A wrong turn.

The next afternoon. Or maybe the one after that. I'm in the kitchen reheating the lunch I made, which started out as breakfast, which was last night's dinner. The phone rings. I look at the area code.

"845."

Jo Weber again.

Ugh. I don't want to pick up. Jo Weber conversations are hour investments, minimum. But I'm lonely up here in the cabin. I wonder, after the thousands of dead-end leads and ideas she has come up with about her ex-husband and the case, at least one has to be true, right?

I pick up.

"I've found it!" she says.

She's panicking. Short of breath.

Found what?

She can barely get the words out.

Found what, Jo? What did you find?

She is sobbing. She isn't paying attention. Tears now. Her shrieks are hysterical.

I scream at her. Get a hold of yourself, Jo, calm down. What did you find?

"The cookbook," she says.

The cookbook?

"In Duane's things," she says. "I went through his things—and Duane, you know, was not much of a reader—and I found a cookbook. Why would Duane save a cookbook, and why would he save a cook-book like this one?"

Well, what kind of cookbook is it?

"I can't tell you," she says.

Goddamn it, Jo. Stop being so paranoid. Tell me the name.

"Well, it's not really a cookbook," she says. "It's just recipes put together."

Okay, fine. Recipes put together by who?

She won't say. She is crying again.

Pull yourself together, Jo. Out with it.

"The Dutch Catholic Order of the Amaranth," she says.

What? Does the cookbook have a name on it? A date on the back?

"The publication date is 1960. The inscription inside the cover is 'Gertrude E. Holmberg.' I tried to find her. I think she is still alive."

Why does she even care?

"Because of the picture."

What picture?

"Of the little girl."

The little girl?

"I don't know if it's Tina but I think it's Tina. The girl looks like Tina. I found it in the cookbook. Mucklow, now that sounds Dutch. And she became a nun. Now Order of the Amaranth, I think that might be in Pennsylvania . . . Tina is from Pennsylvania."

I'm listening now. The hijacker did develop a bond with Tina Mucklow on the flight.

Jo thinks Tina had the cookbook with her on the flight, and inside the pages was a picture of herself, mementos to remind her of home. And being the thief he was, Duane couldn't help but steal the cookbook during the hijacking, just like he had stolen the packets of Kool-Aid he never drank from the Piggly Wiggly.

"I need to meet Tina," Jo says. "Face to face. She needs to see I am real. I need to show her the cookbook."

Where in the cookbook did Jo find the photo? Where was it placed?

"Next to the recipe for cherry cheesecake."

Cherry cheesecake?

"The recipe was handwritten."

Now that's something, I think. Maybe the handwritten recipe is a code of a kind, like the gobbledygook newsprint I saw in the crevices of Duane's ostrich-skin wallet. What if Duane secretly confessed to the crime within the recipe? Ingenious! Or perhaps the recipe itself is another clue that Duane has left for Jo. It could be directions to another safety deposit box—only instead of a *Soldier of Fortune* magazine, this secret chamber contains dozens of stacks of lost Cooper bills! The treasure is mine at last!

Jo won't stop crying.

I have to get tough with her.

"Jo, listen to me now. Take a breath. Calm yourself down. And read me the goddamn recipe for cherry cheesecake."

NOTES

The material and narrative of this book are culled from a variety of sources, mostly interviews conducted by the author and information gleaned from hundreds of FBI case files. Other sources are newspapers, magazines, White House tapes, books, and music lyrics from the late 1960s and early 1970s. There have been several other books written on the Cooper case, all of them worth reading, and some which I relied on to re-create the lives of Cooper suspects and Cooper hunters, most notably *D.B. Cooper: The Real McCoy*, by Bernie Rhodes, research by Russell Calame (University of Utah Press, 1991). The others are *D.B. Cooper: What Really Happened*, by May Gunther (Contemporary Books, 1985); *NORJAK*, by Ralph Himmelsbach and Thomas K. Worcester (self-published, 1986); *The Legend of D.B. Cooper*, by Ron and Pat Foreman (self-published, 2008); *Into the Blast: The True Story of D.B. Cooper*, by Skipp Porteous and Robert Blevins (Adventure Books, 2010), and *D.B. Cooper: Dead or Alive?* by Richard Tosaw (Tosaw Books, 1984).

THE JUMP

Quote: "Bombproof." Found on newsprint in the wallet of insurance salesman and D.B. Cooper suspect Duane Weber.

Nixon quote: whitehousetapes.net.

JULY 6, 2007. NEW YORK, NEW YORK.

Skipp Porteous, Sherry Hart, and Sherlock Investigations: *Jesus Doesn't Live Here Anymore,* by Skipp Porteous; interviews with Skipp Porteous and Sherry Hart.

Kenneth, Lyle, and Donna Christiansen: interviews with Lyle Christiansen; entries from *A Cute as a Bug's Ear* by Donna Christiansen.

The quote from the sociologist ("He comes off as a kind of curious Robin Hood . . .") is from Dr. Otto Larson and appeared in the *Seattle Times,* "Hijacker of Jetliner Steals Public Fancy Here," Ross Anderson, November 28, 1971.

Quotes from sheriff and agent in newsclips following hijacking, FBI file.

Information about D.B. Cooper FBI file: author reporting, FBI agent Larry Carr.

Near death of treasure hunter John Banks, *NORJAK,* by Ralph Himmelsbach.

Journalist's suicide attempt and electroshock treatments: *Son of the Rough South* by Karl Fleming (Public Affairs, 2005).

Charles Manson quote: transcripts of the Manson trial.

Quote from Richard Nixon ("If I'm assassinated . . ."): *1973 Nervous Breakdown: Watergate, Warhol, and the Birth of Post-Sixties America* by Andreas Killen (Bloomsbury, 2006).

Statistics on American skyjackings: Federal Aviation Administration newsletter, January 24, 1971.

Passages on psychology of skyjackers: *The Skyjacker: His Flights of Fantasy* by David G. Hubbard, M.D. (Macmillan, 1971).

Kenneth Christiansen: military records, interviews with Lyle Christiansen.

Lyrics: "D.B. Cooper, Where Are You?" by Judy Sword.

NOVEMBER 24, 1971. ABOARD NORTHWEST 305.

The description of the events aboard Northwest Airlines Flight 305, and of the FBI's response on the ground, is drawn from the FBI files, including interviews with Florence Schaffner, Tina Mucklow, Alice Garley Hancock, Harold E. Anderson, William John Rataczak, William A. Scott, Dennis Eugene Lysne, Hal V. Williams, Robert B. Gregory, George R. Labissoniere, Cord Harms Zrim Spreckel, William W. Mitchell, Nancy House, Earl J. Cossey, and others. Conversations between pilots, air traffic controllers, Northwest officials, and FBI agents are quoted from Teletype reports and transcriptions of various radio communications on the night of the hijacking and found in FBI files and NORJAK. In addition, the author conducted interviews with Schaffner, Hancock, passengers Mitchell, Larry Finegold, Floyd Kloepfer, Patrick Minsch, and others, and interviews with retired agents Himmelsbach, Bob Fuhrman, and John Detler and others; the families of passengers Les Pollart, captain William Scott, and detective Owen McKenna.

Details about Alaska airline jet crash: aviation-safety.net; news clips.

Fear of flying: from *The New York Times*—"Pills, Drinks and Will Power Banish Fear of Flying" by Robert Lindsey, March 5, 1970; "Final Exam for First Afraid-to-Fly Graduating Class: Puerto Rican Flight" by Paul J. C. Friedlander, March 1, 1970; "Pacific Backs Ads on Fear of Flying," May 9, 1967; "Advertising: Stan Freberg Tackles Fear" by Philip H. Dougherty, April 28, 1967; and "Some of the Best People Are Afraid of Flying" by Diane Ouding, August 12, 1973.

Northwest stewardess uniform: *Northwest Orient* (Gallery Books, 1987) by Bill Yenne, *Flight to the Top* (Viking Press, 1986) by Kenneth D. Ruble, and uniformfreak.com.

History of stewardesses: *Come Fly With Us!* (Collector's Press, 2006) by Johanna Omelia and Michael Waldock; *Sex Objects in the Sky* (Follett Publishing, 1974) by Paula Kane with Christopher Chandler.

The United ad ("And someone may get a wife") appeared in the November 11, 1966, issue of *Life* magazine; National's "Fly Me" campaign: *Time* magazine, "Fly Me," November 15, 1971; National's "I'm going to fly you like you've never been flown before" commercials: *Time* magazine, "Fly Me Again," June 24, 1974.

National boycott: *Working the Skies: The Fast-Paced, Disorienting World of the Flight Attendant* by Drew Whitelegg; *The Other Women's Movement: Workplace Justice and Social Rights in Modern America* by Dorothy Sue Cobble.

Air America: *Air-Britain Digest;* "The CIA's Airlines: Logistic Air Support for the War in Laos, 1954 to 1975" by Martin Best, date unknown; and usmcpress.com/heritage/air_america.htm.

John Little, aviation historian and Museum of Flight Assistant Curator, provided information on the Boeing 727 and the habits of airline pilots in the 1970s.

Playboy's Miss October 1971 and Miss November 1971: freeweb.hu/playmate/html/7110.html, and freeweb.hu/playmate/html/7111.html.

Details on Hump pilots and missions found in *The Hump Express,* published during World War II.

Guidelines for stewardesses: reprinted in *Come Fly With Us!*

AUGUST 25, 2007. NEW YORK, NEW YORK.
Kenneth Christiansen: military records, Christiansen's letters home during the war, and interviews with Lyle Christiansen.

Historic currency calculations made at futureboy.us.

Shemya: *Northwest Airlines: The First 80 Years* by Geoff Jones.

Bikini Island: bikiniatoll.com/history.html.

NOVEMBER 24, 1971. ABOARD NORTHWEST 305.

Lewis and Clark: passage appears in *The Lewis and Clark Journals: An American Epic of Discovery* (2003), edited by Gary Moulton. Dark Divide: *Where Bigfoot Walks: Crossing the Dark Divide* (Mariner Books, 1997) by Robert Michael Pyle.

Vietnam War Facts: *Nixonland* by Rick Perlstein (Scribner, 2008).

Tornadoes: *Time* magazine, "Devastation in the Delta," March 8, 1971.

Los Angeles earthquake: *California Geology*, "The 1971 San Fernando Earthquake," April/May 1971.

Animal attacks at the Detroit zoo: *Time* magazine, "Animal Farm," June 28, 1971.

Police deaths, counterculture protests, the Attica prison riot, and Nixon's speech: *Nixonland*.

MAY 27, 1969. SEATTLE, WASHINGTON.

Robert (Barbara) Dayton: medical files of Barbara Dayton; letters and postcards of Robert Dayton; interviews with Ron and Pat Foreman, Rena Ruddell, and Sharon Power; *The Legend of D.B. Cooper* by Ron and Pat Foreman.

Himmelsbach: interviews with Himmelsbach; *NORJAK* by Himmelsbach; Paul Cini, recounted in *NORJAK;* news clips.

Nyrop and life at Northwest Orient: interviews with former Northwest employees. "A bit to the left of Genghis Khan," appeared in "Nyrop, NW and That Aid Pact" by Robert Samuelson, *Washington Post*, September 17, 1972.

Bahamas Charter Jet transcript: *Nashville Scene*, "A Nashville Hijacking 38 Years Ago Set the Standard on How Not to Handle Hostage Negotiations," August 27, 2009.

Skyjacking history: *The Sky Pirates* (Scribner, 1972) by James A. Arey.; *1973 Nervous Breakdown: Watergate, Warhol, and the Birth of Post-Sixties America* (Bloomsbury, 2006) by Andreas Killen.

Ethiopian Air skyjacking: *Washington Post,* "Birdwatcher, Wife Subdued Hijacker," December 9, 1972. Sacramento skyjacking: *Newsweek,* "Skyjacked—And Alive to Tell the Tale," July 17, 1972.

The FAA's secret psychological profile of hijackers can be found in the Report of Proceedings of the National Conference Seeking Solutions to the International Hijacking Problem, July 17, 1970, compiled by the Airline Passengers Association.

AUGUST 25, 1977. HILTON AIRPORT HOTEL, ATLANTA, GEORGIA.

Duane Weber's employment history from 1952 to 1974, as it appeared on a 1974 résumé; his awards and letters of commendation from Life Investors, Annualized Life, Annualized A&H, Michigan Life Insurance Company, Interlock Screw and Bolt Corporation, and American Income Life; and interviews with Jo Weber.

NOVEMBER 24, 1971. ABOARD NORTHWEST 305.

FBI interviews with passengers, stewardesses, Northwest officials, pilots, and others; author interviews with passengers; FBI files and documents; Teletypes and transcriptions between pilots, crew, and law enforcement; passenger statements following hijacking in newspaper reports.

DECEMBER 7, 1942. COVE CITY, NORTH CAROLINA.

Details from Richard Floyd McCoy's childhood, family life, and schooling at Brigham Young University from *D.B. Cooper: The Real McCoy,* by Bernie Rhodes. Details on McCoy's military record: court documents and exhibits from McCoy's 1972 criminal trial.

NOVEMBER 24, 1971. ABOARD NORTHWEST 305.

FBI interviews with Northwest officials Hal Williams, Dennis Lysne, Mucklow, FBI summary reports, transcriptions of radio communications, Himmelsbach, *NORJAK* by Himmelsbach.

Clyde Jabin: Information on Jabin's goof of Cooper's name comes from the *Seattle Post-Intelligencer,* November 27, 2007. Another explanation for the error comes from Himmelsbach, who claims an agent gave the reporter the initials of Daniel Barry Cooper, who was ruled out on the night of the hijacking after police located him.

THE HUNT

Letters from alleged Cooper suspects to FBI, from FBI files.

AUGUST 24, 2007. APPROACHING PORTLAND.

Trip taken by the author; interviews with Himmelsbach, *NORJAK.*

NOVEMBER 25, 1971. WEST LINN, OREGON.

Accounts of the day after: interviews with Himmelsbach. The re-interviewing of the witnesses: FBI files. Search of the plane in Reno: FBI files. Quotes from Walter Cronkite come from footage of the broadcast, courtesy of Vanderbilt Television News Archive.

SEPTEMBER 3, 1969. SEATTLE, WASHINGTON.

Medical procedures come from the medical files of Barbara Dayton. History of Bobby Dayton: interviews with Ron and Pat Foreman, Rena Ruddell, Sharon Power. Postcards and letters of Bob Dayton, from *The Legend of D.B. Cooper* by Ron and Pat Foreman.

NOVEMBER 26, 1971. WOODLAND, WASHINGTON.

Details of search headquarters found in local news accounts and FBI summary reports. Details of the radio communications and pressure bump controversy: FBI files.

Ralph Himmelsbach: interviews with Himmelsbach; *NORJAK* by Himmelsbach.

The passages about local reactions to the hijacking, including quotes and descriptions of local suspects, are drawn from a variety of newspaper sources, including the *Seattle Times*, "Amateurs Hunt Dollars, Not Hijacker," November 27, 1971; the *Seattle Times*, "Money Seekers Join Hunt for Hijacker in State," November 27, 1971; the *Seattle Post-Intelligencer*, "Sketch Made of Hijacker" by Dick Clever, November 28, 1971; the *Seattle Times*, "Hijacker of Jetliner Steals Public Fancy Here" by Ross Anderson, November 28, 1971; *The Columbian*, "D.B. Cooper, R.I.P." November 19, 1976; *The Barometer*, December 3, 1971, classified ads; the *Oregon Journal*, "D.B. Cooper Record Scores In Gresham" by Dennis McCarthy, December 30, 1971; *The Columbian*, "A Party for D.B. Cooper" by Bob Burnett, November 28, 1976; the *Seattle Times*, "$200,000 Question: Who Pushed on Door at Midnight?" by Dave Birkland, November 28, 1971.

MARCH 1995. WEST FLORIDA REGIONAL MEDICAL CENTER, PENSACOLA, FLORIDA.

Jo Weber: The death of Duane Weber and its aftermath are drawn from interviews the author conducted with Jo Weber. The passage and details concerning *Soldier of Fortune* magazine refer to the December 1994 issue of *Soldier of Fortune*. Details about money left in a bucket: "Skyjacker at Large" by Douglas Pasternak, *U.S. News and World Report*, July 24, 2000.

NOVEMBER 27, 1971, SEATTLE, WASHINGTON.

Details of agents' investigation into parachutists: FBI summary reports. Investigation into the parachutes the hijacker was given: FBI interviews with rigger Earl Cossey. Boeing layoff statistics: "SEA-TAC International Airport: Part 3-Boeing Bust to Deregulation" by Walter Crowley, historylink.org. FBI investigation into Air America connection: FBI summary reports.

FALL SEMESTER 1971, BRIGHAM YOUNG UNIVERSITY, PROVO, UTAH.

McCoy's medical condition: *D.B. Cooper: The Real McCoy* by Rhodes. Passages on skyjacker psychology: *The Skyjacker* by Hubbard. Mormon articles: Lds.org. Details about McCoy's home life and idea to hijack an airplane: *The Real McCoy* by Rhodes and news reports from McCoy's criminal trial.

NOVEMBER 29, 1971. SEATTLE, WASHINGTON.

Details about the first sketch composed: FBI files. Details about the Towncraft tie: FBI files. A list of suspects: FBI files. Accounts from those detained: "Hijacker's 'Twin': Looks, Hobby Plague Seattle Sky Diver" by Don Hannula, *Seattle Times,* December 5, 1971; "The Hijacker is Everywhere" by Dick Lyall, *Seattle Times,* December 15, 1971; the letter "I am no Robin Hood," from "Only 14 Months to Live," *Los Angeles Times,* December 14, 1971.

AUGUST 24, 2007. WOODBURN, OREGON.

Interview of Himmelsbach conducted by author. Details of the hijacker's description: FBI files. "A beautiful but moody woman," from *D.B. Cooper: What Really Happened?* by Gunther.

DECEMBER 5, 1971. WOODLAND, WASHINGTON.

Teletypes from agents about the search: the FBI files. Details about suspects and descriptions and investigations of leads: FBI files. Himmelsbach's concern about copycats: interviews with Himmelsbach, *NORJAK.* Everett Holt: "Accused Hijacker Bluffed, FBI Says," the *Hartford Courant,* December 27, 1971. Billy Hurst: FAA reports. Merlyn St. George: "FBI Identifies Slain Hijacker Through Prints," the *Hartford Courant,* January 28, 1972. Stanley Speck: "Hijack Suspect in San Diego Case Arraigned," the *Los Angeles Times,* April 10, 1972.

FEBRUARY 18, 1970. UNIVERSITY OF WASHINGTON.

Dayton medical files, including psychological evaluations, surgical and nurses' notes. *The Legend of D.B. Cooper* by Ron and Pat Foreman. Interviews with Sharon Power, Rena Ruddell, Ron Foreman, Pat Foreman.

JANUARY 6, 1972. MCCHORD AIR FORCE BASE.

Experiment with the aftstairs and SR-71 search: FBI files. The discovery in the cistern: "Young Woman's Body Discovered" by Steve Erickson, *The Oregonian*, March 30, 1972. Army search: FBI files and Bureau Teletypes.

APRIL, 1995. PACE, FLORIDA.

Discovery of "Dan Cooper": interviews with Jo Weber. Summarization of hijacking: *D.B. Cooper: What Really Happened?* by Gunther. Memories and experiences of Jo Weber: interviews conducted by author. "Bloodiest forty-seven acres" and conditions inside Missouri State prison at Jefferson City: "The Wall" by J.J. Maloney, *Crime Magazine*, May 15, 2003. Experiences of James Earl Ray: "James Earl Ray" by Maloney, *Crime Magazine; Truth at Last: The Untold Story Behind James Earl Ray and the Assassination of Martin Luther King Jr.* by John Larry Ray and Lyndon Barstein (Lyons Press, 2008). Conversation of Duane Weber's family members: audiotapes provided by Jo Weber. "Crook, I guess," recounted in "Smooth Talker at Beach Faces Robbery Counts" by Dick Morgan, the *St. Petersburg Times*, July 29, 1957.

AUGUST 25, 2007. SEATTLE, WASHINGTON.

Ken Christiansen's history and childhood: interviews with Lyle Christiansen. Larry Carr and current information and theories on the case: interview with Larry Carr.

APRIL 7, 1972. PROVO, UTAH.

Richard McCoy's hijacking of United Airlines Flight 855, and his parachute jump, his escape, and capture: *D.B. Cooper: The Real McCoy* by Rhodes. The response from neighbors: "FBI Captures Student, 'Evidence' in Skyjack," the *Salt Lake Tribune*, April 10, 1972; "FBI Holds $499,970 in Skyjack Ransom," the *Salt Lake Tribune*, April 11, 1972; additional news clips about McCoy's arrest: Salt Lake City *Deseret News*.

AUGUST 26, 2007. SEATTLE, WASHINGTON.

The trip to Bonney Lake: conducted by author. Ken Christiansen's habits: interviews with Lyle Christiansen. Details of Bonney Lake home: observed by author. Interviews with Christiansen neighbor and Kennth MacWilliams conducted by author. Hubbard "for these men, to command a woman," *The Skyjacker*, by Hubbard. Tracking down stews: Hancock, Schaffner, and Mucklow, interviews conducted by author. Mucklow ("He was never cruel or nasty"), "Search Pressed for Hijacker," *Seattle Times*, November 27, 1971.

JUNE 29, 1972, SALT LAKE CITY, MCCOY ON TRIAL.

McCoy in court; the feds lay out their case; Rhodes attempts to get McCoy's confession: *D.B. Cooper: The Real McCoy* by Rhodes. McCoy's escape: *Deseret News*.

NOVEMBER 23, 2007, SEATTLE, WASHINGTON.

Carr's report on the evidence: interview with Carr. First encounter with the evidence: author. Lyle's response to Kenny's motive: interview with Lyle Christiansen.

FEBRUARY 12, 1980, PORTLAND, OREGON.

Names of suspects: FBI file. Himmelsbach struggles with case: interviews with Himmelsbach, *NORJAK*, by Himmelsbach. Indictment: " 'Dan Cooper' Has One Year to Go Before Statute of Limitations Runs Out," *The Columbian*, December 25, 1975. Money is found: *NORJAK*, by Himmelsbach; *D.B. Cooper: Dead or Alive?* by Tosaw; interviews with Patricia and Dwayne Ingram.

NOVEMBER 23, 2007, SEATTLE, WASHINGTON.
Larry Carr takes the investigation into cyberspace: interview with Carr. Carr's exchange (under the name 'Ckret') on dropzone.com was posted November 6, 2008, and November 7, 2008. Details on dropzone.com: interviews and research conducted by author. Jerry Warner (Georger): interviews conducted by author. Cooper Days: "A Party for D.B. Cooper" by Bob Burnett, November 28, 1976; interviews with bar owner Donna Elliott; lyrics found on newspaper clips on the walls of Ariel Tavern. Ron Foreman and Cliff Kluge present Barbara Dayton: interview by author.

THE CURSE
Snowmman quote ("Jo, you're seeing Jesus in the Toast") posted on dropzone.com, November 4, 2008.

DECEMBER 2008, SIERRA VISTA, ARIZONA.
Tom Kaye gets the money and biography of Tom Kaye: interviews with Tom Kaye. A description of the ranch in Sierra Vista: observed by author.

AUGUST 1988, WASHOUGAL, WASHINGTON.
Living in the woods, biography of Thomas: interviews with Jerry Thomas. Titles, military posts and certificates, copies provided by Thomas. Presenting the canvas bag to Himmelsbach: interviews with Thomas and Himmelsbach.

DATE UNKNOWN, 1978, PUYALLUP, WASHINGTON.
Ron Foreman meets Barb Dayton for the first time: interview with Ron Foreman. Barb is depressed: interview with Pat Foreman. Barb confesses to the Cooper hijacking: interviews with Ron and Pat Foreman, *The Legend of D.B. Cooper* by Ron and Pat Foreman.

AUGUST 2000. PACE, FLORIDA.

Prison records of Duane Weber: provided by Jo Weber, courtesy of Doug Pasternak. Details of *Soldier of Fortune* magazine: found in *Soldier of Fortune*, December 1994. Jo Weber's investigation and memories: interviews with Jo Weber. Details of Robert Kennedy dying near a clip-on tie: *Contract on America: The Mafia murder of John F. Kennedy* (Shapolosky, 1988).

JULY 26, 1972, BRIGHTON, COLORADO, MCCOY.

Richard Floyd McCoy's escape from prison, letters to the judge appealing for a reduction in his sentence, and planning another escape: *D.B. Cooper: The Real McCoy* by Rhodes.

MARCH 1, 2008, CATHEYS VALLEY, CALIFORNIA.

Bobby Dayton and biography of his children: Rena Ruddell. Psychology of hijackers: *The Skyjacker* by Hubbard. Searching the Dayton ranch: author. Life on the Dayton ranch and interview of Sharon Power conducted by author; poem provided by Sharon Power. Billie Dayton's recollection of Bobby Dayton and deathbed confession: interviews of Billie Dayton conducted by author.

AUGUST 2000, PACE, FLORIDA.

Jo Weber's introduction to Bob Knoss: interview with Jo Weber. Jo Weber's recollection of the paper bag floating on the river: interview with Jo Weber.

MARCH 4, 2008, WOODBURN, OREGON.

Search for the cistern and remaining ransom with Cliff Kluge, and Ron and Pat Foreman: interviews and participation of author. Notes of Barb's confession: provided by Ron and Pat Foreman. Medical files of Barb Dayton, provided by Ron and Pat Foreman, courtesy of Rena Ruddell. Larry Carr's discovery of the white parachute: interview with Carr. The discovery of Dan Cooper the comic: interview with Wayne

Walker, aka Sluggo. Details of comic book character Dan Cooper: from *Les Aventures de Dan Cooper,* Volume 1 through 8, Le Lombard Publications. Interview of Albert Weinberg, the Dan Cooper comic book artist, conducted by author with French translation by Valerie Fischer.

AUGUST 10, 1974, LEWISBURG, PENNSYLVANIA.
Details of the prison escape, the flight on the lam, bank robberies, and shootout with federal agents: *D.B. Cooper: The Real McCoy* by Rhodes. Additional details on the shootout: interview with retired federal agent Nick O'Hara.

FEBRUARY 28, 2009, BATTLEGROUND, WASHINGTON.
Following the clues and scientific field work observed by author. The Silver-in-the-Sand theory by Tom Kaye: interview by author. The Missing Minute, by Wayne Walker. Brian Ingram's recollection of finding the Cooper bills: interview of Brian Ingram conducted by author. Controversy over who found the Cooper bills: interview with Himmelsbach; *NORJAK* by Himmelsbach; interviews with Pat and Dwayne Ingram. The fallout between Tom Kaye and Warner: interviews of Kaye and Warner conducted by author. Details of the Fazio Ranch and Tena Bar: observed by author. The fallout over the finding of the Cooper bills: interviews of Patricia, Dwayne, and Brian Ingram conducted by author.

SEPTEMBER 15, 2009, NEW YORK.
Skipp Porteous is convinced Ken Christiansen is Cooper: interview by author. Bills were found in the tree on Christiansen's property: interview with Porteous, and *Into the Blast: The True Story of D.B. Cooper* by Porteous and Blevins.

Barb Dayton loves to fly: "After She Shelves Her Job, She Opens Her Wings," *The Daily,* University of Washington newspaper, date unknown. "All the forces in life converge," *The Skyjacker* by Hubbard. Obituary of

Richard Floyd McCoy Sr. published in *The News & Observer*, October 16, 2008.

Bob Knoss questioned: interview with Don Nichols and R.A. Randall conducted by author. Interview of Bob Knoss conducted by author.

Jo Weber speaks: interview of Weber conducted by author. Cyber attacks against Weber found on dropzone.com.

Jerry Thomas's quest in the Washougal continues: interviews with Jerry Thomas and Charlene Thomas.

Tom Kaye's theory goes bust: interviews with Tom Kaye. Information about titanium sponge and the history of titanium in airplanes: interview with John Little, curator at the Museum of Flight, and experts from the Mining and Metallurgical Society of America. The rediscovery of silver on the bills: interview with Jerry Warner conducted by author.

Patricia and Dwayne Ingram speak about the Curse: interview with Pat and Dwayne Ingram.

Larry Carr is transferred: interviews with Larry Carr.

Karl Fleming attempts suicide: interviews with Karl Fleming, and excerpts from *Son of the Rough South* by Fleming.

Details on Bryant "Jack" Coffelt: *The Last Lincolns: The Rise & Fall of a Great American Family* by Charles Lachman (Union Square Press, 2008). Details on Gossett: interviews with Galen Cook. "A steady third place finisher," from *D.B. Cooper: What Really Happened?* by Gunther.

Jake and Black Bag Jobs: interviews with the source conducted by author. Prison records from Washington State obtained by author.

Cabin experience: East Jewett, New York. Phone interview with Jo Weber conducted by author.

ACKNOWLEDGMENTS

This book couldn't have been possible without the participation, bravery, curiosities, memories, wisdoms, and insights of the following sources, most of whom began a conversation with me several years ago and whom I have met in every time zone throughout the country: Lyle Christiansen, Skipp Porteous, and Sherry Hart at Sherlock Investigations; Florence Schaffner and Alice Hancock; Ron Foreman, Pat Foreman and Cliff Kluge; Rena Ruddell; Sharon Power and Billie Dayton; Jo Weber; Ralph Himmelsbach; Jerry Thomas; Charlene Thomas; Brian Ingram, Dwayne Ingram, and Patricia Ingram; Tom Kaye, Alan Stone, Carol Abraczinskas, and Roberta Burroughs. There are others, many dozens of others, who spent hours with me in person, in coffee shops, bars, diners, libraries, conference rooms, on the phone, and over e-mail. Thank you for your help and your perspectives.

I am also fortunate to have had the help of Special Agent Larry Carr, who was courageous in pushing the case forward. Over the past three years, I have also interviewed scores of other law enforcement sources, including retired FBI agents and state troopers, as well as Northwest officials, passengers, the family members of deceased passengers, air-traffic controllers, and many others; thank you all.

Piecing together the final manuscript has been a challenge. Frankie Thomas is a prodigious editor in the making. Her grooming and pruning skills were exemplary, not to mention her insights and patience with fact-checking. Catherine Coreno is a fastidious researcher, and labored through many waves of copy, offering clarity and organization. Valerie Fischer is a great friend, and her French translation skills proved essential once again. Wayne Walker: thanks for helping try to keep the facts straight and helping others try to crack NORJAK. John Little, assistant curator at the Museum of Flight, in Seattle, knows all there is to know about airplanes; his assistance was extraordinary. John Fox, the FBI's in-house historian, was also helpful in illuminating the history of the Bureau and the era. There were also numerous researchers and aides at the National Archives, Air and Space Museum, Minnesota Historical Society, and New York Public Library who helped me track down materials and information.

At *New York* magazine, executive editor John Homans sent me on the Cooper hunt and was instrumental in the shaping and the telling of it. Like other writers at the magazine, I am lucky to have an editor with his ear and feel for stories and the characters that drive them. Editor-in-chief Adam Moss and managing editor Ann Clarke: thanks again for granting me the time to work exclusively on this project. Carl Swanson and Carl Rosen and others at the magazine: thanks for your advice and support.

Finally, I'd like to thank the talented staff at Crown Publishers, who have made the experience of writing this book, my first, a memorable one. Sean Desmond, my editor, has an extraordinary sensibility about how to make a book work, from the motives of the characters and the historical context in which they interact to the typeface of each font. He's been a tremendous booster and groomer, patient, creative, and inspiring to work with. Stephanie Chan and the editors and designers in the copy, art, and production departments—Mark McCauslin, Linnea Knollmueller, David Tran, Lenny Henderson, and Andrea Peabbles—were also creative and always willing to entertain ideas.

My agent, Richard Abate, saw the potential in this project and worked tirelessly to make it happen. And my friends Allen and Belkis

Hersch, and Chris Delahanty and Dina Badami, were gracious enough to let me camp out in their respective retreats to muscle through various parts of the manuscript. Uncle Wayne: thanks for reading another one. Mom and Mags: thanks for putting up with me. And finally, Dan Cooper: thanks for the story.

INDEX

ABOUT THE AUTHOR

GEOFFREY GRAY is a contributing editor at *New York* magazine. He covered boxing for the *New York Times* and for programs such as *This American Life*, writes for other newspapers and magazines, and once drove an ice cream truck. *Skyjack* is his first book.

HuntForDBCooper.com